Those They Left Behind

Interviews, Stories, Essays and Poems by Survivors of Suicide

Karen Mueller Bryson, Ph.D.

For all of our loved ones, who died too young and left us too soon.

"Keening in Bangor" was originally published by *Sinister Wisdom: A Journal for Lesbians*, Vol. 68/69, Fall 2006, Sebastapol, CA. Reprinted here by permission of the author.

Special thanks goes to Maureen Carpenter for proofreading this book.

ISBN 978-1-4303-0755-6

Visit the Transformational Stories website at:
http://www.transformationalstories.com/

CONTENTS

INTRODUCTION

There are so many of them. They were our sons, daughters, wives, husbands, sisters, brothers, mothers, fathers, nieces, nephews, aunts, uncles, lovers and friends. All of them completed suicide. When I started this book project, I read the statistics. I knew there were approximately 30,000 suicides every year in our country creating about 300,000 new survivors, friends and loved ones left behind. But those are just statistics. When a woman writes about her son and husband who both took their lives, one is no longer reading just another statistic. A real person is writing about their experiences with tragedy and despair.

When I began searching for survivors to interview, I never imagined the overwhelmingly positive response I received. So many people were willing to share their stories—to help others through what they know to be one of the worst things that a person ever has to experience. It helps us to share our stories—it helps us to read the stories of others—to know that we are not alone in our despair.

The thing that was the most difficult was the vastness of the pain—so much pain in so many people. It is a pain that never quite goes away—it's always right there, a little below the surface, waiting to rear its head when you least expect it. As survivors, we wonder why our loved ones did not value their lives as much as we did. The images remain in our minds—our loved one jumping from a bridge, hanging from a rope, bleeding in a bathtub, or with a gun in their mouth. That is not what we would have chosen for them.

As one survivor noted, being a suicide survivor becomes an integral part of one's identity. I feel as though an entire segment of my life was defined by my father's suicide. It colored everything that followed. The tragedy seemed to be like a musical score always playing underneath the action of my life. I was only 25 when my father completed suicide—so I was still in the process of becoming an adult. It makes me sad that my father could not see the person I am today. So much life passed without him there to share it. He left this world just as I left my youth leaving me to become a woman without a father.

Why did I choose to write a book about suicide? I felt the need to create something that would be of use to others coping with the suicide of a loved one—something that would help them realize they are not alone in their pain and grief. I also wanted to provide a platform for people to share their stories—as a way to heal in their own grieving process and provide them with a way to help others as well.

The following interviews, stories, essays and poems were collected and edited by me but the accounts are those of the contributors and the accuracy of their accounts is their own. Some of the individual contributors chose to include their real names with their accounts while others asked to remain anonymous. For those individuals who wished to remain anonymous, I have removed identifying information and used pseudonyms in place of actual names.

CHAPTER ONE
Survivors of Multiple Suicides

"Dorris"

Age: 70

Current Occupation: Playwright

Dorris's mother and son both completed suicide. In 1958, her mother attached a garden hose to the exhaust pipe of her car. Her son jumped from a building in 1980.

In her words...

I was born in the Depression and grew up during World War II, the Korean War and the early Civil Rights movement. My father was in the army during the war. After the war, he was Deputy District Director of the IRS. Then he resigned to become the vice president of a gambling casino in Las Vegas.

My immediate family consisted of two parents, my brother and me. Both of my parents worked. They gave me a lot of freedom and encouraged my participation in school bands and orchestras, as well as writing for school newspapers. They did have rules. I was expected to help with the housework and to either work or go to school every summer, as soon as I was old enough to baby-sit. I usually attended school.

My parents were both quiet people. They came from Kansas farm families. Hard work and fortitude were valued. I felt that they were pretty much like the other parents in my neighborhood, until we moved to Las

1

Vegas. Then my father became wealthy. His associates were later found to have criminal ties. I felt close to my mother but not to my father, who was distant.

My mother was often depressed. Cheering her up was my job. When I made her laugh I felt successful. We did the usual mother-daughter things: shopping, cooking, washing dishes, doing housework, etc. My friends loved her and so did I. She was extremely attractive and kind. She didn't talk much about her feelings. I became good at sensing when something bothered her and would try to help. I think that's one reason I became a social worker.

My son's father and I divorced when my son was quite young. He was a happy baby but not always a happy child. He was in therapy and I was, too. His father wanted no contact with him. This was really difficult for my son. He always said I was a good mother but I felt guilty because I had to work and couldn't stay home with him when he was small. After high school, he enlisted in the Marines but asked to be discharged after a short time. My son also had trouble talking about his feelings. He was very much like my mother, who died before he was born.

The suicides...

At the age of 21, my son decided to work in Las Vegas, where he was born. He called regularly and seemed fine. He had been there for about six months when my brother called to tell me about his death.

Both times I heard about the suicide, I was in shock and on automatic pilot for weeks. I did what I was supposed to do; went to work, cried all the way there and all the way home, but didn't discuss my feelings with anyone but a therapist. I felt that if I did I would probably break down. I did find comfort as time passed in knowing that if I couldn't help my mother and my son at least I could try to help others, and that's what I did.

Neither my mother nor my son ever mentioned suicide. Although they weren't happy some of the time, I had no idea. I think my mother felt abandoned by my father, who had become involved with other women. I don't know why my son took his life. I'll never know.

The bereavement process...

I felt numb much of the time but then suddenly tearful. The anger most people feel wasn't part of my reaction, except for anger at myself for not preventing their deaths. But I got over that as time passed. I felt guilty for years. Why hadn't I been able to prevent both suicides? Finally I realized that feeling guilty wouldn't bring them back or change anything. All I could do was try to live the best life I could.

2

I told others very little about the suicides. Some people felt awkward and didn't know what to say. I tried to let them know I understood. Years earlier a friend's father killed himself. This was how she behaved and I followed her example.

I don't think anyone ever recovers from such devastating losses, but I knew very early that I would not feel sorry for myself and would be as sensitive and responsive as I could to other people and their feelings. For a long time it seemed to me that I needed to live three lives, my own and the two people I loved whose lives ended too soon.

Now I just do the best I can. I feel grateful to have had, despite everything, such a good life. This may sound strange but except for those two tragedies, my life has been marvelous. I'm not saying their suicides didn't affect me. Still, when my mother and my son took their own lives I became determined not to waste mine.

I believe I have come to terms with the losses as much as anyone can. I don't exactly know why, except to say that as time passed I knew they were never coming back and there was nothing I could do about it. I came to terms with both losses gradually, over time. It took years.

Today, I can remember the good times. I think of funny things each of them said. I remember how dear they were to me and still are. I'm grateful for the memories.

Dreams and unusual occurrences...

When I dream about my son, the dreams are always pleasant; he's laughing or playing with the dog or the kids next door. My dreams about my mother sometimes involve teatime. This was our nightly ritual. Also singing together while we washed dishes.

Have you ever considered taking your own life?

No. Quite the opposite. I want to live as long as I possibly can.

Significance of the suicides...

The importance of being responsive to others. I became even more so after my son died.

Helpful coping methods...

I did seek counseling briefly after my mother died but I really didn't find the therapist helpful. When my son died I found a therapist I really liked, who helped a lot. I sought counseling both times because I felt I needed it.

Reaching out to others, not shutting the world out, enjoying my friends' children and grandchildren, becoming part of their lives, attending the christenings, graduations, school programs, weddings, baby showers of all these kids, and now their children. Friends have helped enormously. I have no family left, but my dear friends are like family. I never spend a holiday alone, always lots of invitations, which I return.

Advice or words of wisdom...

No real words of wisdom. I can only say that time will help. There's usually no way of keeping someone from taking his or her own life if that person is determined to do so, and I hope they don't feel guilty, although most of us do. In time and with help, this guilt usually lessens. Being creative is really a marvelous outlet for me. I highly recommend it.

"Maude"

Age: 67

Current Occupation: On Social Security and looking for part-time work

Maude's son and husband both completed suicide. Her son hung himself almost 16 years prior to this interview. Her husband shot himself 14 years prior to this interview.

In her words...

My husband and I were married in 1964. We had a daughter in 1968 and a son in 1973. We were living in an old family house and had lived there with my parents from 1971 until my father died in 1977. Then my mother moved to help my brother and sister-in-law take care of their children in the mid-80s. My daughter moved out on her own in 1988.

We were all very close and I had home-schooled the children from 1977 till the fall of 1987, when my son decided to attend high school.

My husband and I had a good relationship. It wasn't a great marriage but it wasn't a bad one either. My son was extremely close to his father and our relationship was very good also. Because they spent so much time together due to being home-schooled, my son and daughter were also very close with a lot of the same interests.

The suicides...

My son attended his freshman year of high school but stayed home again the following year as he was such an extreme perfectionist that he had "burned himself out" during that year at school. He decided the next year to go back to school and had been in school for about a week when he died. On that day, we discovered his books were still on the dining room table when we got up that morning so we knew he hadn't gone to school but didn't know where he was. About 1:30 that afternoon the police came and asked to see a sample of his writing and determined he was the person who had hanged himself in a secluded park across the street.

My husband died at home—outside in front of our barn. I heard the shot but thought it was a firecracker as it was July 5th. A little while later I found his note on the kitchen table and started to look for him. Something stopped me from going outside and I called the police. They saw him as they came in the driveway.

With my son, for some reason, I was not surprised. When we realized he was missing we looked for him but I wouldn't go up in the barn's attic, as I was afraid I would find him hanging there. As it turned out, he had hanged himself but not there. I think I was in shock and sat in a rocking chair just numb. With my husband, it was almost like reliving my son's death. I was also in shock but in a different way.

I had no idea my son was considering suicide. I knew my husband wasn't handling my son's death well but I had no thoughts of him doing it. I originally thought my son did it because he couldn't deal with his own perfectionism. Later, I was told by a friend who channels an entity that he planned to die at birth but that we made a subconscious agreement that he would stay for a while. The entity was amazed at how long he stayed. In my husband's case, I believe it was mainly his grief combined with financial problems we were having that contributed to his decision.

I was always very open about how they both died. I was extremely fortunate in that I don't feel I was treated any differently because it was suicide than I would have been treated if they had died in any other manner.

The only authorities I had to deal with were the police—local in my son's case and both local and state in my husband's case because there was a gun involved. On the whole, I felt I was treated very well. One of the local policemen came both times just by chance and he was quite upset.

The bereavement process...

After my son's death, I often felt chest pains and hoped I would die from a heart attack. I felt extremely drained physically, emotionally and spiritually.

The two main things I did were to attend meetings of The Compassionate Friends (an international group for bereaved parents, grandparents and siblings, no matter the cause of death) and to write letters to my son expressing everything I was going through. I also read everything I could find on the death of a child and on suicide. Each in its own way was extremely helpful. After my husband died, a group was started in my area for suicide survivors, which I attended in addition to The Compassionate Friends. I now facilitate that group.

I have come to terms with the losses. Mainly through the groups and my writings. I think it was a very gradual process, which I didn't fully realize until my son's 5th anniversary, when I wrote a poem of sorts about my feelings. I think my grief for each of them was really one big grief for both of them. I still miss them both but can understand their decisions.

Dreams and unusual occurrences…

The only striking dream I had (and I believe it was more than a dream) was of a meeting I had with my son in a hospital or hotel where we talked about his death and he told me it was the way it had to be. We cried and hugged, which was very unusual as, even as a small child, he had to be bribed to give hugs.

Have you ever considered taking your own life?

Yes. At the time my husband died, I was seriously considering suicide myself but after he did it I couldn't leave my daughter the legacy of having her whole family wiped out by suicide.

Significance of the suicides…

Very great significance. My life has been completely changed.

Helpful coping methods…

I didn't seek counseling at first because I felt that unless a counselor had been through it, they might have the textbook answers but could never really understand what I was going through. I later sought counseling with my minister, which was very helpful.

Advice or words of wisdom…

I would strongly recommend attending a support group—one focusing on suicide, if possible. I also think writing about what we are going through is extremely helpful.

Ann

Age: 47

Current Occupation: Pre-Arrangement Counselor for Funeral Home

Ann's husband and son both completed suicide. Her husband, Bob, 39, slit his wrists on December 31, 1988. He son, Shawn, 29, shot himself on December 23, 2004.

In her words...

I had a very good childhood. I could not have asked for a better time. I am the middle child of five kids. We had a great time growing up. I had decent, honest parents. My dad is still alive and lives close by.

In the early 1970s, when I was 16, I went a little crazy and ran away from home. I had a rough time after that. My first husband, Bob, was much older. When we met in 1974, I was 16 and he was 25. His family was much different than mine. They lived in the country in Minnesota—they had no indoor bathroom. Bob's parents had five kids. His father was an alcoholic and his mother only had a second grade education.

Bob was a Vietnam veteran. When he went to Vietnam, he was a clean-cut, country boy—a Marine. His drug use started with using pot in Vietnam. He was wounded in action and while he was at the VA hospital, they put him on morphine. He became a heroin addict. He was also an alcoholic. When I met him, I didn't realize he had a serious addiction problem. In the 1970s, many people partied a lot.

When he was sober, Bob was a great, fun guy to be around. But when he drank, he didn't know what was real and what wasn't. Sometimes, he would think people were Vietnamese. Sometimes, he would cry about a previous girlfriend who overdosed. He found her in the bathtub dead. He was a very ill man. I wasn't old enough, mature enough or educated enough to understand how ill he was.

I married Bob in 1975. We were married for 13 years. There were very good times and very bad times. Bob and I had a lot of trouble. We had a very bad marriage. He was very abusive. I denied being beaten to my parents. I left Bob several times but always came back.

Bob and I had three children. Shawn, who was not treated well by his father, also completed suicide at 29. My daughter, Sara, is 29 and my other son, Nick, is 27. The kids were 10, 12 and 13 when their father died. Although Bob was a very hard worker, he didn't have a clue about how to be a father.

8

The suicides...

I actually left Bob about a week before his death. I had a job and I knew I could support the kids. I was actually earning as much money as he was. When he realized I could stand on my own two feet, that's when he knew my leaving was for real.

I had just moved into a new apartment and there was a knock on the front door. It was a police officer. He asked me to call my dad in Wisconsin. I went and called him from a payphone. My dad told me Bob had died. I wasn't shocked. He had tried to die by suicide when I left with the kids. He was hospitalized and put on a 72-hour hold but they let him out early—so I wasn't surprised when my dad told me what he had done.

The psychiatrist who let Bob out of the hospital early called me immediately after the suicide and said he was sorry, "We all tried." I didn't blame him at the time. We are all human, and some things we just don't have control over. I let it go.

Bob was all alone. He was struggling. He couldn't call me because I left him. I moved out on him. I think he took his life because I left him and he knew I wasn't coming back.

My son, Shawn, is a different story. I was ashamed to say I had a son in prison. Why would I want to talk about it? I think it is helpful to remember the good times with Shawn. All families have problems—we are all human. I don't hesitate to tell people what happened when they ask how Shawn died.

My relationship with Shawn was very odd. When I moved back to Wisconsin from Colorado, Shawn didn't want to come back. He had friends in Colorado—three or four boys from across the street who enticed him. The boys were older and were drinking, partying and smoking. This was in 1992, after Bob died.

Shawn registered at an Alternative School when he was 18 years old. He got into some trouble in Wisconsin for breaking and entering. He left Wisconsin and ran amok. The police caught up with him in Nevada or Arizona.

Shawn was in prison in Southern Colorado for more than three years. I never went to see him. We wrote letters back and forth faithfully. We spoke on the phone—often—and he said he didn't want me to see him in prison. I didn't want to, either. I regret that he didn't have a visitor the whole time he was there. I'll never forgive myself for that. Everyone told me to follow tough love, that he did the crime and he should have to pay. Shawn finished his diploma in prison. He was released in Denver and put on probation for two to three years.

He got settled in an apartment in Denver and I went to visit him in August 2002. I got to meet him when he was totally drug free and alcohol free. He was very strong. He was in the best of mental and physical health then. We had a perfect week together. I had prayed he would change and when I left, I had felt he had changed a little bit, but more so, I had a feeling of acceptance. I though he was going to be okay.

When I went to see him again in 2003, everything had changed. He had completed probation but he lost his job and was back on drugs and alcohol. He looked terrible. He had a shaved head and Mohawk, different color hair and dark circles under his eyes. He was staying with one of those boys from across the street—only now the boy was a 37-year old man. Shawn was sleeping in his basement.

The first night I was there, Shawn went to work as a bouncer at a bar. He left at 9pm and never came home the next morning. I called my husband and he asked me to come home. I told him I wanted to help Shawn. I went to visit a friend in the mountains and while I was gone, Shawn came back to his home, slept the day and left again by the time I returned at 7pm.

I thought he was normal the next morning. He had his girlfriend with him. He had gotten a job on a pipeline where he would make a good living and have some security. I took him shopping but he could not keep his eyes open. I was totally disgusted with him. I thought I did everything I could. But hindsight is 20/20. I should have offered to take him back home with me but I didn't think I could do anymore. I did everything humanly possible to help him. But he was a handful and often made the wrong choices.

In October before he died, he said he was working construction and that's why he kept missing my calls. I left messages but he never called back.

Shawn had gotten into drugs very heavily and was dealing. He didn't show up for a court date because of the drugs. When he didn't show up, a bounty hunter found out where he lived because a neighbor turned him in. At about 3 pm, the bounty hunter was following him in a car and Shawn starting shooting at him. Shawn went into his house. The bounty hunter called the police and the police had a SWAT team surround the building. Shawn wouldn't come out. The police never called me to help get Shawn out of the building. Shawn didn't call either. He didn't want to go back to prison. Maybe he thought I wouldn't help him because I hadn't in the past. Around 11 or 12 pm, he shot himself.

On December 21, I got a phone call from Dottie, an old neighbor from Denver. She said "Shawn's been shot." She didn't know what happened. Dottie gave me the name of the hospital. I just knew what had happened and fell apart. My husband, George, took the number and called the hospital. They told us that Shawn had shot himself and was brain dead. His body was still alive at that point but they said he would probably be dead in four hours. We got the family together but it was impossible to get a flight. The weather was very bad.

The doctor told us not to come to the hospital because he would not survive. If he did, he would be in a vegetative state. We had to decide if we should take him off life support or not. The doctor told my husband that they could keep him on life support if we wanted to come out to see him. The family said it was my decision. At the time, I felt if I did go, there was nothing that could be done. I decided not to go. It is my biggest regret that I didn't go.

Shawn didn't die alone. His girlfriend, Linsey, has been with him the entire time he was in the hospital. When Shawn was taken off life support, the family gathered around my daughter's table and we said our goodbyes over the phone. When Linsey put the phone to Shawn's ear, she said a bloody tear came out of his eye. Shawn died a day later, December 23, 2004.

The police report stated that Shawn tried to kill himself two other times. I don't know why they didn't try to contact me—I would have been very easy to find.

The night after Shawn's dad died, he popped pills. Another time, he called me to say goodbye. He said he just couldn't deal with things anymore. He had called me to tell me he loved me. I had no idea where he was— what state even. Somehow he survived that time. I'm not sure how.

I wish I would have tied Shawn up and forced him to come home with me but I was worried about destroying the family I had at home. Shawn was a reckless person.

The bereavement process…

I didn't grieve when Bob died. My number one concern was my children. I wanted to make sure they all got counseling and that they knew everything was going to be okay. We all had to talk about Bob's death. We did a lot of counseling. I did not feel the counseling was very effective because the counselor had not dealt with suicide. People are now becoming more educated about suicide.

I really didn't process Bob's suicide. You don't really grieve someone you're afraid of. I grieved for my children. The children reacted horribly to the death. All three of my children, at the moment their father died, emotionally stopped growing.

My youngest, Nick, hurt the most. He was 10. He is my quiet, gentle child. After Bob's death, I could never find him. He would hide in a ball on the top shelf of the closet. At school, he would hide under his desk and not come out.

Shawn was extremely difficult to handle. He was 13 when his dad died. He became defiant. He would not cooperate with anything. He would destroy everything. He began drinking and smoking pot.

Sara was 12 when her dad died. She knew her dad wasn't that good of a father but she didn't know he was a bad father. She was humiliated by his death.

I didn't figure out for years, until I saw a counselor in Wisconsin, you don't grieve for someone who beats you. It was such a complex relationship. When Bob died, I was relieved because I wasn't going to have someone hurt me anymore. I don't think I ever told anyone I was relieved.

I am very sad that Bob took his life. He was suffering so much. He was in a lot of pain. He was so troubled with his family, Vietnam, his experiences with drugs. But there was a good Bob deep inside.

I don't miss Bob. He was a very ill man. The whole thing—our life together—was too bad. I feel sad. I was as responsible for things as he was.

I was really in shock when I got the news about Shawn. There are blocks of time I can't remember. I can't remember moving from our apartment into our house that we were building at the time.

We had Shawn's funeral but I still have his remains. I don't know what I want to do with them yet. I think I want to put a park bench in front of a lake and put his remains there but I haven't done anything yet. The bench is the one thing that feels right. I want to do that and maybe take the rest of his remains to Colorado. I deal with this type of thing all of the time with my husband's funeral home. I don't know how people make these types of decisions so quickly.

Shawn's brother quit his job in Wisconsin, put his things in storage, and left for the mountains in Colorado for an entire summer. At the time I thought it was Nick's way of closure. Then he went from Colorado to live in Florida in the national forest. He had become a bum, totally depressed. My husband and I went to Florida and asked him to come home. Two weeks later he called and said he would like to come home. Nick is doing better now. He is on medication for depression, going to counseling and is employed, after being unemployed for over a year. He is living with us at age 28, but I would rather have a healthy, happy son than a dead one.

I feel sorry for Shawn. I love him more than anything in the world and I feel sorry that he had such a rotten life growing up. We did things with him like soccer and Boy Scouts but his father would get drunk and abuse him. I feel so responsible. I always wonder if it was his destiny. I knew Shawn would die before me. I didn't know how—but I knew he would.

Dreams and unusual occurrences...

I have had the same dream eight times since Bob's death. I have a dream that he is alive. He is back in town and is coming to see me. I'm horrified and very fearful. In the dream, I know he's coming back—that he never really died.

I didn't see him for three of four days after he died. I didn't believe he was dead until I saw him at the funeral home.

About Shawn, whenever I am in the doctor's office and they ask me if I have heart problems, I say no but inside I say, "Yes, it's broken." As far as dreams go, it seems like when I dream of Shawn, it's always when he was a little boy, never as an adult.

Have you ever considered taking your own life?

Sometimes, I think I'm surrounded by suicide. It's been such a part of my life. But I don't think I'd ever do it. I would never do that to my children, husband and grandchildren.

Significance of the suicides...

If there is a God, I know I'll see Shawn—if not, it won't matter anyway.

Helpful coping methods...

After Bob's death, I got busy improving myself and helping my children through counseling. As for this time of grieving for Shawn, in the beginning, I would talk to my husband, George, because he understands much about the grieving process. I didn't want to be on any medications. I thought I could do it myself. After a year of crying every day, and sleeping a couple of hours every afternoon, I did go to my family doctor as was put on an anti-depressant. Now that I have been on this drug, and feeling so much better, I realize I have been depressed since Bob died in 1988. That's how long I have been tired.

I now attend a Survivors of Suicide (SOS) group. The group doesn't suit everyone but it has helped me tremendously. In the group, we can talk about everything—things you wouldn't normally talk about—the guilt, the whys. Not that the other group members have all the answers but it is someone to talk to.

Advice or words of wisdom...

I have no wisdom but plenty of advice. The biggest thing is to get into a group that specifically deals with suicide. Don't think about the group as public grief. Everyone there is in the same boat. It is natural to feel guilty. There is no time limit to grief. Everyone grieves at their own pace.

There is nothing more important than your own family. If you see any sign of depression, or pick up on any suicidal thoughts from a loved one, just do whatever it takes to help the person. It could mean a lifetime commitment to that person, but it would be worth it rather than losing them.

CHAPTER TWO
Sons and Daughters

"David"

Age: 65

Current Occupation: College Professor

David's son completed suicide in 2001 at the age of 31. He hung himself.

In his words...

I had a normal family. My parents stayed married. My dad lived into his 80s—my mom lived to her 90s. They were always there for us. I have a sister eight years younger.

There were four of us. My wife is four years younger—61. She is a psychologist. She teaches and has a psychotherapy practice. My daughter is married with a husband and two children, seven and four.

My son was my best friend. We liked many of the same things. We were very close. We have a summer home at the Jersey Shore. My son liked to hang out there. We always provided a refuge for him when he was having problems—he came home.

My son was our buddy, our chef, our film companion. He was a filmmaker. He made a feature film at 28. The film was screened at the Toronto Film Festival and won a few awards. My son had a great capacity for work and to achieve. He possessed great charm, enough to get perfect strangers to invest in his film making projects. Yet, with all his vibrant potential, he took himself out. We have since had several showings of his film as fund-raisers for his university alma mater.

I thought I'd carry on his work in filmmaking, but I'm not a film-maker. It didn't take to long to learn I could not do that.

The suicide...

My son's fiancé called. She was in Chicago. She was the first to learn of my son's suicide. She asked a friend, who had an apartment nearby, to investigate. He discovered my son's body.

It was an experience from hell—a parent's worst nightmare come true. We never felt as low or as completely devastated, as we did during the first three months after his death. We've come a long was since then.

We didn't really have any idea he was considering suicide. Six weeks before—for the first time—he attempted suicide. He swore he would do everything possible to never have anything like that happen again. After-wards, he seemed resolute to avoid any future flirtations with suicide. He sought counseling immediately thereafter and vowed to never, ever con-template such a dreaded deed. After he died, the autopsy suggested his suc-cessful suicide was probably associated with a down cycle linked with co-caine use.

He had a traumatic experience as a college student. His girlfriend, at that time, took our rowboat out from our summerhouse on a mild and un-usually warm January morning. He and a group of friends were spending a winter holiday weekend at our Jersey shore summer home. Then the wind came up and the water went from glass calm to rough and our son lost his girlfriend. He never forgave himself for not preventing her death. That was eight years prior to his death.

He liked to shine brightly. He liked to think of himself as a filmmaker and could not conceive of himself in any other kind of work. Yet, three years after making his debut feature film, with nothing promising happen-ing in his film career, he felt like his career was over. He struggled with fail-ure and was terribly shortsighted. He adopted a permanent solution for a temporary problem.

He was a party person. He was very infantile in a lot of ways—he was jealous of his cousins and friends who seemed to have an easier time. He was super-sensitive. He was the wrong person to be in film—he took things too seriously and personally.

My son had a wonderful but demanding fiancé—high maintenance. She's a very striking woman and he was proud of her. But she was impatient and lacked an understanding of addictions. She wanted to go to parties—do social drinking—she didn't understand that at certain times he had to refrain altogether from any drug use. She never wanted to accompany him when he went to AA or NA meetings. She did little to help him get free of drugs, though she did not inspire much drug use in him, she did little to help him stop drugging.

After his first suicide attempt and getting psychiatric care, he was getting different doses of (prescription) drugs—Zoloft and Paxal. Then, he grabbed cocaine to get some peace from his girlfriend—not knowing the impact of the other drugs. We think he had no immediate impulses to kill himself, but it was the unanticipated interaction of cocaine with the other drugs taken at the time that brought him down.

We were always aware of his smoking. We knew he was trying to quit smoking. Yet, he still smoked while he was wearing nicotine patches. We were dimly aware of his struggling to stop taking cocaine. He was a mass of self-delusions. He kept thinking he didn't have an addiction problem.

The bereavement process…

At first you're in shock—you don't want to talk about it. Then you want to talk about it. You go around in big circles. There is a tremendous sense of hurt, confusion—I don't think the hurt of suicide will ever end.

At first, we were in a daze—nothing anybody could have said or done would have made a difference. The authorities were very nice—responsible—we were there when his body was taken out. We were permitted several hours later to attend the city hospital to view the body prior to the autopsy. Then we had the burial. And next, three days of people traipsing through our house; we were warmed by some of the caring responses of family members and good friends; it was a blur. Then, there were the bureaucratic details of dying; moving his things out from his apartment; closing out his checking account and needing to verify his death with the death certificate; giving many of his clothes away, ugh! There is no greater sadness.

It was hell to deal with. To see how sad you become. You know your life will never be the same. The hopes and dreams you had have to be replaced—the second best—not as meaningful. You never want to see yourself outlive your children—it's a very hard experience.

My wife is doing as good a job as any person as closely involved and as psychologically acute as she is. It has been the most incredible failure in her life. As a practicing psychotherapist, not being able to foresee the dangerous state your child was in left her with acute feelings of ineptitude. She blamed herself for a while and wanted for a spell to change careers. Yet, we have since learned that people in the behavioral sciences and treatment fields are often surprised by suicides. For every completed suicide there are between 100 to 250 unsuccessful attempts; it is so very hard to tell the difference between an innocuous attempt and the real thing.

I initially had trouble sleeping—after a while the difficulties subsided. My wife became more needy of things to put her to sleep. She sometimes took medication in the evenings. We're in better health now than when he died. We participated in the American Foundation of Suicide Prevention Out of Darkness Walk—it was 20 miles throughout the night—in Washington, DC. We trained for the walk and we still do a lot of fitness walking; we're in pretty good physical shape.

Have I come to terms with the loss? It's not ever done—not ever a settled issue. There is a sadness and disappointment in our life. We'll always wonder why. We think we know—but who knows?

I don't see it ever getting fully settled. We don't want to feel anger but we sometimes do. Sometimes I curse him out when we visit his gravesite because I'm pissed he's not here now to share in our triumphs and tragedies. I love him just as much, though. I'll always love him. I do what I can to remember him.

Have you ever considered taking your own life?

I have thoughts every now and then—fleeting impulses—like everyone—then they are overcome. If I ever have a suicide impulse I think of the harm his suicide caused all of us survivors and I vow never, ever to hurt people like that.

Significance of the suicide...

We're not going to be making long-term future plans—if we want to go to China—we should go now. Things change so quickly. You have to seize the moment. I am much more aware of the transient nature of things.

My whole life has changed. Suicide issues have become important on an intellectual and personal level. I will only keep friendships with people whom I can bring these issues up with ease.

Some people have a knack of saying insensitive and uncaring things. One good friend said why don't you go out dancing instead of attending a suicide support group meeting. People can sometimes say hurtful and stupid things. I'm glad some of the jackasses are gone—pseudo-friends and kin who are unable to handle anything like this—good riddance.

Helpful coping methods…

We attend a peer support group—monthly; there we meet people with recent suicide losses. We know how devastating the new hurt can be. We feel better when we can offer some support to new survivors that the deep hurt they are feeling will eventually pass; in time, people come to a better place. The initial sense of agonizing hurt eventually dissolves; it gets to assume a more dormant position, never completely disappearing. It's a process.

We attend a suicide support group and will continue to do so for as long as it seems to be helpful and useful to do so. I went to a bereavement counselor two or three times. My wife went six times. It was okay. Support groups are more meaningful. I haven't felt a need for therapy.

Advice or words of wisdom…

You just have to look inside yourself and find what you have—what strengths you have. You have to do something good—as a way to tell the person you lost—you fool, look at what you're missing. Life matters; even though we sometimes put up with a great deal of crap, there is a point to it all, to living and to making things better for the people you care about. And we're doing it without you! We want you to know you made a huge mistake by killing yourself; you should have stuck it out. Yet, despite your awful deed, we will always love you and try to keep your memory alive, even though our brains lose the ability to retain all those beautiful memories we once had.

You enter a new chapter that is so different from anything else you've ever experienced. But, we suicide survivors are in very different place. Being a suicide survivor pulls you apart from conventional experience—it changes you profoundly.

Mary Anne Burke

Age: 49

Current Occupation: Housewife

Mary Anne's son, Matthew, completed suicide on November 25, 2001. He shot himself.

In her words...

We were a family of four. My husband is retired Navy and I am a five year Veteran. Matthew was our oldest and we have another son, Brian, who is two years younger.

Being a military family, we moved every two to three years with my husband away for extended periods. The boys and I were close but the moving and not having Dad around was a strain.

I think Matthew and I had a fairly normal mother/son relationship. As Matthew got older there were the normal teenage conflicts. No matter what was going on, he always told me he loved me before bed. The last few years of his life we grew closer.

The suicide...

I was informed of Matthew's suicide by the county sheriff. Since Matthew was in the military we were very upset that they did not follow procedure and notify the Navy that they had found Matthew. They found his military ID card on him. It should have been the Navy that informed us.

For some reason, I knew what I was going to be told. I knew it was going to be that Matthew had died of suicide. Still my world stopped. It was like the life had been taken from my body. It was like I knew my life as I had known it was gone forever in that instant. I had so many questions running through my head and yet I thought this could not be real.

I knew that Matthew was not himself the day before. I knew something was terribly wrong but I did not know what. He had come home on leave for Thanksgiving and he was going to take his car back to Georgia. When he called earlier in the Thanksgiving week to tell us he was coming home I had a feeling that I didn't want him home. It was a very strange feeling and I didn't know why. He was quiet all weekend and did not eat much, even on Thanksgiving Day, which was not normal for him at all. He didn't go out to see his friends; he said that he wanted to spend time with us. Saturday he was very quiet and I finally got him to talk. The one thing he did say to me was, "I have done everything that I have wanted to. I went

20

to boot camp and did well. I went to Sub School and excelled. I am stationed on a ballistic submarine in the world's greatest Navy and I'm not happy and I don't know why." (He had also told me earlier that if he had it to do all over again he would have gone surface Navy, that the qualifications that he had to do on a sub were overwhelming.) He told me he didn't know what he was going to do and he would figure it out for himself. His father and I told him that many people go for years looking for the job that they would be happy with. We told him it just takes time and he would be okay. If he was still unhappy when his enlistment was up, he could get out and go to school. This was not going to be the rest of his life. We thought it was not something unusual for a young man to be thinking. Having been in the Navy both of us thought we knew how he was feeling. You always feel overwhelmed when you get to a new duty station, job or even a new year in school and we thought he would get through this time.

We have never been anything but honest with others that Matthew took his life. Most people were very good to us immediately following. We were so surprised to hear so many others tell us that they had been touched by suicide. I only had one person avoid me at work. I found that people just didn't know what to say to me.

The county sheriff's detective was wonderful to us. She would check up on us and was very helpful with any questions we had. The military had assigned a Bereavement Officer, LTCDR Street, to us and he was an angel. He was always there to take care of whatever was needed. He took care of all the paperwork for us. We only had to make a few decisions on our own. I truly don't know how we would have made it through without him. We also had a chaplain that we could call on day and night if needed. I just can't say enough about LTCDR Street. Even his wife came out once with him.

The bereavement process...

The first six months or so I know I had to be in shock. I just functioned, how I don't know. I cried all the time. I didn't think I would ever stop. Concentration was gone and I knew my priorities had all changed. Nothing was fun anymore. I couldn't sleep and if I went to bed not ready to fall asleep I would just lie there and cry. I learned that if I stayed up until I couldn't keep my eyes open and then went to bed I would sleep a bit easier. I prayed I would have dreams about Matthew. I did not want to be around people. I quit my job and knew that I had to spend time alone and try my way to get through all of this. The first year was just surviving, day-to-day and sometimes hour-to-hour. If it weren't for the fact that we had two dogs that had to get out in the morning, I am sure I would have spent days in bed.

The second year was the worst. I think it was the realization that this was all real and Matthew was not coming home. Up until then I thought if Matthew would walk through the front door I would not be surprised. I still spent most of my time at home. I had started yoga and was forming new friendships. I found that my circle of friends had grown very small. Midway through this year, I realized that I needed more help than the grief counseling to get through. I was having thoughts that I only wanted to be with Matthew again and the route to that was dying. I did not want to take my life but if I was in a car crash or had a terminal illness, I wouldn't do anything to help myself. This is when I started antidepressants. They helped me tremendously. I do feel that this is my life now and I will never get over Matthew's death. It is going to be a lifetime of "getting through it." I really hate it when people talk about closure. There is not such a thing for me.

I had heard so much about the terrible pain of heartbreak. I now know the true meaning. There was a tremendous pain, ache really, in my chest that stayed for a long time. Of course, there was the depression. I just did not care about anything. Forget memory; that was gone. There was always a bit of a headache, sometimes I think from sinuses being swollen from crying. My concentration was gone. I could drift off in mid-conversation so easily. Sometimes when talking to people it was like word processing was gone. I knew they were talking to me in English, but the words just did not make sense.

I have come to terms with the loss and achieved a peace. It is what it is and no matter how I feel about it I can't change it. Matthew did what he felt he had to do for him.

One month after Matthew died I felt I needed counseling to get through. The same week Matthew died, my uncle was given a terminal diagnosis of lung cancer. I just could not cope with all of it. I could not live with the guilt I felt, as a mother, the feeling of being alone and all the other feelings of having a child take his life. I went to one on one grief counseling for about nine months, then went back after four months or so. I also began group counseling which my husband and I continue to go to.

I only really came to peace with Matthew's death and the way he died after I began antidepressants and group counseling. I realized that there was no changing my life and I may as well look at it head on and see it for what it was: my reality. If I were to keep on denying or feeling sorry for myself, then that is all Matthew's death was for. I chose to live my life the way he would be proud of me and do some good with it. I wanted Matthew's death to lead to some good. His life was not going to be wasted and do no good.

Matthew's suicide is always going to be a mystery. We have theories but no answers. We see the signs of depression now that we did not realize was rampant in our family. Also we think that he really just wanted to be with family, not living his life so far away and on his own. We also think there may have been steroid use as a teenager that may have played a role in the depression. I also think he may have been tired of starting at the bottom all of his life. So many questions but no answers. And believe me I have searched everywhere for clues.

I feel so much closer to Matthew today. I believe that he is always with me and helping me. I still have moments, especially on holidays, when I miss him so very much and get angry that our holidays now always have this sadness to them.

Dreams and unusual occurrences...

I have had several striking dreams about Matthew. One dream Matthew came home and of course I was so happy to see him. I hugged him and held on to him and said I knew he wasn't dead. I knew it was all a mistake. He told me how someone had car-jacked him and he was afraid to come forward and say that it was not him they found in the car. He had answers for all my questions. The next thing I knew my husband and I were in bed and I was telling him about when Matthew came home and I could see Matthew in his room packing his sea bag. I went in and asked him what he was doing, he couldn't go anywhere. He said he had to go, that he wasn't going to spoil his brother Brian's Christmas by being back. This was his Christmas.

Another very vivid dream began by me going down a long white corridor with many doors. I passed up all the doors on the side and when I got to the end of the corridor I opened the door. There was Matthew with a big smile and a bright light behind him. I grabbed on to him, holding him tight, and I could feel his arms around me. I was not going to let go. Behind him, out of the light, came my uncle who had recently died of lung cancer. He looked younger than he did when he died and he was smiling. Then came my aunt, his wife, who had died a few years before in a car crash. She was smiling. Then my grandfather and grandmother, gone for years, came out of the light. The light dimmed and behind all of them were many people I did not know but somehow I knew they were all relatives, who loved me deeply, and who had gone before me. Then they all faded away and I woke.

Have you ever considered taking your own life?

When I was about 14 or15 I did make an attempt at my own life. It was not really a very serious one, I took a handful of aspirin, hoping to just go to sleep and not wake up. I woke up and never told anyone about it until after Matthew died. As a teenager I spent many days in my room crying, thinking I was not loved. My family was not one that was really demonstrative with affection. I have three brothers and one sister and my mother was always busy with the younger ones. It seemed to me that nothing was ever about me, even though I was an A student in school and swam on the swim team. I never had anyone at any of my swim meets or at school when I was inducted into the Honor Society. I felt as far as my family was concerned I was a built-in babysitter. I know realize how depressed I was. There were times after Matthew died that I don't think would have taken much for me to take my life had it not been for my husband and son. I just could not put my son especially through that pain again.

Significance of the suicide…

Matthew's death simply tore my life apart. I felt as though I was truly destroyed. I was given a chance to begin my life over and become who I wanted to be. I am a much more sympathetic person. The priorities in my life are no longer the same. Matthew's death has brought our entire family closer. Family is the priority. I want to do what I can to help people now, where as before, I am ashamed to say, I would say, "Oh that's too bad" and go on with my life. Now I want to do all I can to help. I feel as if I am living the life I was supposed to be living from the beginning. I am really alive and feel so much more deeply. I trust my intuition so much more. I am a person that Matthew is now proud to say, "That is my Mom and I am so proud of what she has done with her heartache."

Helpful coping methods…

For me it was just working through, going through all of the feelings head on. So much soul searching. I also journaled, which worked very well for me. Yoga has also been a great help to me.

Advice or words of wisdom…

For me it was going through the pain head on. You cannot run or hide behind work or anything else, it will come back. Just know the pain will always be there, it will soften but never go away. I do feel it is very important to seek out support groups. It is a safe place to be with others on the same ship.

Marie Dudek

Age: 49

Current Occupation: Marketing/Operations Manager

Marie's daughter, Natalie, hung herself on June 13, 2003 at age 22.

In her words...

I was raised in a two-parent family, with four children. There is a 17-year age difference between oldest girl, 13-year age difference with next girl and me and a 9-year age difference between me and my brother. I don't remember my oldest sister living at home, the next sister I remember living at nursing school and she would come home for weekends. We had a lot of family in the Chicago area and would spend time with them every couple of weeks. When I was 17, my father died of a heart attack. When I was 18, I left home and did not have much contact with anyone for about eight years. My son was born when I was 24. My daughter born when I was 25. Natalie was a premie, born at seven months. Natalie's brother is 15 months older than Natalie. When they were growing up, they were often thought to be twins.

I was a single mother with two children. The children's father was born in Belize, and had been in the United States for over ten years when I met him. We were together for eight years, with the children coming along near the end of the relationship.

When the children were one and two, we left their father and came to live with my mother, a widow, in the house I grew up in. I left the relationship with their father due to physical and emotional abuse. I did not want my children growing up in an unstable atmosphere. Because we were living with my mom, I was able to give my children more opportunities than if I was living on my own. The children's father died when they were 10 and 11 years old. They saw him on an inconsistent basis when he wanted to see them. We did not have close family in Chicago anymore. They were spread out around the country. We did have my mother's sister nearby, and we did many things with her.

My son had been away at college for four years and had moved to Florida about 15 months prior to Natalie's death. Natalie had been attending the School of Visual Arts in New York for two and a half years. She was studying photography. She was home for 18 months before her death.

Natalie and I had a very close relationship. We were described as two peas in a pod. She shared some of her pain with me, but was worried she

25

was a burden to me. We did have a few talks about her suicidal thoughts and she said she had a plan, but would not tell me about that.

The suicide...

It was horrendous. I found Natalie in the garage at about 8 pm. I had talked to her around 4pm on the phone. She told me she was at home. I had thought we were going to meet up and go to the aquarium, but when I talked to her, she told me she missed her interview and never did get downtown. I could hear that she was crying, and I thought that was a good thing, because she did not cry much and I thought she would get some relief by crying. I called her at 6pm, but there was no answer. That was not unusual so I didn't think anything more about it. I was backing into the garage when I saw her. I screamed and ran over to her hoping she was alive. My neighbor heard me and ran over. He called the police and then got a knife to cut her down. I held her and held her, stroking her hair as I cried and cried.

The police came and told me my mother was in the house wondering what was going on. They said they told my mother that something happened in the garage. I could see my mother though the garage window, but knew she wasn't able to see into the garage. I called my therapist and she came over right away. The police allowed me a good amount of time with Natalie. I overheard on one of their radios that there was another suicide in the area. It made me wonder if there was a full moon. When I walked out of the garage to meet my therapist, I looked up and saw that it was a full moon. And it was Friday, the 13th. My therapist asked me if I wanted to pray. I looked up for awhile and finally said no. After awhile, the police told me I needed to leave the garage until the detectives arrived. I went into the house to tell my mother and some friends that heard the call over the police radio. At some point, I was calm and realized that there was no way I could change this. I hated it, but there was nothing I could do about it. I went in and out of the garage many times that night. Her boyfriend came into the garage and spent time with me there. We cut two of Natalie's dreads. He was in the garage for some time alone. I could not look at her neck. I recalled that two weeks prior, while cleaning the garage, we came across the rope and our eyes met and held for a few seconds.

Natalie told me twice that she was having suicidal thoughts. She was hospitalized both times. I told her I didn't think she would tell me if she was having these thoughts again. She promised she would tell me. Someplace deep inside of me I knew Natalie would complete suicide. I was so afraid of receiving a call telling me that Natalie was dead, or coming home and finding her in her bed, or the bathroom. I never considered the garage or for her to die by hanging. That day was one day that I did not have any thought of her completing suicide.

I think of Natalie as a diamond with many facets. No one facet caused the suicide, it was a combination of nature and nurture, her own individual life experiences and her thought processes.

I told others that she took her own life. That her pain was too much. Many people were aware of her depression. Natalie shared her struggles with some of her friends. I shared them with other family members. People shared love, care, concern, and support. I was amazed at the number of people's lives Natalie had touched in her 22 years.

The authorities treated me very well. They were very comforting and concerned.

The bereavement process…

I was not able to pray that night, but on Sunday morning, I went to church. I wanted to go. I sat in the Mother's room, which was empty at the 8 am mass and allowed me space to cry. I spent time with family and Natalie's friends on the porch of our home. My son was home at 7am the next morning. I spent time with him and he helped me make funeral arrangements. My siblings all came to Chicago as soon as they could. Afterwards, I spent some time at their homes in Memphis and Ft. Lauderdale. I went back to work about two weeks afterwards and was able to work as much as I could. Some days it was a few hours, and other days it was longer.

I felt an intense emptiness in my heart. I made the effort to take good care of myself. I went to the YMCA and walked or rode at an easy pace for at least 20 minutes five days a week. I was in a store and knocked over a CD. I picked it up and it was called "Moving through Trauma." I bought it. It's a Feldenkrais CD and I found the individual that made the recording held group sessions in Evanston. I participated in those weekly. I went for a massage once a month. I continued going to my therapist and I talked as much as I needed to.

I found counseling extremely helpful. I went to the Loving Outreach for Survivors of Suicide (LOSS) support group offered through Catholic Charities in Chicago. I first attended one of their monthly meetings, which is an open meeting. This was just one month after Natalie's death. My mom and aunt attended with me. They offered 10-session groups where the same individuals met for eight weeks in a row, and then once a month for two months. I participated in two of those sessions, the first starting in late August. Now in Florida, I am participating in Left Behind After Suicide (LBAS) offered through Hospice of the Comforter in Orlando. We meet twice a month as an open meeting. I continue working with my therapist, now over the phone bi-monthly.

I accept Natalie's death and find some days I can speak about it without tears. There are other days that tears flow quickly. I let them flow. I continue with a support group as well as continuing on in discovering and exploring my own journey.

I believe I came to terms with the death in the garage on that night. I had to accept she was dead because there was nothing I could do to change that fact. I know I did everything I could to be the best mother I could be for my daughter. At one point, she told me that. There are days when I think back and wonder what if, and I let the tears come. I know she did everything she was capable of and so did I. There is no blame. We both are responsible for our actions; tragically, one action of hers is irreversible.

I miss my daughter immensely. I will love her for eternity, just as she will love me. We remain connected to each other.

Dreams and unusual occurrences...

I had a dream of Natalie's face; she was smiling at me with tears streaming down her face. There were beautiful red roses falling towards me. Another time I had a dream of Natalie dressed in a short white toga outfit with gold trim. We were all in a lounge and they were going to have women's wrestling. The current champ was a petite blonde. Natalie volunteered to take her on...then I woke up.

Once while driving to work in the morning, I was thinking about a conversation my son and I had about Natalie the night before. I was crying as it was a very deep conversation and his love for both Natalie and me was so very evident. As I was getting on the crowded expressway, I looked at the car in front of me and saw the license plate was "NATLEE." I felt her presence so near to me that I was laughing and crying at the same time.

I recently returned to Chicago for my mother's funeral. I was out for a walk on a hot morning near the hotel and a man came up to me asking if I could help him. He was a large man dressed in a white tee shirt and had a white head covering on that looked as though he was in the desert. He proceeded to tell me his dilemma and how he needed a few dollars to take the L train. I had just purchased a bottle of water and had a couple of dollars in my hand, so I opened my hand and said this must have been meant for him. He smiled and was grateful. We continued walking along and he told me of his mother and how her Alzheimer's was getting worse and how he wanted to care for her. I listened quietly as I had just gone through the death of my 92-year old mother. As we turned the corner, he started singing the Intruders song, "I'll always love my mama, she's my favorite girl." Tears started streaming down my face and he wasn't sure what was going on. I shared with him that I had lost my daughter two years ago and that I was amazed of all the songs he could sing, he chose that one. We hugged each other and continued walking along arm in arm and talking. When I returned to the hotel, I realized this man was actually dressed in all white and I believe Natalie sent me a message through the song he sang. I laughed and cried again all at the same time, feeling such joy in receiving a message from Natalie.

Have you ever considered taking your own life?

I have thought of it through the years. I have not planned it out. Once I remember being in the passenger seat of my car with my son driving on the expressway. We were having a terrible argument. I thought of opening my door and falling out. I thought that the seat belt was in my way, holding me in. I have wondered if the seat belt wasn't there if I would have actually opened the door.

Significance of the suicide...

It has brought my understanding of the preciousness of life to a whole new level. I am living in the present, making the choice to continue on in my journey knowing my beautiful daughter remains a part of me. Natalie's photographs have been displayed several times in an exhibit a few of her friends and I created called "Not Unnoticed" to honor Natalie's 24th birthday. Since then, we have had an exhibit with 11 other artists' work (all completed suicide) in Chicago and are planning another exhibit in Florida. I want to continue creating this display for others to participate in to help in their healing process. This art is the gift our loved ones left for the world to see. See http://www.notunnoticed.com.

Helpful coping methods...

I had been participating in some personal growth workshops for about eight months prior to Natalie's death. I experienced an amazing understanding of community and their love, care and support because of doing this work prior to Natalie's death and afterwards...through the present.

Advice or words of wisdom...

Take it day-by-day, hour-by-hour or minute-by-minute...whatever it is you need to do to take good care of yourself. Join a support group, even if you don't want to talk. Listening helps, too. Know that you are not alone. Allow yourself to embrace your pain and work through it, pushing it aside will take care of the moment, but it still remains. The pain will always remain, but it will soften. Take time to recall some of the beautiful memories and fun times you had with your loved one. They are no longer physically here with you, but they remain forever in your heart.

Holly Hobbs

Age: 50

Current Occupation: Customer Service Coordinator

Holly's daughter, Stacy, completed suicide on July 18, 2005, six week prior to this interview. She died of carbon monoxide poisoning.

In her words...

    I had a very dysfunctional family growing up. My mother left when I was about four and my two older brothers and I were raised by my father. Then my mother's name was forbidden. Somewhere along the way I heard she died. She didn't die; in fact, she lived quite close to us for many years. When I was 26, she did finally die of alcoholism.

    My father was an ironworker and lived that lifestyle to the fullest. He was married eight times and there was always some unsavory type of woman around between his marriages. None were the motherly type. I grew up being the youngest and only girl, feeling a sense of shame for being different in my own family. My father was also an alcoholic and we moved a lot, following his work (dams and bridges). I probably attended a new school or two a year until my sophomore year in high school. From that year until I graduated, I got to stay in the same town and go to the same school. I had a tremendous sense of isolation growing up, feeling different because I didn't have a mother or any acceptable substitute. My lack of a decent role model actually made me who I am today. I knew very early on what I didn't want to be like.

    I was a single parent for over twenty years. My son, Jason, was ten and Stacy, only four, when I divorced. From that time, until about four years ago when I remarried, it was always just the three of us. We were close. Jason and Stacy fought like most brothers and sisters do, but Jason always looked after his little sister. He took on more responsibility than he should have back then, and most of it centered around Stacy. She was a social butterfly until about the fifth grade and ours was always the house the other kids came to. There weren't many weekends that didn't include a sleepover, and there were always giggling girls around. The phone was constantly ringing and it was always for Stacy. Somewhere, sometime, that all changed and Stacy became more surly and withdrawn. At around 12, she became so rebellious that she refused to go to school and when I put my foot down, she ran away. At 14, she came back home to live. During this time, the stress was barely manageable. Jason spent several years harboring resentment at Stacy for causing such turmoil for us and worry for me. I still feel guilty for

31

not giving Jason the time and attention he deserved because I was busy dealing with Stacy.

Stacy was a very sweet and loving young woman. Although she was what I called a high maintenance child, she could be very giving. She loved animals and seeing old people alone made her cry. In all the chaos and turmoil of her preteen and teen years, she never treated me with any disrespect. Even when she ran away from home and I didn't know where she was going or how she'd end up, she always hugged and kissed me goodbye. Our parting words were always "I love you". We never argued. I never heard her utter a curse word in my presence. It was also very frustrating because she was so stubborn and never listened or took advice from me or anyone else. My litany was "I don't know whether to hug her or slap her!" I was present when she gave birth to both of her children and spent a good deal of time with her the last several years of her life. Our relationship was always close, always loving.

The suicide…

I listened to several voicemails when I got home from work, each one more frantic. The last one was from her fiancé, saying she was gone.

I was alone. My husband was about 100 miles away fishing. I knew by the tone of the first couple of messages that something was terribly wrong. The school called saying nobody picked Bailey up from kindergarten. When I got to the last message and heard the words, "She's gone." My whole body got still and I could have heard a pin drop. I physically felt and heard a whoosh in my chest. The next thing I knew, I was on the floor yelling "no", shaking so badly I couldn't dial the phone. I felt like I was going to throw up. I managed to get up and I just walked in circles doubled over in pain until Jason got there.

Hindsight can haunt you. Initially, I told people that we had no clue and didn't see it coming. Now that I've had time to look back, I wonder why I was surprised. And that's where a great deal of my guilt comes from. If I'd have only done this, said that, etc., etc., ad nauseam. When Stacy was in fifth grade, a female student at the school died from a brain tumor. From that point on, she thought she had it all: cancer, tumors, AIDS, ulcers, you name it. I spent a lot of time and money making sure she didn't have all the things she thought she had. At around fifteen, she developed debilitating anxiety and was borderline agoraphobic. She put up black curtains and spent all of her time in her bedroom. When I found out she was cutting herself, I took her to counselors and psychiatrists for that, too. At eighteen she announced that she wanted to have a baby. When I pressed, she said it would give her a reason to live. I immediately put her in the psych ward of the nearest hospital. She and her boyfriend did have a baby and life was great until they broke up about a year later. She got very down and dabbled in drugs for a while until she met her fiancé, James. The four years they were together were the happiest I'd ever seen her. Somewhere along the way, though, she got into online gambling. The last month of her life, her gambling had gotten so bad that James moved out, hoping it would force her to get help. She spiraled downward very quickly. I saw her at her daughter's second birthday party the day before she died and there was nothing in her demeanor to give away what she was thinking. I thought she'd made an appointment to see someone at a mental health clinic about her gambling. She told me her appointment was August 1 but she called another clinic to see if they could see her sooner. She was waiting to hear back from them when she killed herself.

I believe Stacy's pain was greater than the love she felt for those of us she left behind.

After a lot of internal debating, I decided to others the truth about Stacy's death. Many of my coworkers avoided getting near me. Ninety-nine percent of people didn't know what to say to me and were visibly uncomfortable.

The male policeman at Stacy's apartment was very compassionate and warm. His female partner was the opposite, cold and aloof. The medical examiner was very nice and took time to answer my many questions.

The bereavement process...

So far, I've just put one foot in front of the other, one day at a time. I took time off work (my return being open-ended) and saw my primary doctor. I have read several books on suicide and suicide survivors. I attend survivors of suicide support meetings and have an appointment to see a counselor. I spend a great deal of time with both of my grandkids. I looked at several cemeteries and finally found the place where I want to put Stacy to rest. I'm shopping now for a headstone. I can't be at rest a lot of the time so even though I'm going in circles, I'm busy. The rest of the time I'm a lump of clay, mindless and immobile.

I feel sick to my stomach most of the time. I'm so restless I can't sit still. Other times, I'm running through molasses, numb. I have times of feeling like life is overwhelmingly surreal, like looking into a pond where you just dropped a rock. The ripples distort everything. All of it is punctuated by periods of deep agony so hard to bear I want to jump out of my skin. I was so out of touch with everything, including my body, the first few weeks, I couldn't feel my bladder. I wet the bed one night. I feel a lot of anxiety, too. My sleep pattern is totally gone and I probably average about four hours sleep a night. I can't concentrate and I'm powerless over the thoughts and images that pop into my head. I've lost count of the times I thought I might be going crazy.

I don't know that I'll ever come to terms with the loss. I spent twenty-six years with two children, my youngest, my only daughter. How or when can I come to terms with now having one child, my son? I'm a recovering alcoholic and have been on antidepressants for years. Did I genetically doom my daughter?

My best friend of several years told me the other day how she envied my relationships with my children. She went on about what a good mother I'd been, even citing specific times and conversations. All I could think was, if I'm such a good mother, why is my daughter dead?

Do I believe I'll eventually come to terms with the loss? Yes, I believe I'll get there. I'm a survivor; I don't know how to do it any other way.

I have an appointment tomorrow with a psychiatrist. I'm seeing him because I believe the only way to get past it is to go through it and I'm leaning into it as I go. He was referred to me by my primary care doctor and I didn't have the capacity to shop around.

I love Stacy and I miss her. But, O, for the touch of a vanished hand and the sound of a voice that is still.

Have you ever considered taking your own life?

I've had those thoughts once or twice in my life but never was it an option.

Significance of the suicide...

My life as I knew it is over. And then there were two. Am I the mother to two children? Or one? My dream of being the mother I never had to my daughter is gone. I have two grandchildren who have no mother and the best I can hope for is to be a less than perfect substitute. The photo albums no longer depict my life as it is today.

Helpful coping methods...

Talking about Stacy, her life, her death and everything in between brings the only real relief. Focusing on her children and their needs has been effective in easing my pain.

Advice or words of wisdom...

Seek out others who've experienced this kind of loss. Talk about your loved one, their life and their death until you can't talk anymore.

"Frannie"

Age: 52

Current Occupation: Retired Sales Manager

Frannie's son shot himself in the head with a gun six years and nine months prior to this interview.

In her words…

I was married (one time) for seven years to my children's father. Once divorced, their father had nothing to do with any of us—there is no contact from him still. The boys grew up in a single-parent household. They were very involved in all sports, had lots of friends, and were very popular. Both boys delivered newspapers for extra money. We took family vacations every year with their grandparents and aunt, uncle and cousin. The boys had chores around the house.

I was very close to my son until he went into high school where he started to rebel. He stopped playing sports and then his grades dropped. In elementary and middle schools, he was in the accelerated programs, and always on the select teams. Academics and sports came very easy to him at a young age. Once he got into high school, he lost interest in participating, although he was still very popular and funny with his friends. We went through phases of getting along and not even being civil. I tried counseling but he would not participate.

The suicide…

My oldest boy was there. He witnessed the suicide. He called the police, then me. I knew it was my fault; my son and I had just had a fight about his lack of care for his grandmother. She was just diagnosed with stage four-lung cancer in October of that year. We all were taking turns taking care of her. They were very close.

My oldest son took his brother home to his house. I was in a panic. I kept asking God to let me take back what was said.

When we were going through the high school years I used to talk to my friends about worrying that my son was depressed. They would say he's just a teenager; it's a phase. I'd ask my oldest and he would tell me my youngest was fine, "You just aggravate him."

I always felt like I did something wrong, I should of pushed for an intervention of some kind. I think a mother always knows in her heart what is going on. I had doubts but let people talk me into thinking everything was okay.

The bereavement process...

I think the first two weeks it was like an out of body experience. I could watch myself going through the motions. I got good at faking it—if someone came over I'd pull myself together but in reality I didn't sleep, eat or get out of bed for months. I felt like someone blew a huge hole right through me—like just empty.

I refer to the two to three years after my son's death as "my crazy" years. I couldn't really go out in public. I felt everyone was either judging me or whispering to others behind my back. I really don't remember many details of those few years. I sought counseling; I went to two support groups Compassionate Friends and Survivors Group.

I told others the truth about the suicide. My friends would check on me ALL the time. I got to a point that I didn't answer the phone or the door.

The authorities treated me with kindness. I went to a Licensed Social Worker for one and a half to two years. I felt safe, not being judged. But I had to stop because I began to think I was using it for a crutch. I needed to get going with my life; I had another son, a wonderful partner who did everything for me. I needed to stand up for myself. It was time. I didn't like the idea that I was on medication. Anti-depressants and something to allow me to sleep. I used to joke that I was in *The Valley of the Dolls*.

I don't really think I've come to terms with the loss—more like I have gotten use to it. I have had moments of happiness. I can think clearer now and participate in life. I just started going to the food store—my new attitude is I don't care what anyone thinks.

How do I feel about my son today? Some days I'm angry, most of the time I miss him and feel empty.

Dreams and unusual occurrences...

For a long time I would dream that my son was calling out for me and I couldn't find him. I could hear him but couldn't see him. Occasionally, I have the same dream.

Have you ever considered taking your own life?

My mother died two weeks after my son. It was about two months after my mother passed. I was trying to clean out her house I pulled into her garage and was working in the kitchen; I could hear a car running. I opened the door in the kitchen to the garage and it was my car. I had a remote starter and I had to hit it in order for it to start. But I thought it was a sign for me to get into my car and just end the pain. For a few minutes, I really wanted to be done with it all. But I didn't want to do that to my oldest son.

The significance of the suicide...

I don't take anything for granted. I don't do anything I don't want to and have a lot more understanding of difficulties in people's lives.

Helpful coping methods...

If someone is opposed to counseling, they should get in touch with a chapter of Compassionate Friends and/or find a Survivors Group in their area!

Advice or words of wisdom...

The one thing I learned is there is no timeline in grieving. What you are feeling is okay. Do not try to be at a certain point in the process by a certain date/year. Let people help, you probably need it.

Nancy Laird

Age: 61

Current Occupation: Retired

Nancy's daughter completed suicide on July 21, 2001. She shot herself. She was 28.

In her words...

I have two daughters, two sons, two ex-husbands and am currently married. I was a single parent a good bit of the time and worked. I got no child support, so money was tight. After getting married the third time, it got easier. The house was full of kids and their friends.

My daughter, Kassandra, and I had a relationship, which was stormy sometimes—not as close as I would have liked.

The suicide...

I was taken to the emergency room and told there had been an accident. I was then told there about the suicide. When I found out, it was devastating, horrible, and sad.

My daughter had threatened it several times, even telling me how she would do it. She had been diagnosed bipolar five years earlier.

I tell others that she died of suicide. They have been loving and sympathetic. The medical personnel treated me with compassion.

The bereavement process...

Tears and talking. I have had chest pains, panic attacks, depression and sleepless nights. Most of the time, I believe I have come to terms with the loss. It happened in the second year after the shock had worn off. I went to a few sessions of counseling and it was helpful. I love my daughter and miss her.

Dreams and unusual occurrences...

After weeks of nightmares and no sleep, I cried out to God for just one good night sleep. That night I dreamt of my daughter and a Jesus-like man walking down a path in a field. They were walking away from me and they were talking. She kept leaning toward him and laughing. That was the end of the nightmares. Another time, I woke up and saw her sitting in a chair watching me sleep. I asked her why she had to leave me and I heard her say, "You know why and now I am happy."

Significance of the suicide…

I have been active in suicide awareness prevention.

Helpful coping methods…

Internet support groups. I built a memorial website and my faith in God.

Have you ever considered taking your own life?

No.

Advice or words of wisdom…

Search out others who have lost someone, who has lost a loved one to suicide. A loss to suicide is so different from any other loss. Only someone who has suffered a loss to suicide can truly understand your loss.

Write in a journal.

Write poetry.

Don't dwell on the "why."

Don't beat yourself up with "if onlys."

Grief is a personal thing. Each of us does it at a different pace. Don't let anyone tell you when you should be "over it."

"Georgia"

Age: 55

Current Occupation: Teacher

Georgia's son completed suicide on July 31, 2003. He shot himself with a 12-gauge shotgun. He was 33.

In her words…

I was born in 1949 and raised in a small town—the same town I live in now, in fact, the same house. My husband and I bought my parents house and remodeled it. My dad was a logger; my mom was a stay-at-home mom. I have two brothers who live close by and who I am close to. My dad worked hard and had an average lifestyle. I was very close to my dad. He loved his grandkids—he adored them. I'm not too close to my mom but we have a regular, cordial relationship. I do not talk to her about Jeff's suicide and my feelings. She does not deal well with tragedies. I also don't feel comfortable with her. My dad died in 1995.

I was married in 1968 to my sons' dad. We divorced when my sons were almost six and almost two. They never saw their father again when he returned to his home state, New York. I remarried my present husband. He raised my sons. We also have a daughter, who is 26. We are a close family and have a close extended family. I was an at-home mom and always there for my kids—very involved in their activities. I went back to school when my daughter was 6. I got my teaching degree. My husband was not home often. He worked long hours in his logging-construction business. I was the main adult in their lives and my parents were a big part of the kids' lives.

I feel my relationship with my son was very good. I feel good about my relationship with all three of my kids. Of course, my son was an adult, a husband and a father, at the time of his suicide. He lived close by. We saw him and his family often. We'd talk on the phone. But I also know my son was not one to openly talk about his problems or emotions. My children were close and got along very well, especially the brothers.

The suicide…

I got a phone call from my son's boss early in the morning. He drove a dump truck. He was very dependable—never missed work and loved his job. My son's boss is also a friend of my husband's—they have done road building and logging jobs together. My son worked for his dad, too. My son's boss drove out to his house when he didn't show up for work or an-swer his phone. He called us concerned as he was on my son's front porch and no one answered the door. He could hear music and he said the music was loud enough that he could hear the tune and words. He said it was a sad song. (It turned out to be "Indian Summer" by The Doors.) We played that song at his memorial and I have since gotten a tattoo that says Indian Summer. My son's boss said the house was locked and asked if we knew where a key was. My husband answered the phone and I listened to the one sided conversation. I knew something was wrong. My first thought was that he was passed out and had possibly drank too much the night before since I knew he was troubled over his marriage. So I called his wife, who was staying at her mom's with their two sons. She was really concerned—she told us to tell my son's boss to slide open a window. She wanted me to call her back immediately. My husband called my son's boss using his cell phone and told him to go through the window. He soon called us back and I knew then just how serious it was. I have never seen my husband look like he did or had I ever heard his voice sound as terrified as he sounded. It is very difficult to explain the feeling I felt. It was like it wasn't real. We drove immediately to the house and my husband called 911 so all the authorities were there when we arrived.

The suicide was a complete shock. I knew my son was upset over his failing marriage and knew he had some problems with drinking but it did not seem any different than the many troubled marriages in today's society.

Why did he take his life? I believe it was a combination of misfortunate events. He should never have been alone and he made an impromptu, permanent decision. A failed marriage—I believe his wife told him that day she was not coming back—weeks of little sleep, long work hours starting at 4am and drinking several beers after not drinking for weeks. He was also probably battling alcoholism—listening to a sad song over and over. It all added up to feeling helpless and hopeless.

The bereavement process…

It felt unreal—like it wasn't happening. I was in total shock. I was going through all these emotions, doing what was needed, but it felt so surreal. But I remember every detail. I remember crying so hard and then recovering. Calling my other son was so very difficult. He told his sister and my mother.

When my husband and I arrived home our house was full of family members. There was so much pain involved just to walk into the house and see my daughter and son. I will never forget that painful look on their faces. To this day, I don't know how I made it through that day. All in one day, we got the news that changed our lives forever. That same day we were making arrangements for a memorial service and writing an obituary. I have come to realize that a person can do what he or she must do to survive. I think I had some internal defense mechanism that took over so I could do what I had to do. I think to this day that internal mechanism still takes over. But I have some real bad, rough days. I use a "road" analogy. I am on this road called "grief". The road will have many ups and downs—turns—but as long as I am traveling in the right directions I'll be okay. But the road will also never end.

I'm still very much in my bereavement days—months. Immediately after I just overwhelmed myself with books—finding support groups— making calls—using the Internet. I had to keep going to Jeff's house— walking through the house—going into the bathroom where he shot himself and just standing. Going into his workshop—always at the cemetery— looking at pictures—continually immersing myself with him. It is almost as if I overdosed on it. I had my grandsons. They would talk about their daddy. I worked so hard at keeping myself strong (I continue to do so). I continue to attend a suicide support group. I have attended two national suicide conferences and am sure I will attend many more. I went to a psychic and spiritual healer.

I have felt dull pressure on my chest/heart area. I never knew what real sadness felt like until now. I get agitated and work hard to make myself maintain control. I tried Paxil but went off of it. I wasn't for me. Keeping busy and work help. But there hasn't been a day gone by that I wasn't thinking of Jeff—the suicide—the past—the great memories. Some days the thoughts are much more—some days just briefly—but for sure every day I am with him somehow.

I told others the truth about the suicide—I just did not elaborate in the details—only with those very close to me.

Persons close to me were very compassionate and willing to talk. They continue to be so. Casual friends and colleagues sent cards and attended the memorial service but then it just ended. But I may be part of that response. I think I give the message that I want to be left alone and in a way that may be true. If I don't know a person well, or if I feel out of my comfort zone, then I don't want their sympathy or to talk about it. Maybe that will change when I get further in my grief and more time goes by. There are some relatives who avoid talking about it but I'm sure it is because they just don't know what to say and they don't want to bring me pain.

Police, medical personnel and other professionals were extremely kind and compassionate. I tried a counselor I believe too soon after the suicide. It did not go well. I waited and used support groups and a grief support group. Then about a year and a half after the suicide I again tried a counselor and felt more comfortable and liked her. I have felt good about it and continue with it. I went to a counselor because I felt the need to talk to someone unattached to me and the suicide. I felt the need to talk to someone unattached about how my husband is dealing with his grief because we are dealing with it completely the opposite. It has been a struggle and we have had some difficult times. My husband has had anger outbursts (none physical or violent) but very much anger from pain and frustration.

Today, I feel extreme overwhelming sadness and sorrow about my son but I have never felt anger.

Dreams and unusual occurrences...

I have had quite a few dreams but will only elaborate on a couple. I would end up writing a book if I wrote about all of them. My counselor and I have talked about them and she helps me to try and reason out why.

I had a dream in which I heard a loud bang thinking someone was lighting fireworks. I quickly saw myself standing in my son's yard when I heard him fire the gun.

I had another dream in which I took a motorcycle for my son to a local spot and left it there so he would have a way home when he came back. But I realized I forgot to leave the key (or I hid the key and didn't leave him a note to tell him where the key was). So, I was panicking because he wouldn't be able to get home.

Have you ever considered taking your own life?

NO.

Significance of the suicide...

My life will never be the same.

Helpful coping methods...

Support groups, national suicide conference, American Foundation for Suicide Prevention Northwest (AFSPNW), Survivors of Suicide (SOS), the Internet, close friends and family.

Helpful advice or words of wisdom...

You are not alone. Seek help. Reach out. It's not your fault. Don't carry the blame.

I got a tattoo in memory of my son. I wear a necklace (heart-shaped) with two pictures inside, one of him as a child and one of him as an adult.

I have a mini-purse filled with pictures, the quotes (or sayings) that help me and other miscellaneous items that I keep in my purse so I have it with me always.

I have many songs I listen to that remind me of my son—how he may have felt, etc. I need to connect to him. I visit the cemetery often. I left a box of pictures at the cemetery. I keep a journal and I write to him like he can read it. I have a corner in a spare bedroom that I made for my son with pictures, memories, etc.

I receive a monthly newsletter from a local suicide support group. I attend meetings when I can.

I physically work out every day. I've always worked out on a daily basis and found since Jeff's suicide that the workouts and jogs on the beach are a way to help me deal with my grief.

Cathy Gettle

Age: 50

Occupation: Housewife

Cathy's son, Jon, completed suicide on April 16, 2002, at 14. He hung himself.

In her words...

My family consists of my husband Mike, my daughter Jenn, my in-laws Jess and Olga, my parents James and Marjorie, two brothers and their wives, five nieces and one nephew, plus lots of cousins, aunts and uncles.

When I was growing up, we lived in a small community where everyone knew everyone and knew what he or she was doing. My parents were devoted Christians and we attended the local Baptist church every time the doors were open. My parents were also both teachers, so I couldn't get in trouble at school without them knowing about it. I grew up in era where personal computers were non-existent and it was nothing for me to ride my bicycle to the local store a mile away and my parents not have to worry about me being attacked. I went to a small college in Alabama (University of Montevallo) and after graduation, got a job with a bank in Birmingham, Alabama. That is where I met my husband, Mike.

I had a loving relationship with my son, Jon. I always made sure that I was available to take him to his activities, if he couldn't ride his bike there. He was always ready to give a hug or ask if he could help with some chore.

The suicide...

On April 16, 2002, our son, Jon was supposed to go to school early for a jazz band practice and was supposed to furnish donuts for the students in jazz band. When I realized that he wasn't at home and the donuts were there, I decided to walk to the school to deliver the donuts. That's when I found him hanging from a beam leading from the school.

When I realized that it was Jon hanging, I started screaming and was attempting to undo the rope. One of the students came around the corner to help lift him up to take off the pressure, but to no avail. Then a couple of neighbors came and we were able to get him down. But, when I first saw Jon, I knew without a doubt that it was too late to save him because of his color and the marks on his neck and the body fluids dripping from his nose.

We had no idea that Jon was considering suicide. The school was in shock as well. All of the warning signs (change in clothes, friends, grades, loner, etc.) were not there. He had tried to change his clothing style, but we wouldn't let him. His friends had changed because we had just moved to a new community. His grades changed because of the different grading scales. He always had a bunch of friends around him at lunch and seemed happy. As we look back on it, the clues that we missed were: (1) he had started being aggressive toward our dog; (2) he was possibly not wanting to do swimming, scouts or band; (3) his sleep habits had changed and he seemed tired a good bit before his death.

The circumstances surrounding Jon's death (hanging himself at his school; leaving a note that said bullying was a problem and depression was a problem) caused the local media to have full rights to publish it as a suicide. It was no secret.

The community really reached out to us after Jon's death. Between the visitation and the funeral, there were about 1,000 people in attendance. In the months and years that followed his death, we had several people do things for us and in memory of Jon, and that actually was a little over-whelming.

The police, medical personnel and/or other professionals treated us very well. The coroner and I kept up contact for a couple of years afterward and he also would let me know on the sly if a certain person had died of suicide or not. They handled the entire situation in a very professional manner and began the investigations immediately and did not wait 24 or 48 hours to do so.

The bereavement process…

Each family member has handled the bereavement process differently. I personally began relying on God to get me through each day. I realized that I could not bring Jon back, but life did go on and I needed to do so as well. By August, I had written a speech titled "Teasing, Bullying, & Teen Suicide" and contacted the local schools to give my speech. Some schools only allowed me to talk to the school boards, while others allowed me to talk with the students. I turned my bad situation around to try to make something positive out of it.

I personally only went to one counseling session and that was more for my marriage than anything. My husband still requires some counseling sessions because of depression that overwhelms him at times. On several occasions, I attended the session with my husband, because I knew that he would go into the doctor's office and tell her that he was doing okay and to cut back on his medication. But I knew things were not okay enough for him to be taken off of the antidepressant. My husband went to a psychologist who could prescribe medications. I think for my husband that the counseling did help him, because it wasn't me telling him that things weren't so bad and that he would survive. I did not choose to seek counseling because of my faith in God and that He was in control of everything.

I was extremely sad that my son died and that he had not felt comfortable in telling us that he was having problems, either physical or emotional. Since I have a very strong faith in God, I had to turn everything over to Him. At the visitation and the funeral, I made it a point to hug each teenager and tell him or her not to let anyone or anything bother them.

I have come to terms with our loss, because I have been able to make something positive out of this situation by talking about why my son decided to die rather than live. I actually believe that I came to terms with the loss very quickly—within six months of his death. (That is when I had my speech written and went into the schools.)

I still miss my son and so often I see him in another person. That person will have some trait (such as a haircut, glasses, walk or body language) that is just like my son. I believe without a doubt that he is in heaven. The signs have been too many for us to deny otherwise. I know that he is at peace, which in turn makes me feel at peace.

Dreams and unusual occurrences…

I did not have any dreams before the suicide and it took a while following the suicide for me to have any. My daughter and my husband both had dreams immediately after Jon's death letting them know he was okay. One dream that I did have was that we had caught Jon in time and I asked him if he was glad that we had and he emphatically said no, he wasn't glad.

Significance of the suicide…

My son's suicide has made me direct my focus on suicide prevention and to emphasize that it is okay to ask for help when you need it.

Helpful coping methods…

My method of coping consisted of daily prayers and just accepting things with a positive attitude. I would like to share through my own book things about my speech, about Jon's life, about things that we didn't know and things we now know.

"Tammy"

Age: 46

Current Occupation: Transportation/supply clerk for mental health facility

Tammy's son completed suicide on November 13, 2002, at age 21. He hung himself.

In her words...

I was raised in a large family of six kids. My dad was a marine and we moved four or five times before I was eight. I was a middle child. I would consider us a dysfunctional family. My father was an alcoholic and abusive. He died in 1985 at age 54. My parents divorced when I was 15. We were poor.

I moved out of my mom's house when I was 17. I married when I was 20 and had my son when I was 22. Josh was born with clubfoot and had to have casts on his foot monthly to correct this. He also had to wear corrective shoes with the bars between his shoes. He absolutely hated wearing them. It was so restrictive. He would cry. I divorced his dad when I was about 24. I then married when I was 26 and had a daughter, Lindsay. Her father was an alcoholic and I divorced him in 1992. I guess I didn't break the chain of dysfunction.

I loved my kids but I felt tied down and did a lot of partying when I could. My mother babysat and I paid sitters for my freedom. The dads really weren't much help with the kids physically, mostly financially. I always worked. We always celebrated birthdays with parties. We had family cookouts and we got together on the holidays. My kids had friends over a lot to play with and spend the night. I went to school activities and as many school trips as I could with my children. My son failed kindergarten and was diagnosed with Attention Deficit Disorder in the second grade. School was a struggle for him but not because he wasn't smart.

My son went to live with his father in the 6th grade but hated his stepmother so he moved in with his dad's parents. In the 9th grade he moved back in with me but got in a little trouble at school. I thought it would be best if he lived with his grandparents because that school wasn't as academic as the one where I lived and I wanted him to graduate. He did graduate in 2001. I was so proud of him.

My son tried to join the army but couldn't because he had a rare allergy called Urticaria. He would get this terrible rash when he chilled or sweated. There is no known cause and he took Allegra for the symptoms.

While growing up, my son also developed Vitiligo, a disease in which one doesn't have pigment. His eyelids were white and he had white spots all over various parts of his skin. People always used to ask what it was. He had to wear t-shirts when he swam as it would sunburn easily. Kids made fun of him because of this affliction. They said things like he had eye makeup.

My son was a very good-looking man. He was six feet tall. He didn't have any self esteem though. I remained close to my son with phone calls and visits. He only lived 12 miles away. My son always had problems with lying. I don't think he thought he was lying. It used to really irritate me. We had some family therapy through the years. The first I was aware of the seriousness of how deep Josh's problems were was when he was 19 and had broken up with his girlfriend. He called a suicide hotline and told them he took pills and drank booze. The ambulance and police went to his grandparents and took him to the hospital. He wasn't admitted but he sought counseling. Then in August 2002, after another break-up, he took over-the-counter sleeping pills and beer. His grandfather found him. He could've died but he made it and his dad and I had him sent to a mental hospital for 72 hours. I was scared to death. I wanted my son to live. I wanted him to want to live. I found out that when he was younger he took rope to his grandfather's barn and threatened to kill himself a few times. No one ever told me that. I don't know why I wasn't told.

I was always a worrywart about everything and I think I passed that on to him. I wanted my son to be responsible and maybe I pressured him too much with my advice. He was a good kid but he had severe depression, which runs in my family. Bipolar disorder runs on his dad's side.

It wasn't the greatest situation for my son I am sure. We all loved him. I would definitely change things knowing what the outcome would be. My son had a lot of resentment for his dad. His dad could've been in his life more over the years but he let his wife run the show basically. I don't blame his dad because I know I made major mistakes where my son is concerned. I feel badly that he never had the normal childhood he wanted with his mom and dad together. I feel I failed him as a parent and it hurts terribly.

My son and I loved each other but we didn't see eye to eye. He told me what I wanted to hear whether true or not so he wouldn't have to listen to my nagging. I didn't mean to nag. I felt I was always looking out for him. I worried about him all the time. I don't think anyone but me really knew my son, the one who made up far-fetched stories even at a young age. His grandparents couldn't see it and his father never dealt with it. I didn't deal with it enough perhaps.

The suicide…

My son seemed to be doing okay and then in Nov. 2002, he signed a lease with some minors for an apartment. I told him to wait until he was in better financial shape but he already signed the lease and said it was time for him to be on his own so I turned supportive. He moved in the first Friday of November. I had warned him not to buy booze for his younger friends. On Saturday night he bought beer and had friends over, none of which were 21. An irate mother of one of the visitors came over and raised holy hell with my son about a truck her son had there. Her boy wasn't there at this time. My son told her he wasn't there and she could take the truck. She kept on with her tirade and my son told her to get off his property or he would call the police. She jumped my son when he turned to go in the house. My son was nothing but nice to her at first. She left and even though she denies it I am sure she called the police and said there was a drug party.

The police came and they all got arrested including my 15 year-old daughter, who was supposedly "helping them unpack." They went to city lock-up and I went to get my daughter who was released to me and went in to talk to the kids and told them they knew better than this. I also told them it wasn't the end of the world. When I got home I called the jail to tell them about my son's recent suicide attempt and they said they would call the county jail with that information. My son's dad bailed him out the next day. It was Sunday and the last day my son was ever in my house. He was leaning on the TV stand and he told me the jail had his information and was going to notify his counselor. I said good. I didn't tell him that I also called. He was rounding up money to get some of the girls out but never asked me to help.

The next day my son left his job at the trailer factory and went to court where they sentenced him to 60 days in jail. He didn't get a lawyer and I didn't go because he never asked me. He was okayed by the court to have work release but the jail screwed that up so he lost his job. I didn't know that until after his death. The jail never documented the phone call about his suicide risk. His intake information at the jail should have classified him as a risk but that was overlooked unbeknownst to me. I knew I would have to worry about him when he got out.

I went to visit him on the November 13, a Wednesday evening, with his dad and my daughter. I was first to talk to him. I told him I would help pay his rent or get him out of the lease if he liked. I told him I called the car place to get his car and fix it and that they had said they would work with him when he got out. I told him the girl who lived with him wanted to move because the other two boys weren't doing anything to help. She wasn't his girlfriend, just a friend. I told him the boy whose mother came over lost his job and moved out. My son was upset about the information I gave him but I tried to assure him I would help him. He wanted me to tell the other two boys to get a job by Monday or move out. I told him that might not be possible. I told him I would have them visit the next week so he could talk to them. My son told me he lost everything except his clothes. He didn't even have his guitar. My response was that he had money to buy the booze and he was mad at me for saying that. At the time I didn't know my son had told the boys to pawn all his stuff for money so they could buy food. I wondered how the boys were renting movies and other stuff. My son didn't have a lot of common sense about things.

My son didn't have commissary money so I had mailed him a money order on Monday and asked if he had received it yet and he said no. My daughter then talked to my son and then his dad. I saw a tear roll down my son's cheek and I tried to get his attention to see me point to my eye, my heart and to him, meaning I love you but he didn't see me. We left and went home.

My son called his grandparents after we left and was very upset. They tried to calm him down but eventually were disconnected. After that, inmate witnesses say my son tried to get help and was denied more than once. He was even threatened over the intercom to stop it or he would be put in lockdown.

I reviewed the jail tapes and my son went to his cell around 10:10pm and they found him after midnight. They weren't consistent with their hourly checks at all. My son had had a cellmate up until that evening. He was also located in a cell upstairs at the end where nobody ever walks by. He was in jail on a misdemeanor but put in the felony block. Everything the jail did was wrong. I thought he would be safe in the new state of the art jail. I just couldn't believe it was such a "Mickey Mouse" operation. They didn't document the welfare call. They didn't share his mental health information. They denied him access to get help when he reached out for help. I feel he would still be here today if not for their stupidity. No compassion. Nine days in jail, out of 29 to be served, and he hung himself. He was given all the tools to do it. So senseless.

He was severely depressed. I think he acted in the moment because he couldn't get the help he asked for so he felt helpless. I sometimes think he thought he would be found and saved, like he was before.

The bereavement…

At 4:27am on November 14, 2002, three sheriffs woke me up. I opened the door asked if there was a problem. I just knew without hearing it what had happened. I knew my son was dead.

I was in shock and disbelief. How could this happen? They had no answers for me but there would be a full investigation, I was assured. They kept asking me for phone numbers they could call and I finally let them call my boyfriend at his mom's. Then when he arrived they left. My boyfriend called my sisters and my daughter's father because I just couldn't tell her. She slept through my whole tirade. My one sister went to get my mom and tell her the news. My house was flooded with family and friends and coworkers but I was unresponsive to them. I just wanted to crawl in bed and stay there forever.

I felt shock, denial, and guilt. I was finally forced to accept he's gone forever from my life. I have anger towards the jail. I experienced Post-traumatic Stress Syndrome. I kept waking up with a jolt at 4:27am, believing I heard the doorbell and I would go look and nobody was there. It was so real.

Of course I knew it was a risk but I thought he would be safe in jail because they had his mental health information. I believed the real worry would be for us when got out. Had he been classified properly at the jail chances are he would be alive today. I blame them for not following their own policies, everyone of which I have read.

It was on the front page of the newspaper that day. The statement from the jail made it obvious to me they were nincompoops. They said it was tragic and he was not on suicide watch and there was no indication he was suicidal. DUH! That same day I also received the money order I had sent my son returned from the jail unopened. I just didn't understand that.

I received a letter from some woman who had lost two children in accidents. I thought it was kind of her to reach out to me, a complete stranger to help me through the most difficult time of my life. My friends, family and coworkers were very supportive. Support has tapered off over time. I can still reach out to Parents of Suicide (POS) and get support.

I felt the police were cold about my son's death. They were scared about getting sued I guess. They have to know they messed up even though they will never admit it. After they notify you about the death, that is it. They will never apologize because that would be admitting to wrongdoing. I guess they are right because I am suing them. I want answers but I have been told by my lawyer that isn't going to happen. The most we will ever get is a monetary settlement. Of course, you have to pay out the nose to sue. I don't care about money but our world is based on the almighty dollar. (That's another story in itself.)

I just live one day at a time. If not for my surviving daughter and grandchild I am not sure I would want to live. I think about my son every-day.

I saw an EAP counselor a few times. My daughter had counseling for a year. I went to a group called Mourning to Dancing once a week for eight weeks. It made me realize there are so many people hurting by losing their loved ones.

I don't think we ever come to terms with the loss. We are forced to live without them. We are helpless. Nothing we do or say will bring them back. Put on a happy face for the world while dying inside everyday.

I love and miss my son and I can't stand that I will never see him on earth in my lifetime. Never hold him again and tell him I love him. I will never see him get married or have kids. It is over, period, and it hurts badly.

I worried about him all the time. I wasn't the perfect parent; no one is. We all try to look out for our kids but sometimes what happens is just out of our control. If it was in my control, he would still be here. It's hard when you think a situation is safe and come to find out nothing was further from the truth. You can't change what happened though. You have to take one day at a time. On one hand where my son is concerned my life is over. On the other hand if I totally give up I could not bear the pain I know I would be placing on my surviving loved ones. So I choose to go on. It is hard. There are no black and white answers to losing a loved one by suicide. It's all a very gray area. I thank God I have a living daughter and granddaughter. When I see my grandchild smile at me my heart just bursts with joy. There are still blessings to be thankful for, even with the tragic loss of my son. He will always be with me and I can only hope we will reunite again someday.

Dreams and unusual occurrences...

A month or so after my son's death, I had a dream. A coworker (ac-quaintance) and I were walking around the high school and we got into a big elevator, which doesn't even exist, and sat on these bench seats. I looked to my right and there was my son right next to me. He said, "What ever happened, Mom, it's okay." Later I had a nightmare that he was mur-dered. He was in a bed sitting up with a rope around his neck but it was murder not suicide. I had another dream of being in a car and his grandpar-ents were in the car and police were involved and I can't remember the rest. That's the only three dreams I can remember about him.

Have you ever considered taking your own life?

I live for my daughter and grandchild. If they weren't here I honestly don't think I would want to live.

Significance of the suicide...

He's not here. I can rarely think of the good times because of the devastating way he left. My life is not whole.

Helpful coping methods...

I joined an Internet group called Parents of Suicide (POS). That helped me. I also became the Memory Tree coordinator for Indiana. I helped raise money for a book our POS group is having published about our loved ones by selling magnets that said, "Every 40 seconds someone dies by suicide. Please support suicide awareness."

Advice or words of wisdom...

Most people do not know what to say to you. Some people will say dumb things. Overlook it. People won't talk about your loved one because they don't want to hurt you. Let them know its okay to talk about them, if it is. There are groups on the Internet such as Parents of Suicide (POS), Siblings of Suicide (SOS), Family and Friends of Suicide (FFOS) and compassionate friends that may help.

Tracy Stack

Age: 49

Current Occupation: Post Office

Tracy's son, Kent, completed suicide September 1, 2002. He shot himself with a deer rifle. He was 16 years old.

The following is an excerpted version of Tracy's story.

In her words...

Kent had two brothers, Jake, three years older and Micah, three years younger. His father is self-employed in heating and air conditioning and I work for the post office. His Granny and Grandpa live a half of a block away.

Kent was a difficult baby. He bit his fingernails at a young age. He always wore a hat, since he was six months old. He was very cute and people were always drawn to him. He had a very unique personality. He was very popular in school. He was very intelligent—a good "con"—he knew what people wanted to hear. He and I communicated pretty well. He had a quick temper but would always come back to apologize.

Every picture we have of Kent he is looking straight into the camera smiling. A person would never know this kid had a depressed day in his life. Even when we went to family therapy while he was in treatment, he didn't tell us how badly he was hurting inside. The only friend who may have had a clue was Bryan. Everyone else couldn't believe it. How could he hide it for so long from so many?

Kent was never diagnosed but I know in my heart he was bipolar at a very young age. As a preteen, Kent started having problems. He ran away, got violent, starting experimenting with drugs and alcohol and eventually graduated to intravenous methamphetamine usage. He was sent to treatment a wonderful place in Minnesota in May 2002 and he successfully completed the program. I feel blessed because we did have our old Kent back for the last summer anyway.

The suicide...

The night Kent shot himself there were three parties in town. He had gotten drunk and picked up by the police on the way home. He got his second DWI but was released to his grandmother. His dad and I were out of town at the time.

The arresting officer harassed Kent about not having his driver's license. He was on probation yet was allowed to refuse a blood or urine draw. He was not taken to juvenile detention. His probation officer was not called. He told the cop to call his grandma, so they did. They allowed a drunk child to call the shots. No one bothered to call his father or me. The police knew of Kent's history (violent, drinker, past IV drug user) and still released him to his arthritic grandma. Major, stupid, idiotic mistakes were made.

Kent went home and shot himself with his deer rifle. His grandma was on the other side of the door pleading with him not to pull the trigger. I believe Kent was panicked, drunk, scared and felt doomed.

I told others the truth about the suicide. I went to talk to the high school kids three or four days after the funeral. I think I made others feel uncomfortable. People would avoid me. There seemed to be a social stigma.

The bereavement process...

I made sounds I didn't know a human being could make. There was a smell in the house from the seal that they used on the walls to keep blood from seeping through. I still dream that smell.

Trying to get back into a "normal routine" again was very difficult. It took weeks to come out of that dream state. I know now it was nature's way of letting in a little bit at a time as one can handle it. We had this huge mirror upstairs in the bathroom. Every day for a month when I walked by it, it was like my peripheral vision would see a person. When I looked to see who it was, I realized it was me. Then I would think in horror, "God, this really happened."

I felt overwhelming sorrow. I never knew when it would hit. It was hard because I was also dealing with law enforcement and then a divorce. When I moved out six months later, I started gambling. I was angry and stuck.

Six months after Kent's death, I moved into a small apartment. Things started going from bad to worse. I was taking Prozac but I had been diagnosed bipolar years earlier. It had taken months of fighting just to get police reports. We had talked to lawyers but it felt like I wasn't communicating the right words to them. They said it would be an uphill battle for a lawsuit. All I wanted was a damn apology or an admission of guilt that there were mistakes made. Where was the accountability? It was so frustrating.

Divorce proceedings started and my gambling was out of control. I would wake up at midnight, get dressed and go play video-lottery until 2am. It would be nothing for me to get up Sunday morning and play for 12 hours. It didn't matter if I won or lost. It was an escape. It was just me and the machine and it seemed like there was a protective shell around us. I cashed in CDs I had inherited and maxed out my credit cards. I was fighting with my mother and my sister and cutting myself off from friends. Another holiday season had come and gone and it sucked.

I found out my mom was going to move to Madison, my sister's town, and I had no say in the matter. When she moved, she offered me her house until I got on my feet again. It was then I hit bottom. I felt like such as failure— so beaten, misunderstood, let down and broken. I had gambled away my inheritance, maxed out my credit cards. I signed divorce papers without fighting for any of the business. I was left with a Suburban and a Harley Davidson motorcycle. I had lost the respect of my remaining two sons. I hadn't slept in I don't know how many nights. My mind was telling me it would be nice to go to sleep permanently. It would have been so easy just to close my eyes. I thought my son, Jake, could use the insurance money for college and my son Micah wouldn't have to be embarrassed about having a mom in the "nut house." Then my heart took over and I'd think of the devastation Kent left with his suicide. My struggle between heart and mind seemed to go on for hours. Then, just that quickly, my mind won out. My spirit was broken and I felt I had nothing left to give and no fight left.

Once I made the decision I was very calm. I got my pajamas on, wrote a quick note, grabbed a bowl, poured about 200 pills in it and started taking them. I waited 23 minutes then I called Steve, now my husband. I didn't tell him right away bit it didn't take him long to figure out. My speech started slurring then I told him.

Maybe unconsciously, this was my cry for help. Consciously, having been an EMT for years, I knew how long it would take them to get there and I knew it was a 35-minute drive to the hospital. I was going to let God decide if one hour and 15 minutes was too long.

I was told I spent three days in the ICU. I was told I came about as close to death as one can get without dying. After I was out of danger, I was sent up to the 4th floor (for the "nut cases"). It was my third time.

I was taking a shower feeling dirty and weak from ICU. When I came out of the shower, there were two policemen waiting. I was told to get dressed. They had a signed order to take me to the state hospital. I couldn't believe it. They asked me if I was okay with it. All I said in disgust was no. Then they put me in handcuffs. It took about one and a half hours to get to the state hospital. I didn't say a word. I was angry and uncomfortable.

As they were giving me my admittance physical at the hospital, my speech staring slurring and the left side of my face started drooping. The woman giving me the physical took my blood pressure, went into another room, got on the phone and said something like, "I damn well better not have anybody drop on my shift." I had a slight stroke. My whole left side drooped and dragged for a while. I now take blood pressure pills. Luckily, one can't tell now that I suffered a stroke. I stayed in the hospital for 10 days.

When I got out of the state hospital, there were two things I was hanging on to: (1) I was going to see my counselor again and (2) I had a near death experience in the hospital.

I admitted myself to the "4th floor", where I started shock treatments. I had three done on that stay. I found them to be very helpful. They somehow buried the "horribleness." The only drawback was that I would forget how to do my job. I would have to reteach myself my case and my computer terminal each time. But I was so used to being a scattered brain by then, it was worth it.

About a month later, I was arrested. They came to work, cuffed me and took me to jail. I was charged with possession of the controlled substance, Phenobarbital. It had been in storage at the post office, along with other stuff like aspirin and salt, in old brown glass medicine bottles. When they were thrown away, I took them out of the garbage because I liked the bottles. I was facing a 10 years and a $10,000 fine. In December 2004, I got three years probation.

I started with a line of medication for bipolar disorder. I saw my counselor weekly. I joined a grief support group and took an eight-week bereavement class. I continued with my shock treatments. I also filed for bankruptcy.

There was one lady, my court services officer, and I was ordered to see her before my sentencing. At this point I had lost all hope. I didn't care what happened to me. I looked terrible. She told me to tell her everything from the beginning. I said no, it wouldn't matter, it was too long of a story and she wouldn't believe it any way. There was no way I could prove it. She kept at me and didn't give up, so finally I gave in and told her the whole story. She listened, nodded her head and smiled in acknowledgment. That's all I needed, somebody within the system, not only to listen but believe me, too. It took over an hour. It was emotionally draining. I had a half hour drive home and I cried all the way. My court services officer said later that it was emotional for her, too. I report to her once a month. When I saw her on October 2, she said she couldn't believe how well I was doing.

It has been almost three years now and what a journey it has been. I think I have finally figured out that all of the "if onlys" and "what ifs" and guilt trips aren't going to change a damn thing. I feel I have come to terms with the loss. I had to give my anger over to the injustice; the way things were done wrong, then hand them over to God for my own survival.

I ache for Kent every day but I know he is at peace with God. Attempting it myself, I understand how far down one can get. I feel forgiveness and peace.

Dreams and unusual occurrences...

In January 2005, the week Kent would have turned 19, he came to me in a dream. It was awesome. Dreams are so hard to write about but the heaviness has been lifted.

Have you ever considered taking your own life?

I attempted suicide in May 2004. I took an overdose. I messed up and didn't know how to fix it. My own suicide attempt finally led me back to my counselor, who I had previously seen for bipolar disorder. I looked for him but couldn't remember his name; someone in the ER knew him and contacted him right away. I still see him to this day. He has been my lifeline.

Significance of the suicide...

I don't know the answer to that yet. I just know my gift is sharing my story with kids. If it helps one person, then it gives Kent's death some meaning or purpose.

Helpful coping methods...

Shock treatments, meditation, sharing my story, talking to kids and being there for new survivors.

Advice or words of wisdom...

Don't be ashamed to ask for antidepressants. Get involved with a group of suicide survivors. Be patient with those trying to help. At least they are trying. Be patient with yourself. It is okay to have down days (even years later).

Everyone connected to that person who died has their own path (or trail) to travel, to find their own way. Some make the trip—some don't.

CHAPTER THREE
Mothers and Fathers

Nick Shelton

Age: 19

Current Occupation: Author

Nick's father completed suicide five years prior to this interview. He shot himself.

In his words...

I have a close family of five. I have an older brother by another father. We all get along well; though my dad was out of town on business a lot. My family taught me good morals and gave me a good education. I felt like I had a great childhood.

I was very close to my father. I was as close to him as anyone else in my life. (Everyone says how we were exactly the same.)

The suicide...

I heard the gunshot. I was in complete shock. I did not think anything like this could ever happen to me or my family. He seemed to be living a great life and there was not any clue it was coming.

I tried to keep quiet about; it embarrassed me to talk about it. I just said that my father passed away. If they asked anymore, I would just say he completed suicide and leave it at that. Others tried helping, but it was a very uncomfortable situation talking to them.

The police and other professionals tried to keep everything professional; however, I tried to escape from seeing these people as much as I could. It did not help being reminded about what happened.

The bereavement process...

At first, I was totally withdrawn from talking to anyone; however, I eventually started sharing more of what I felt months afterward. Finding a solid home in the church and turning to God for comfort was the largest help.

I was in an emotional state of depression like I had never been before. It was hard to even do the little things in life feeling this way.

I did not seek counseling except from a youth pastor at my church, who initially came to me. He was very helpful. He had a father, an uncle, and a brother also do the same. It was great for someone who had already battled suicide.

I did not receive professional help because I thought professional help was for those with serious problems. I did not want to consider myself with a serious problem.

I believe I have come to terms with the loss. I can talk about it comfortably and have completely put the loss behind me. It occurred when I realized that I no longer had an earthly father in my life, but I had a spiritual Father in heaven that could help guide me in my life. I still respect my father; I just do not respect what he did.

Have you ever considered taking your own life?

Yes. It was when I became so depressed after the thought of my father. I did not follow through because I saw how much pain that my father's suicide caused others.

The significance of the suicide...

It has completely changed my life. If he would not have completed, I may have never taken the steps of committing myself to the Christian faith. If that would have never happened, I doubt I would ever have tried to write any books. Now I have seven completed books, and I am pursing a career as a full-time author.

Helpful coping methods...

Becoming closer to God. I found that he could ease all the pains, worries and sorrows that I had.

Advice or words of wisdom...

Do not be afraid to seek help (it does not have to be professional help; maybe just talk to someone who was gone through the loss of a loved one this way). Personally, I would tell the individual that believing in God has had the greatest impact for me. I would stress to that person how much having God in one's life can turn around any situation.

I would like to stress how much religion can take away the burden which one bears after suicide. I believe my own life is a testament that shows how one can leave the depression and grief and start living an even more joyful life than ever before. In a time when one is hurting, they can find no better comfort than finding God in their lives.

Terese Rigodanzo-Adom

Age: 47

Current Occupation: Home Care Corporate Director

Terese's father completed suicide on August 1, 2004. He shot himself.

In her words…

My parents were to celebrate their 50th wedding anniversary less than one month before my father died. My father was orphaned at a young age and my mother became an only child after her younger sister died at age six. There were three children in our family; my older brother is 21 months older than me, and my younger brother is five years younger.

We had a stable upbringing with our parents putting us as priority given their goal of creating family. We were provided with many opportunities, given much responsibility and encouraged to fulfill our dreams. Family and community have been strong influences for each of us. Quiet time alone is equally important to us, especially with nature. Being the only daughter, I was my dad's princess. My dad was a quiet man who enjoyed his privacy, but he was a good friend to many including his children. He taught me many things as I was growing up. Even after I became an adult, he was always there to lend support and a guiding word.

The suicide…

My mother called me shortly after he died. It wasn't until her second call, or perhaps when I called her back later that night that she told me of the circumstances surrounding his death. Although my mom remembers this night differently, I'm going to stick to my story acknowledging that she is the best; she gave more than her all that night, the days, months and years before and continues to do so with every passing day.

I was shocked, devastated and saddened in a way that has not gone away; shocked because I thought he had at least a year of some quality of life, devastated because he died so ill and alone and saddened because I loved him so much.

Sadly, honestly and honorably, my father discussed his thoughts with me a little more than a week before. He had just undergone an extremely difficult few months medically with no favorable prognosis. Due to major changes in his medication, as well as other health related influences, he was feeling and expressed feeling psychotic at times. My personal experience of working with seniors for more than 13 years gave me some expertise about the aging process; I shared honestly that given his prognosis, life would be a challenge with probably more downs than ups. He agreed and cried about how proud he was knowing the care others might have gained through my work. My dad had a close affinity with nature, which gave him a philosophy not compatible with today's modern medicine, which can prolong life beyond its natural course with little or no quality of life. That philosophy, coupled with his traumatic military experience, gave me a sense that suicide might be a realistic option when he faced his death. I felt like the suicide note.

My dad expressed not being able to face the suffering he had gone through especially with little chance of a good recovery. He did not want to be a burden to any of us nor to become demented. I believe he was overcome with too many dark and evil spirits to be completely rational in taking his own life; his death occurred during a full moon, which I believe has a great effect on the human psyche as the lunar pulls all of earth's water (the human body being made up of a large percent of water).

We were very honest from the beginning that he took his own life. Coming from a small town, the community outpouring of love and support was phenomenal. People shared our loss. Without glorifying his death, most people so understood his suffering and did not hold any judgment about his choice.

How were we treated by the police, medical personnel and/or other professionals? Very, very well according to my mother. My parents' parish deacon arrived soon on the scene to lend a strong spiritual presence. I saw him a few months later and he was equally as kind, personable and supportive.

Coincidentally, the day following my dad's death when I arrived at my parents' house, an elderly friend who was visiting had her hip break and went down on the back stoop forcing us to call 911. The same team arrived as for my father so we had a chance to hug and exchange mutual support; the team so dreaded coming to our address again because they shared in our loss.

The bereavement process…

Being the diplomatic middle child, initially I was concerned for others. It was my strong suggestion, which pulled together the immediate prayer service at our home. The first three months I knew I was in shock. I attended a survivor's support group within a month or two, an art therapy session in December with exhibit in February, and included my father's handmade and self-designed model airplane in an April art exhibit.

As the shock wore off, a sense of being mildly psychotic settled in. I still went to work, kept up with some relationships and provided more support to my mother, but cried a lot in my private time. One year has passed; although I allowed myself to grieve, I'm only just feeling like I can acknowledge my dad's death in a natural way.

I can clearly describe my major symptoms as coming out through my female reproductive system; I hemorrhaged severely for the first three months. Because I knew my grief had to release itself somewhere, I understood the process, but now a year later am struggling not to go into early menopause.

Have I come to terms with the loss? Yes and no. I've done my best for the first year, but knew it wouldn't be until Dad's first anniversary that I could really begin to grieve. Fortunately, I have a very supportive husband and friends beyond compare.

Although I did call a suicide hot-line one night, it wasn't the appropriate referral at the time. In general, I've found friends, books and prayer to be the most helpful means to aide in my coping and healing. For a while I felt the daily need for a psychiatrist; I instead turned to Jesus, our Wonderful Counselor.

I believe I will come to better terms with the loss of my father for several reasons: 1) My loving husband also misses my father and needs my love and care, 2) My birth daughter was able to be with my father shortly before he died and she, too, needs my love and care, 3) My two step-sons will be with us by the end of the month and also need my love and care. Lastly, I sense my father's presence from the spirit world that he does not want me, my mother, brothers or any of us to be sad.

I love my dad and simply miss him so much. I'm sorry he suffered so and that I wasn't more of a faithful support to him. We all miss him and wish he were still with us in the world to share our lives.

Dreams and unusual occurrences...

The night before my dad died this is what happened. I woke up around 2:30am after I heard myself repeating aloud to my husband, "Did you call Rachael (my daughter)? Did you call Rachael?" That was immediately following my dream in which there was a man with dark hair about 30-40 years old. He had a bomb-like thing, which he ignited. The only reaction was that his body totally disintegrated in an ashy dust. Nearby, there was a big group of us in a sort-of classroom/house, both friends and family. I kept trying to get us into showers because the dust had completely covered us including getting in our mouths and eyes. I had a clear sense that the dust permeated everything and we had to be cleansed. Before any showers or cleansing, I woke up.

To me this dream is totally symbolic of Dad's death. I didn't think much of it at the time, because I was still unsettled from the previous week being at my parents', our reunion, the hospital, etc. The entire Sunday was a relatively quiet, peaceful day, which meant God was in control, but right now I wish I would have been totally unsettled so I might have reacted.

Have you ever considered taking your own life?

In this age in which depression, anxiety and suicide are at an all-time high, I'd be lying if I said that a suicidal thought never crossed my mind. I believe these thoughts can be attacks from negative forces over which we seem to have little rational control. I take them in stride, recognizing that I am a perfectionist and the world in which we live is highly imperfect.

Significance of the suicide...

About 15 years ago, I thought of attending a suicide support group because I had met so many people whose lives were touched by suicide. The first was when I was 17 in high school, one of our classmates took his own life; although as a child I was also mildly aware that a distant relative had died by her own hand. My dad's death forced me to finally attend a support group. I have become active with others who lost a loved one to suicide and hope to offer all I can for other's healing which in turns brings my own healing. I pray more and open myself up to others in hopefully a kinder and more patient way.

Helpful coping methods...

In addition to participation in the art therapy and art exhibit, I also wrote a few poems and stories. What I did not do was take my usual long healing walks; perhaps that, as well as playing with my boys, will be my strategy for the upcoming year.

Helpful advice or words of wisdom...

God forgives in His great mercy. We must be strong in this age of spiritual bombardment.

"Dawn"

Age: 59

Current Occupation: Writer

Dawn's mother completed suicide in 1965. Her mother took Nembutal with vodka.

In her words...

My parents split up when I was five and I never saw my father again. My mother never remarried; it was only she and I. I was a very lonely kid and became a classic bookworm, which was easy since we always had books around. My mother was very intelligent.

I really loved my mother with all my heart and wanted to please her. She was about 10 years older than the moms of kids my age, and after a long day at work she would come home tired out. I was always in fear of her getting mad at me because the house was messy or something. On the weekends, when she was rested and feeling okay, she was hilarious and fun to be with.

The suicide...

I was at work—my first job right out of high school. My fiancé called me on the phone and said, "Babe, you need to come home, I think your mother's dead."

I sort of went very calm; I told my boss something was wrong at home and I had to leave. I drove home in five minutes, just quiet and numb. My fiancé was there at the house and wouldn't let me go in, he just held me and talked to me.

Things were so unbalanced at my house the only clue about the suicide I would have gotten was a sandwich board on the front porch. My mother was lonely, depressed, had lost her job and was surrounded by drunks and losers.

I told others that my mother died of a drug and alcohol overdose. It wasn't a big secret. All my friends were very supportive and my fiancé was terrific through the whole thing. Funny thing: we ended up getting married about two weeks later at the city hall; he was in the Navy and that way we'd get a monthly 'dependent allowance' for me. All my mother's friends thought we got married so quickly because I was pregnant. I was furious when I found out.

I dealt with the mortician, the city clerk, and a bank manager. They were all very polite.

I did not seek counseling. It was the 1960s and therapy wasn't in style yet...I was busy getting my life together, getting married, and moving out of the area.

I've always missed her. I wish she had been able to get a grip on things. She always told me, "Nothing bad lasts forever." I will always treasure the things she taught me to appreciate—good books, music, good food and a sense of humor. And how to make a crappy little apartment look great for next to nothing.

The bereavement process...

I felt numbness...thinking "this isn't really happening...I'm going to wake up and this will just be a nightmare..."

After the numbness wore off...I felt horribly guilty. The previous two years of my mother's life had been an ugly slide into alcoholism. I stayed away from home as much as possible to avoid confrontations with her or her drunken boyfriends—not easy since I was a senior in high school and had to sleep somewhere. The night before she died we got into a raging argument. Not a good final memory! Then over time I began remembering the good times my mother and I enjoyed together; a sense of sadness and loss replaced the guilty baggage and, like a traumatic bloody wound, gradually everything began to sort of heal over.

Do I believe I've come to terms with the loss? It's been forty years—I'd be pretty screwed up if I hadn't by now! (That's my mom's sense of humor channeling...)

After a couple of years I was able to look at the situation as more of an adult and objectively realize that things happen over which we have no control and that we need to get our act together and get on with life.

Dreams and other unusual occurrences...

About a week after my mother died, I dreamed I was back in the kitchen of our house with my back to the back door. I turned around and she was standing at the sink. "Mom—you're here!" I said in the dream. She laughed and walked over to the stove and started dinner. "Of course I'm here." I could hear her voice as though she was right next to me.

Have you ever considered taking your own life?

It seems I inherited more than just outward resemblances to my mother; as I got older I began having periods of depression and I realized that most likely she had felt the same. While it didn't make me feel any better, it did help me understand her actions. I had times when I vaguely felt that if I went to bed and never woke up, it would be no big loss to the world. But I never took it any further than dark thoughts; I suppose I had a deep-seated sense that I might eventually be okay.

The significance of the suicide...

Well, it gives me tremendous insight regarding individuals in the same position. I have, however, always been sad that she never knew my son.

Helpful coping methods...

Humor. Example: one day some friends were discussing their parents' marriages—some of them had been married before and some hadn't. I said my mom had been married twice. Someone said, 'Oh, yeah, my mom was married twice but she's divorced again. So, what's your mom now?' meaning of course, married or single...Without missing a beat, I replied, "Dead." The looks on everyone's faces were priceless, and if there's a Hereafter, I know my mother was laughing right along with me.

Advice or words or wisdom...

First: It's not your fault. IT'S NOT YOUR FAULT! Don't waste your emotions beating yourself up. Second: Don't hate them for doing what they did. To them it seemed the best solution to the situation; don't judge them. Third: Remember ALL the good times, the happy times. Keep them in your mind and in your heart.

Twenty-three years after my mother died, I met an easygoing interesting man one evening at a concert. We really hit it off and stayed up until 3am drinking coffee and talking. At one point he sighed, and said, "Well...I have a confession to make." Swell, I thought...he's a parolee? He's married? He only has six months to live? What? "I'm a recovered alcoholic. I go to AA meetings about four nights a week." I began laughing and jumping up and down; he thought I was nuts...We've been married for 15 years now. And it was my husband who persuaded me to get help for my depression, which had sucked me into the dark rut in which my mother spent her last days.

"Leah"

Age: 19

Current Occupation: Cook in healthcare facility (dietary aid)

Leah's dad completed suicide just over a year prior to the interview. He shot himself.

In her words...

My parents got divorced when I was about 10. I have a sister who is three years older than me. After my parents divorced, my dad, my sister and I moved to another state and only saw our mother about once a month and sometimes only on holidays, so my dad pretty much raised us girls and we were really close.

Growing up in my family was good for the most part. When my parents were still together they fought a lot and my dad could be abusive sometimes. After they divorced it was mostly good. My dad drank more than I know he should have, but he treated us well.

My dad was my best friend. I loved him with everything I have and we had an awesome father/daughter relationship that I believe a lot of families miss out on. He trusted me to the fullest extent and let me make mistakes so I could learn from them. If I were to ever get in a real bind I knew I could count on him to help me out of it and get me back on track.

The suicide...

It was the day of my cousin's wedding. When my dad didn't show up and didn't answer his phone I decided to go find out what the deal was...so I found him.

It was surreal. Even though it was right before my eyes I didn't believe it. It was by far the worst experience I had never imagined. Every emotion one could think of probably ran through me in a half hour.

I didn't find out until it was too late that my dad and his girlfriend had broken up. I know there were a lot of other things that had an impact on his decision. Maybe if I would have thought about all that he was going through I might have thought about it, but I didn't. It didn't ever cross my mind until it was too late.

Because I was the one who found him I was the one who informed most people. After the funeral and stuff I basically tried to avoid the conversation as much as possible because it was too hard to tell people what happened. It's like when you tell someone that he completed suicide they don't even know how to react, what to say, how to feel, how to treat you and it made it awkward. If somehow it came up in conversation with people who didn't know him well, I would just tell them that he passed away and try to leave it at that.

Different people had different reactions. My close family didn't treat me much differently. They are caring and treat me with respect. I have friends who choose not to talk about it, as they were also close to my dad. I also have friends who understand that I need to talk about it sometimes and that I need to let loose and cry. They will allow me to do that. On the other hand, people who don't know me and my family, if they know what happened, they act differently towards me. Like, some people who never would have glanced in my direction before, talk to me like we're best friends and I know it's because they feel sorry for me and I don't like that.

I know how much my dad was going through and had gone through in his life, but I can also believe that he honestly had no idea what he was doing. See, my best friend once jumped out of a moving vehicle and she literally had no idea what she was doing. The doctors said it was caused by a chemical imbalance in her body. After my dad's death, I learned that he had opened up the car door, like he was going to jump out of the car, while traveling down the highway about two weeks prior to his death. His girlfriend asked him what the hell he was doing and he replied, "I don't know." Maybe he didn't know what he was doing when he did it.

I love him just as much now as I ever have.

The bereavement process…

Crazy. It's an emotional roller coaster. Some days go by just fine other days I don't even feel like getting out of bed.

Physically, I was drained of my energy and the months following the suicide I lost about 20 pounds. Emotionally it's kind of hard to explain…emotionally I didn't know what was going on with anything. Every emotion ran through me at the most unexpected times.

I didn't really seek counseling. I've never had good experiences with counseling in the past so I just didn't want to go through the trouble for someone that wasn't going to help me anyway.

I am part of an online support group and was on an anti-depressant for a while. The support group helps because I realize that I'm not alone and that I'm not crazy for the emotions I go through.

I have not completely come to terms with the loss and I don't know if I ever will, but I don't really know how to explain why.

71

Dreams and unusual occurrences...

I've had some dreams with my dad in them that really get to me. One that sticks out in my mind is where we sold my dad's house. The striking part was that my dad was there with us and we took one final walk through the house before we left it for good and my dad left with us. More recently, I had a dream about our vacation. My sister, dad and I always took a one-week vacation in August and visited other family. In my dream we were on our vacation sitting at my aunt's picnic table. My dad stood up and said, "Well, I gotta go now." (He was going back to heaven.) I got up and hugged him and I cried and I woke up crying. It was really weird because it was like he came back to visit from heaven.

Have you ever considered taking your own life?

It has crossed my mind, but I have never seriously thought about it. I could never put my friends and family through that again. I want to get married and have kids still and I will never put my kids through what I go through everyday as long as I can help it.

The significance of the suicide...

I grew up more. I came to understand that people are the way they are for a reason. I learned to deal with change a little better and I learned that even the people closest to your heart aren't going to be there forever and that you have to be able to accept that when they are gone.

Advice or words of wisdom...

Try to get your life back to a so-called normal, a new normal, as soon as you can after your loss. I believe if you don't go on right away it will be harder to later. Take everything one day at a time, don't push yourself. Let yourself grieve at a pace you feel comfortable with. Everybody grieves differently and that's okay. Find your own way to deal with your pain and don't worry about what other people say or think about you. Those are the little things. You will find good in your life again, be patient. It's a challenge and you can make it. The best advice I can give is to take everything one day at a time don't worry about the future and don't live in the past.

CHAPTER FOUR
Spouses and Significant Others

"Paula"

Age: 50

Current Occupation: Freelance Technical Illustrator/Graphic artist

Paula's significant other, "Karl" completed suicide on September 11, 2003 at age 53. He shot himself.

In her words...

I grew up in small Midwestern industrial town in a middle class, white collar, Catholic family of French, Irish and Swedish descent and Karl grew up in an East coast mill town in a poor, blue collar, Catholic family of French, Irish and English descent. The only reason I mention this is that he felt we came from similar backgrounds and were very much alike. He has six siblings and I have three.

Karl, my significant other, and best friend of over ten years, was fifty-three when he took his life. We met at work in 1988 and began dating in 1993: Karl has been with the company for many years before I was hired. We were both living in New England at the time, and both of us had devoted many years to our careers in the high tech industry. We found we had similar skills and interests; we were not only teammates but also officemates for six years. Not only could we finish each other's sentences, we could finish each other's artwork so that it looked like it was created by a single artist...yet I has no idea what he has planned for September 11, 2003.

In 1997, after many downsizings in the company, Karl decided to start a freelance graphics business. Things were going fairly well until January of 2001 when the economy in New England took a downturn. After that time, Karl was unable to find work. I remained with the company for two years after Karl left to start his business. In 1999 the company was purchased by another high tech firm; many organizations were downsized and I volunteered to leave based on Karl's advice. I freelanced for a year then returned to the same company was a full-time employee in October of 2000 when I was offered a terrific opportunity to further my skills.

I believe Karl took his life on September 11, 2003 as a statement to the world. Words in his last note to me read: "The events that happened on September 11, 2001 along with all the crooked business and investment scams have stalled the economic momentum that this country needs to be able to keep people working and prosperous. You win some and you lose some." He had been unable to find work since January if 2001.

During our years together, Karl spoke frequently of marriage. I didn't want to get married until he was out of debt and our lives were somewhat stable.

We had apartments in the same complex but did not live together until October 2002, when he could no longer pay the bills. We put most of his things into storage, and he moved into my apartment. My apartment was very small with half of it devoted to my home office. We turned my living room-dining room into his home office. I also had two cats at the time, we were living on top of each other but we tried to make the best of it.

The company that rehired me began downsizing again in December of 2002. In September of 2001, the week before September 11, the company announced a new manager and rumor was that my organization would be downsized. It was stressful working long hours (12 hour days plus two hours of commute) and worrying about Karl's mounting bills, his bad luck (it seemed drawn to him) and my impending layoff. I felt like I was drowning in problems, so to a certain extent, I withdrew. We didn't fight very often; I kept trying to encourage him to find any work because soon I would be looking for a new job too.

With so many companies moving their operations to Asia and India, it was difficult to find work, especially in our specialized field. After the first merger, the Vice President of our organization was downsized and could not find work. He completed suicide. One of the other technical artists, who was also part of our team, had a nervous breakdown and attempted suicide.

The suicide…

He walked across the street to a wooded area outside of the local airport, called 911 and told the police where they could find him. He stuck the barrel of a 38-caliber Smith & Wesson in his mouth. Later, when his family arrived, I found a graphic notepad; he had drawn a self-portrait with the gun in his mouth. Weeks later, I also was able to track sites on his computer where he found out how to plan his suicide.

Karl called me at work that afternoon and asked me what I would like for dinner. He told me he loved me very much and I responded that I loved him very much too. He did this every day around lunchtime, so I did not think it unusual.

When I arrived at our apartment; there was a business card on my door from a detective. I called the detective and got his answering machine. I thought Karl might have been in a car accident. As I stated earlier, he seemed to attract bad luck. A secretary from the rental office stopped by the apartment and I asked her if she knew what had happened. She told me that she wasn't supposed to say anything, but seeing how distraught I was, she told me that Karl had completed suicide and I should call the detective. Karl had planned his suicide for 3:30pm, knowing that with my one-hour commute I would arrive home around 4pm. The news hit me with such force that initially all I could do was moan in pain.

Why do I think Karl took his life? Depression—lack of job—feeling of no self-worth, and anger at the world. Several months later, while I was packing my apartment for my move to the Midwest to care for my parents, I came across some papers that Karl had written back in the late 1980s. There was a reference to having toyed with the idea of suicide back then. He had been playing with a sharp knife and had run it across his throat and was having trouble stopping the bleeding. He often complained about winter being so depressing and wouldn't it be nice to move to Arizona. I wondered, "Was he always depressed in the fall and did I just not see it?"

Karl had somewhat of an erratic temperament. Many of his friends were frustrated with him. He liked to argue with them and play devil's advocate. He was very smart and loved to have heated discussions, but he often ended up irritating them, not knowing when to stop. He had a hard time looking at the world in a positive light, or I should say he tended to carry the weight of the world. Karl liked the fact that I, for the most part, understood many of his frustrations. (I had many of the same but chose to approach my solutions differently.)

How do I feel about Karl today? Sad. Such a waste of a talented, interesting, smart man. I think of him every day and miss him. I feel as though half of me is gone.

The bereavement…

Complete and utter grief—chaos. I think I was in shock. I felt like moaning. I just wanted to be with him. I kept wondering what I had done to trigger his suicide. He had been crabby the previous evening because I had asked him to find out why our power bill for the month was three times the usual amount. Karl refused to call stating he would be busy the following day. I wondered why he would be busy because he wasn't working and his reaction was so contrary to his usual nature. Then he picked a fight and went outside to talk to a neighbor. I had been unable to sleep that night because I couldn't understand his anger and unwillingness to help in any way. I couldn't remember whether I had kissed him goodbye the following morning. He had recently decided to shave his head because he was starting to go bald. I didn't realize that this was all part of the plan.

I was in Never-Neverland. I don't remember much but feeling like I was going through an out-of-body experience. I went through the range: extreme grief, disbelief, anger and acceptance.

At his mother's funeral, one month earlier, I thought Karl was acting strangely. He had a coin collection and was giving some of his coins to his family. (I did not find out about this until after he had passed away.) He had always given me coins on every birthday, anniversary and Christmas, but had to sell all of the ones he had given to me in order to pay some of his bills. He also met up with an old high school friend at the wake and introduced me to his friend with the comment, "I hear you don't want to get married…this is my girlfriend and she doesn't want to get married either…I think you would be perfect together." I did not know what to say except that I was willing to get married once our jobs were stable and he was out of debt. I was alarmed that he would say something that that, and when I confronted him later, he said it was only a joke.

I called one of his sisters and let her know that Karl had taken his life. She contacted the rest of his family. His sister lived about an hour and a half away. During the time that I was alone waiting for her to arrive, I found his final letter to me, and notarized will in which left all of his belongings to me. While waiting for her, I walked around in a trance. I called my mom, sister and best friend in Wisconsin. My sister, mom, one brother and brother-in-law made plans to arrive the following day.

I also called the two other artists I currently worked with and my manager because he knew Karl and had worked with him in the past. The detective called and I read the letters to him. He was compassionate but ran me through a business-like interrogation. When he found out that I was not married to Karl, he said he would not discuss anything further with me but rather would only discuss things with Karl's immediate family.

When his sister arrived at my apartment, she read his letter and his will and went into a RAGE. She blamed me for his choice and then called Karl's brothers from various parts of the country and one of his best friends, who was a police officer in Karl's hometown. She read the letter and the will to them and asked them how she could keep me from getting his possessions. I then told her I didn't want any of Karl's things, and that she could have everything except his letters to me and the books we purchased together. I was not interested in his possessions. Mind you, Karl and I had been together for ten years and we had been very generous to members of his family. I was in such utter shock at her reaction; I just could not believe what I was hearing. I kept thinking that Karl just killed himself and she is thinking about his possessions? It did not make sense to me – they were just things, mostly books, tools, kitchen items, furniture and some coins he was unable to sell.

The following morning when Karl's siblings arrived, the first thing they did was wave a copy of the will in my face and declare that it was not binding because there was one witness. (It was notarized with the signature of one witness but the state we lived in required two.) Not that it mattered; I had planned on turning all of his possessions over to his family anyway. It was the principle. I was buried in grief and they were looking through my apartment at all of MY things and discussing how they were going to take them. Most of Karl's possessions were in a storage facility and as it stated in his will, the reason he wished his possessions to me was because I had been supporting him: "I wish everything I own, all my worldly possessions, to be given ownership to Paula, who can do what she wants with those items: to sell or keep–repaying her for the debt I owe her. She paid my bills, housed, clothed, and fed me during my unemployment to the present day. I gave her my promise to repay her when things got better and I was back on my feet."

Karl had several members of his family the year he took his life: a brother to multiple sclerosis in January of that year, a nephew that summer to a military accident and finally his mother to an illness a month before his suicide. At the time I wondered if that much sadness in a family causes such callous behavior or was it that they were once so poor that is all they know.

Once Karl's brothers arrived, they began to remove Karl's clothing and possessions from my apartment. Karl's wishes were that he be cremated and his ashes scattered in the ocean. The family allowed me to go to the funeral home and discuss Karl's wishes, which were in the letter to me. The family decided that I was not allowed to view his body. One of his brothers was very kind and compassionate towards me, as were his nieces. The brother who barely knew me and the sister we had done so much for were cruel. Although they did allow me to attend the scattering of his ashes, I was not included in any other family activities. In the following weeks his family and I moved his things out of storage and to his sister's home. I gave the few pieces of jewelry Karl had given me to his nieces. I had several calls from bill collectors looking for Karl and they were told that he had passed away and to contact his immediate family.

Our cats sat in the window and cried for days and days (they were used to Karl being home and interacting a lot with them).

I did not have any idea he was considering suicide. The weekend before the suicide, Karl pulled me out of my home office and said we needed a family picture. I kept telling him I was busy with work, but he insisted. In the picture, each of us is holding a cat. He downloaded the picture to his pc and wrote "MY FAMILY" and the date across the top. After he passed away I found out that he had emailed this picture to all of his relatives and friends. Karl had an uncle who had completed suicide rather than go to a nursing home and Karl would sometimes talk about it. His uncle had passed away around the time Karl and I first started dating. Karl always felt what his uncle did was a good choice for his situation because he took control of his destiny. Karl often spoke about the book *Hawaii*, he felt the Hawaiians were making a wise choice drowning babies who were not healthy. After he passed, I often wondered if he suffered from depression and considered himself unhealthy.

The only alarm I had was prior to Karl's death was he applied for a security position about a month before his mom passed away. He said he wasn't hired because he needed a gun. I asked him if he really wanted to do that type of work and I told him I felt really uncomfortable with a gun in the apartment. He told me not to worry; he didn't get the job and didn't own a gun.

He often commented that he could not understand why his brother had a gun collection. After his mother's funeral he often talked about this particular brother and felt that this brother had given up on life. I asked why and he said that he though his brother "gave into the rat race." I found out later he had sold a scanner to a friend and with the money he made, purchased the gun. I still don't know what to think. But in his will, besides leaving all of his possessions to me, he specifically mentioned the gun. I asked the police department to destroy it and the clothing he was wearing at the time.

The officer who took the call about Karl's suicide happened to be getting her hair cut at the same hair stylist I used. My hair stylist heard the police call and knew about the suicide before I did. His shop is only a half block away from where the suicide took place. Because of the call to the police ahead of time, I did not go through some of the horrible treatment I've heard others have gone through.

I told others Karl completed suicide because he was distraught about not finding a job in the field he had worked so hard to master. I did not see the extent of his depression—neither did his friends or family; he put on a front.

Following the suicide, people didn't know what to say. Many were angry. My sister is still very angry and feels that Karl "took my sister away from me." Some avoided me while others were very compassionate. Some wanted to know exactly what happened and others wanted to know nothing.

I returned to work after one week off and was advised to see an EAP counselor. For me, it was a waste of time. She told me all about her problems, so I listened; she felt I was doing fine. I was pushing myself to keep going as I did not want to lose my job earlier than the planned layoff. I also met two times with a counselor through my HMO. That was a strange experience because the counselor was Asian, and it is my understanding that suicide is more acceptable in Asian society. She did not think I needed a counselor. She thought I was handling everything very well. I do not talk about it to anyone except closest of friends (or Survivors of Suicide members) as I don't like to make people uncomfortable.

Recently I joined the SOS group here in the Midwest. I needed to have a place where I could speak freely. As stated before, my sister is very angry and sometimes lashes out at me. Also, I felt guilty about the pain I had brought onto my family.

I'm not sure if one ever gets over the loss and sadness of the situation. I find that I can only study what has happened in little bits. Within eight months of Karl's passing, my whole organization was laid off. I found out my mom had terminal cancer and my dad was rushed into emergency bypass surgery. On the surgery table he had a stroke, which left him partially paralyzed. He had been working full-time up to that point. So, God provided me with a diversion from my pain concerning Karl. The following August (11 months after Karl's passing), I moved to my parents hometown. (I had been in New England for 30 years.) Currently, I take care of my parents and work at my freelance graphics business.

Life goes on. I have other critical things to attend to. I doubt that I will ever marry.

Dreams or unusual occurrences...

An odd thing happened on the day of the 1st anniversary September 11, 2004. A friend of mine and I went to a resort where an innkeeper allowed us to check in early. The innkeeper was wearing a t-shirt with the famous Michelangelo painting of God creating Adam and the t-shirt read, "Pull my finger." That was a joke that Karl tried to play on me shortly after we began to date. Not falling for it, I told him I would only do it on his birthday or a special anniversary. I burst out laughing because it was just so coincidental. The innkeeper apologized for the shirt, which even brought more attention to it. He had been out on the grounds gardening, which was one of Karl's favorite pastimes.

Have you ever considered taking your own life?

No, I have not. I have had bad and sad days and have been frightened about the future. After all, I am on the same career path as Karl was, but I look at things differently than he did. Life changes constantly and I know things often swing from good to bad to good again.

Significance of the suicide...

I would like to help others who have been through similar circumstances. I think the "shame" aspect needs to be removed. Every day I think of Karl and how he would do something. I try to honor his memory, especially at work.

Helpful coping methods...

I began to take Kripalu yoga, joined a new church and SOS. It helped to have a place to talk openly about my experience. I decided to focus outward more than inward, but it was not always easy. I decided to do my best to "fix" myself and move forward in my life.

Advice or words of wisdom...

I read as many books as I could find on the subject. Many gave me solace and stressed that it was not my fault. I realized that there was really very little I could do in my situation and I had to accept it.

"Ruth"

Age: 35

Current Occupation: Civil Servant (Policy Adviser)

Ruth's boyfriend, Peter, completed suicide in June 2004. He hung himself.

In her words...

My family is comprised of mum and dad, who separated March 2004, after nearly 40 years of marriage, and one older brother. My mum and brother both live near London (about 400 miles away) and my father has moved to the South of France (about 1000 miles away) with the "other woman."

Growing up in my family was mostly happy. I fought with my big brother, like lots of kids do. I idolized my dad. Childhood memories are mostly good—my dad building us a wooden castle in the garden, damming streams, going on holidays, camping, Gran teaching me how to bake and so on. Mother and apple pie sort of stuff. The worst thing about my childhood was being picked on at school—I was this geeky, exceptionally bright kid, who just didn't fit into a failing school.

When I first met Peter, we both just fell completely for each other. It was all pretty intense stuff, and we spent most of our spare time together. We adored each other.

Our backgrounds were very different. We both came from fairly ordinary working class families, but I had been to university (and have a Ph.D.) and had a responsible and well-paid job in the government. Peter had left school with no qualifications and worked in the demolition industry. His previous serious girlfriends had had various emotional and addiction problems, and had 'helped' him get into debt.

I think in retrospect, we probably offered each other stability. On my side, I found Steven loving, dependable and capable. He could turn his hand to any practical problem—he could plumb in a bathroom, plaster a wall—you name it—and to an exacting standard. He was also a nice guy—if all he had was a potato, he would cut it in half and share it with you. He was immensely generous, and would help other people out where ever he could. I felt comforted by the thought that he would never hurt me (though of course he did). I trusted him completely.

On his side, he had someone 'decent' back—I wasn't going to gamble the electricity bill money or come home off my head on drugs. I think I offered him the chance of a stable, 'normal'—if there is such a thing—life. We got engaged, and we talked about having children. Reading back this post-justification sounds rather unromantic—which isn't an accurate reflection of how it felt at the time—we were engrossed with each other.

The differences, which pulled us together, however, ultimately pulled us apart. Probably because of the difficulties in his past, he was a terrible liar. I know I said I trusted him—but it was a little like Tom Sawyer's aunt famously said: "I'd trust Tom with my life, but not with a pot of jam!" We had big rows over undisclosed debts and other things. Peter's horizons were also rather narrow —the only thing he really seemed interesting in doing (besides staying at home, work and DIY) was propping up the bar at his 'local'—a rough pub about 15 minutes away. I had nothing in common with his friends there—and he felt uncomfortable around my friends. I wanted to go for long walks in the country, sit in the sunshine, travel to exciting cities, go to museums—and all Peter wanted to do was sit in a dingy bar. It caused more tension between us than other subjects.

The suicide…

Peter and I had been together for 23 months, and living together for about 18 months. At the time of his death, I was trying to break up with him.

I'd told Peter on the Sunday night that I wanted to end the relationship. He took it very badly, and spent the next few days drinking excessively to the point where he would collapse. He was very angry and kept smashing glasses against the windows. There was broken glass everywhere in the house. He ripped a cupboard door off the kitchen unit, and threw it against the opposite wall with enough force to rip the plasterboard. At points I was genuinely frightened for my safety, though he never assaulted me at any time in our relationship.

Eventually on the Friday morning, I told him I couldn't take it anymore, and was going away for a few days. I told him when he got back I wanted him to be sober so we could talk (about how we split up). During this week he said a lot of things—he was going to come to my work and cause a scene; that he couldn't cope without me, etc. He showed me some razor blades at one point, and told me this was now his only option. At the time I didn't take it in because my initial assumption was that he was going to cut me. It didn't occur to me that he was threatening suicide—this seemed very unlikely as he had never expressed suicidal thoughts before, had never had any mental illness, etc. The last night I saw him, he also took the safety harness and seemed to be trying to hang himself off the banister—but was so drunk he couldn't really do it—I took the harness off him, and told him not to be so silly.

In the morning, when I left him—he was distressed and begging me not to go. He said he understood why I needed the time, but that he would 'give his right arm to be with me.' I held him while he sobbed in my arms. When I tried to leave he got angry—I had to run out of the house. My last memory is of something smashing against a wall as I left and ran to the train station.

When I came back several days later, I remember wondering what would happen next. I wondered if he would be drunk or sober or not there. It never even crossed my mind that he would be dead.

When I arrived back he had locked all the doors. I was really angry that I couldn't get in, as I assumed this was so I couldn't sneak back and get more clothes and things without seeing him. I looked through the window. In slow motion, I remember thinking, oh good, he is in. Then, Oh God, I saw he was hanging. I phoned the police.

He hung himself in the dining area of our home. We were renovating the house, and planned to pull down a nasty 1970s style pine ceiling. We'd already taken some of the ceiling away in order to put in plumbing and wiring. He took one of the pine planks out of the ceiling in the very middle of the room to expose the rafter. He hung himself off the central rafter. He had wrapped a tea towel around the rafter and used a safety harness that we had for working on the roof as a ligature. I was told later that the tea towel would have been to lessen the chance of the ligature snapping. He also put the pine plank that he had removed from the ceiling out in the rubbish pile. It was very dramatic. I've heard of hangings where people have done it off doors, and been just off the ground—but he was about a foot off the ground—just hanging in the center of the room.

One of the things that really upset me—though it took a while to figure out why—was that the ambulance came, but just went away again. No one took his body down—they just took pictures and examined it hanging from the rafter.

I told others that Peter killed himself. It never occurred to me to be ashamed or to feel any stigma about it—it seemed a petty consideration compared to the real awfulness that was that Peter was dead. His sister kept telling people 'he'd passed away suddenly.' I found this rather offensive.

I think Peter killed himself because he was an idiot. Peter did rash, irrational things all the time—and this was just one of them. In this sense, I believe it was an accident. I know he meant to kill himself, but I don't really think he had weighed up properly what this would do to us all.

The bereavement...

July and August 2004 were just a haze of pain. I kept trying to go back to work, but I couldn't. I kept seeing my General Practioner to get signed off, but that was all that seemed to be on offer. They wouldn't diagnose anything or offer any treatment or referral. I had all the classic PTSD symptoms (flashbacks, constant anxiety, feelings of impending doom, suicidal ideation). All I could think about was suicide—if I walked in the woods, I would be thinking, a person could hang themselves on that branch. If I saw a tall building, I would wonder if someone was about to jump off it. I would constantly look around to check there were no dead bodies. My nerves were shot, and my concentration was literally so bad, I could only cross the road at a pedestrian crossing with lights.

In September it got really bad. It's not just the absolute pain but also the unrelenting nature of the misery. I totally fell to pieces. I kept saying I just wanted to die. My 'friends' had me arrested for breaching the peace, and put in a police cell for a night because they thought this would stop me killing myself. In reality, they just let me out in the morning, and then I was totally terrified. Just imagine—You'd never been arrested before—you're suffering PTSD and flashbacks and you're dragged along the ground, by police who say you're a load of trouble, we HOPE you do kill yourself. They also called the police who broke down my door and dragged me over for a psychiatric evaluation at a mental hospital—before letting me go immediately. This is because they would diagnose PTSD, which is a psychological problem, and not sectionable.

In the end, my girlfriend came and got me, took me to her house, and fed me tea and sympathy for five days. This was a turning point—because after it being so bad, I could see this was a little better, and it was possible to recover.

October 2004 was very difficult, but November was bearable. December was the first month that I really believed I was going to recover, rather than "have" to die too because the pain was so unbearable. I think I've improved a lot in 2005, but I'm still not quite normal.

Very few people could handle the suicide. I would say I lost most of the people I thought were my friends. My close relationship with my father broke down. He couldn't understand why I was upset when I had been in the process of splitting up with Peter anyway. Until the suicide I thought I had a close family, but we have found all of this very difficult to deal with.

84

We all used to pull together and support each other, now we can barely talk without arguing.

A number of my friends and relatives actually got very angry with me. I developed PTSD and people would talk as though this had been my choice—and I was choosing to be upset and annoying. People at work stopped talking to me. I found this upsetting—I knew all these people well, and had been contributing to birthday cards, birth presents, etc., and they didn't even send a wreath or a card or anything. When I came back after three and a half months off sick, my line manager told me that he was very uncomfortable around me, and so were other people—sensitive, huh!

How was I treated by the authorities? People were pretty insensitive. Mental health provision to tackle my PTSD was practically non-existent.

I have not come to terms with the loss. It was just so senseless and unexpected. How can you ever accept this?

The Employer Assistance Program offered a counselor. I had one session and didn't go back. The counselor seems better qualified to deal with relationship break-ups or mid-life crises, etc. The counselor clearly didn't have a clue about suicide.

I had several psychiatric referrals—two psychiatrists, two psychiatric nurses—my doctor and friends kept chucking me into the system, because they thought I was in such a state. Everyone was very nice, but all they could conclude was I had PTSD, which was a psychological problem.

By the time I got referred to a psychologist I was already getting much better and coping on my own. I stopped going after a couple of appointments, because it didn't seem to help. However, I still see our work counselor about once a month. He has no special training and was always rather humble and reluctant to talk about the suicide, as he said that he didn't feel qualified to tackle it, but in reality he has been better at helping me with it than any other 'professional.'

I do not think it was Peter's choice—because no one would choose to do this. He obviously just felt so desperate that he couldn't see the other options he had. But after months of obsessively thinking about it all, I've accepted we will never have an answer as to why he did it. I honestly believe that if he was here now, he wouldn't be able to tell us either.

It has gotten easier with time, and I believe and hope it will continue to do so. The difficult thing is how long it takes. I still long for the day when I forget that I am a suicide survivor just for a little while. At the moment it feels like an integral part of my identity.

The house where he hung himself is on the market now. I was never able to live there again. The last time I was there, I felt a sense of peace (strangely enough). Is there a ghostly parallel universe where things were slightly different and have turned out the opposite? The house I have for sale is half way through a renovation but in this ghostly other world is it finished and bright and full of laughter. Are we still together there? Do we perhaps have a child? I leaned out the window, and could almost sense that he was about to walk around the corner from the front garden. I found myself murmuring, rest in peace my love.

Since Peter died, I've felt every emotion—from anger to complete pain. Now I just feel tender towards him and hopeful that our pain is passing.

Dreams and unusual occurrences...

I remember dreaming that Peter was comforting me and explaining that he'd had to kill himself because his body was riddled with cancer. My interpretation is that this is probably the only explanation that I would have considered okay.

Have you ever considered taking your own life?

I was suicidal for about a month, a couple of months after Peter died. I didn't WANT to die, I just couldn't take the pain anymore. When I realized and understood that things could get better, stopped feeling suicidal.

Significance of the suicide...

It is the worst thing that has ever happened to me. I think one of the scariest things is finding out how vulnerable you are. One day I was pretty much okay—just a bit stressed and upset—and in a blink of an idea I'd become a gibbering wreck.

I've also discovered that when really bad things happen to you, the people who you trust will probably let you down. (I think that's a pretty common occurrence now.) I've also discovered that getting ill is scary because society suddenly treats you like a second-class citizen. Also that people are frightened of mental illness and direct a lot of anger at the sick person (as though they have chosen to be ill).

Helpful coping methods...

For me, classic CBT (Cognitive Behavioral Therapy) stuff—from day one. I made an effort to try eating, going for walks, being nice to myself, giving myself treats, taking exercise. The shocking and depressing thing is that even with all that effort it still took months to feel anywhere near human again.

Talking and posting on suicide discussion boards.

Advice or words of wisdom…

Be gentle with yourself. Accept that the world is full of people who will be ignorant and unsympathetic, who will judge and say unkind things. It is probably a good idea to stay away from these people (aka bastards) for a while. Try and find people who will support you. They are there—go look!

Expect to feel terrible. But do expect to get better—you will.

"Wanda"

Age: 46

Current Occupation: Office Manager/Hair Salon

Wanda's significant other, Harry, completed suicide on September 18, 2005 at age 38. He hung himself.

In her words...

I am the single mother of two sons, ages 21 and 14. My parents are deceased. In 1987, when I was 28, my mother, born in 1923, died of cancer at age 64. In 1972, when I was 13, my father, born in 1908, died of alcohol related liver disease in 1972 at age 64. I have a sister who is 59, a brother who is 53, and a sister who is 50. I am the youngest.

My father was an alcoholic who was both physically and verbally abusive to my mother. He also suffered from mental illness, resulting in his being committed to mental institutions in the middle 1960's. Our lives were disrupted with terror and violence on a daily basis by my father's drinking and mental disorders.

Harry, my significant other, and I had a very close relationship. He was extremely intelligent and articulate, having a gift for poetry. He was very loving, considerate and respectful. However, he had what I believe to be bipolar disorder, and had been addicted at one time in his life to crystal methamphetamine. He was adopted, which caused him great distress, and he also suffered from a neurological disease known as polyneuropathy. He had, on top of that, a drinking problem. He had severe mood swings. I have found quite a few notebooks filled with his poetry since his death, all of which convey a very dark side, with apocalyptic thoughts, as well as mention of "voices" in his head, telling him he was not good enough to live, among other things.

Incidentally, just for the sake of discussion, he and I met in a chat room online. I was 43, and he was 35. He lived in Salt Lake City, Utah, and I, in Shreveport, Louisiana. After getting to know each other online and by phone, we decided to meet. We made several trips to each other's hometowns, and as the relationship progressed, he decided to move down here to be with me. (He was raised Mormon, but had separated from the Mormon Church as a teenager.)

Harry struggled with world problems as well as his own. He literally bore the weight of the world on his shoulders. He was extremely sensitive to other people's plights, as well as the wrongs being done in the entire world. He just simply could not understand hate, greed, prejudice, and all the other negative aspects of humanity, and struggled constantly with feelings of hopelessness.

On the other hand, regarding the bipolar comment above, when he was up, he was delightful. He was witty and charming, just a beautiful human being. But when he was down, his whole body—his face, his posture, his voice—conveyed defeat. His despondency was heartbreaking to witness. His drinking was a concern of mine, as were his mood swings. My youngest son witnessed these incidences, and also found a journal of Harry's, from 1995, just full of suicidal writings. My son brought me the book, and was quite upset. I was increasingly having second thoughts about our relationship and instead of focusing on Harry's positive attributes, unfortunately, I was focused on his drinking and mood swings. I was concerned about my son and the impact these episodes were having on him. I decided in July to leave. Two months later, Harry hung himself in his shed behind his house.

The suicide...

I do know that Harry's best friend, who was also one of the guys who found Harry dead, was the last one to talk to him before he died. It was Saturday night, September 17th. His friend said Harry was drunk. Harry wanted to go to his friend's house, but his friend talked him out of it because he was afraid Harry would either wreck or get pulled over by the police. His friend offered to come over instead but Harry told him no, that he would just sleep it off. Of course, his friend feels responsible, that if he had gone over to Harry's house, he could have stopped him.

One of Harry's co-workers called me on September 19th at 2:40pm. He told me that two other co-workers had gone to Harry's house to check on him since he didn't show up for work that day. They found him 10 minutes earlier. The co-worker told me the two other co-workers had just found Harry hanging in his shed.

At first, I was just unable to respond. I said something stupid like thanks for calling me. I hung up the phone, and proceeded to get my purse to go to Harry's house. On the way, the impact of the situation hit me. I literally screamed and cried uncontrollably the whole way there.

When I arrived, the police wouldn't let me near Harry's house. There was an officer in a police car parked on the street, and I gave him Harry's parents names and the city where they live. I didn't have their phone numbers but I figured they could find their number in order to notify them of Harry's death. I also gave him my name and number in case they needed it. I waited 24 hours before calling Harry's parents, thinking they would have already been notified of Harry's death by then. But when I called them on Tuesday, September 20, they had not been notified. I had to tell them what happened. I was horrified.

The whole ordeal has been a nightmare. I barely know Harry's parents, having met them only once. I had talked to them on the phone briefly when Harry and I were together, and wrote a letter or two, but hadn't really had much contact with them. I'm sure they hold me responsible. That phone call was the last time I have spoken with them. I sent a flower arrangement to Harry's funeral, as I couldn't afford the expense of going to Utah for the service. They did send me a thank you note, stating that although they were very sad about Harry's heartache over me, they wanted to thank me for making him happier than he had ever been in his life while we were together. Last Sunday, October 16th, I sent them a letter with my heartfelt sympathy and apologies for causing them pain in any way. Whether or not I get a reply remains to be seen.

I wonder if Harry's birth mother may have been addicted to drugs. I've heard since his death that polyneuropathy can come from formaldehyde ingestion, and one way for that to happen is if you lace your pot with formaldehyde before smoking it. I wonder if Harry's mom did this when she was pregnant with him? I wonder if Harry may have been addicted at birth. I wonder if he was bipolar. I think Harry's polyneuropathy, the fact that he was adopted and possibly bipolar, all played a part in his depression. He was a small man, and that bothered him tremendously. I know what crystal methamphetamine does to your brain, so I wonder if that played a role in his depression, as well. His poetry mentioned "voices" more than once. He was an alcoholic. He moved down here to be with me, hoping our relationship would "save" him. Instead, it only added to the pain he was feeling. He simply lost all hope, and felt as though there was no other choice but to take his own life. I think he just wanted to get rid of the pain once and for all. There was too much pain in this world. He couldn't take it anymore. I think he was just tired of trying.

I read Harry's suicidal journal. Why didn't I try to get him help? I have gone over and over the whole thing in my head ever since it happened, and the only thing I can say, sadly, is that I failed Harry. Instead of reaching out to him and trying to help him, in my fear, I abandoned him and ran. My failure to help another human being in his depression will haunt me for the rest of my life. I cannot describe the guilt and shame I feel for not reaching out to a beautiful man who was obviously in pain. Harry told me, on numerous occasions, that he was "damaged goods." I was not there for him.

I have read a lot of books on this subject since this happened, and I am aware that some people have a hard time relating to suicide survivors' pain. However, I must be surrounded by angels, because I have had such a tremendous support system since this happened, I have been truly blessed. My family and friends have been so very supportive of me, and if not for that, I don't think I would have been able to function.

There was one instance in which a girl I work with made some comment about not knowing what was in Harry's heart, so she couldn't speculate about where he "is" now. She was referring to whether or not Harry was in heaven or hell, considering that he took his own life. This girl is what I call a "holier than thou" Christian, and her comment did not surprise me in the least. I have had nothing but positive support from everyone else in my life, though.

The bereavement process...

My life changed forever after hearing of Harry's suicide. I have begun counseling with a professional dealing with grief, and I start this Saturday going to a group suicide survivor's meeting. I meet with the counselor once a week, and the group meets once a month. I have read every book I can find on suicide survivors, grief and grieving. The first couple of weeks I cried constantly, couldn't eat or sleep. I've lost eight pounds. I didn't go to work for the first week, but realized that I needed to try to get some structure back in my life, because I would take my son to school, and sit in my house and cry all day. My co-workers have been so supportive since I went back to work. Two weeks before this all happened, I had given my notice at work, because I had planned on going back to school full-time on a grant. Now, however, I am so emotionally unstable, I can't think straight, so I decided to just go back to work until I can figure out what in the hell to do. I can't make even the most insignificant decisions now.

My appetite is gone. I cannot eat solid food. I can only take liquids. I've been eating soup, because I can't swallow solid food. The first couple of weeks, I cried so much my body ached. My stomach hurt. I can't sleep. I wake up several times a night, and of course, the first thing I think of is Harry. My mind starts racing, going over and over every little thing I ever said or did that I consider now to be uncaring. I imagine him the night he took his life, and what happened.

Anyway, I wake up all through the night, and can't go back to sleep. If I do happen to be able to go back to sleep, every morning I wake up at 4:30am. Every morning.

I've let myself go. My hair, usually colored to hide the gray, has two inches of gray roots showing, and my nails are horrible. I wear the same thing to work everyday. I just wash it at night and put it back on the next day. It's easier than trying to decide what to wear. I just keep telling myself, "What difference does it make?" I have thought of joining Harry on more than one occasion, but, now that I have first hand experience of what it does to loved ones when a person takes their own life, that is just not an option for me. My children are what keep me from doing something like that. I can't be responsible for causing that much pain in the people I love.

I have tried to "contact" Harry in several different ways, using "automatic writing", and also, a lady who used to be a member of the Wiccan society, told me how to burn certain scented candles while relaxing in a tub to "connect" with the deceased and talk to them, but nothing so far has worked. I am even considering using a psychic. If I only knew he was at peace and free of pain, maybe I could begin to heal. The fact that I played a part in another human being's decision to take his own life is something I cannot describe. I am absolutely heartbroken, guilty, ashamed and I feel like a failure. I don't think my life will ever be right again. I am simply putting one foot in front of the other, day after day.

I feel guilty if I smile. I feel guilty if I complain about how sad I am, because, after all, Harry was so sad he killed himself. Who am I to complain? I feel like I don't deserve to be happy. Or to have fun again. Or to love again. Or to live even. But as I said earlier, I simply cannot take my own life, even though I wish I could.

I don't believe I've come to terms with the loss. Because of the part I played in another human being's despair. I abandoned someone whom I was supposed to love. And I don't think I can come to terms with the seriousness of such a callous act of abandonment on my part.

Some people say that they start to feel anger at their loved one that took their own life. However, I know I will never feel that emotion concerning Harry. This man possessed the purest heart I have ever known. The struggles in his head were in no way connected to the goodness in his heart. I have also read in books that, in a lot of cases, the survivors have a way of just remembering the good qualities of the one who took their own life. That they cannot "speak ill of the dead." I realize that, as you read what I have said about Harry's pure heart, that you may have a tendency to speculate that I am one of those who can't bear to suggest that the deceased even had any bad qualities. All I can say is this: Harry was the most kindred spirit I've ever encountered. I wish he had been someone I could be angry with. Then maybe I wouldn't have such a struggle with healing. This man knew what love is, and he knew *how* to love. I have never been treated with more dignity and respect in my life. Gentle, sweet, kind and intelligent all described Harry perfectly. His problems had nothing to do with his character.

I believe Harry had mental illnesses that tortured him throughout his life, and according to his writings, they began long before I came into his life. He had been drinking and had a car wreck when he was 25. He broke his back in three places. He had a hematoma on his brain. He was in a coma for weeks. His recovery took a very long time. In his poetry books, I found a poem that talked about this wreck. From what he said, this wreck was an attempt to take his own life that was unsuccessful. So many of his poems talk about his sadness, grief and despondency.

How do I feel about my loved one today? I miss him terribly. I look back on everything, and I realize that I will never find a heart that pure again. I know he suffered from depression, and that his mind was tortured. But the kindness this man possessed was something that you're lucky if you get to witness even once in your life. I had it, and I let it go. For that, I will never forgive myself.

Dreams and unusual occurrences...

Before Harry's suicide, and, coincidentally, I feel that this added to his depression, Hurricane Katrina hit. Looking back, I had a feeling of impending doom. I said to friends, more than once, that I had a really bad feeling that something worse was going to happen. Now, I wonder if it was some sort of premonition about Harry.

Since his death, I have only had one dream about him that I can remember. In the dream, I remember talking to him. He told me "sunsets were even more beautiful." That was comforting to me. I wish I would have more dreams about him. Or a visitation. Or some kind of sign. Anything. I can talk to counselors for the rest of my life, but I can't talk to Harry, and *that* is what I need.

Significance of the suicide...

I have never felt so alone in my life. Even though I know there are millions of other people who are experiencing the same thing I am, I still feel alone. I go through my day, business as usual, going through the motions, dealing with people, etc., but in my mind and heart, I am alone. This feeling, however indescribable, is with me always. I am forever changed. My heart is irreparably broken.

I am not, nor will I ever be the same again. I feel as though all my innocence is lost. I have been told that everything happens for a reason. That there is some lesson to be learned in this. The only thing I can come up with is that I failed to recognize the deep depression and misery in another human being, that I turned a deaf ear to someone who was in dire need of help, and the realization of my failure has taught me that I should try, in my life, to look for deeper meaning, to tap into my soul when it comes to people in need and go the extra mile to reach out to someone who needs my help. I have definitely turned my focus to understanding my soul, and how I am connected to every living being on earth, that we're here to help one another. My prayer is to ask God to help me do a better job here on earth, so that, hopefully, one day, I can be reunited with Harry and make up for the mistakes I made with him in this life.

Helpful coping methods...

I mentioned earlier that once a week I am going to a counselor, who specializes in grief. And I am starting to attend a suicide survivor group meeting that will meet once per month. I'm reading anything I can find on this subject as well. And I am really looking to spirituality to help me cope with the grief as well. I will continue counseling indefinitely. I knew I needed help. I feared that I might decide that my own suicide was an option if I didn't get help.

"Connie"

Age: 40

Current Occupation: Nurse

Connie's fiancé completed suicide seven months prior to this interview. He ingested poisons.

In her words...

I was one of five kids, the middle child. I am a single parent of two teenagers ages 13 and 18. My fiancé was like my soulmate. As a single parent, he helped me out in a lot of different ways. He showed me a lot of love. I was with him from the night I met him, five years ago. He is such a big loss in my life.

The suicide...

I was beside myself, especially when I got him to the hospital and pleaded with the crisis team not to let him go and they did. Horrible pain.

He did lose his job one month before suicide. He was hopeless, embarrassed and ashamed. He drove for a living. He had lots of friends to reach out to. He had a big family. He was one of ten. He panicked in a lot of different ways.

Two days before the suicide, he was really agitated at me. He did say bring him home to die. He was jumping out of the car on the highway. He said he was having weird thoughts. He didn't tell me the thoughts. I regret not taking more time. I did do the final step. He called me and said he was going to do something to hurt himself.

I work right in the emergency room that the police brought him to, so everyone at work knows. Others, I say he took his life. People who ask who I don't know, I say he died tragically. Others feel really bad for me. It was sad for him to get to that point. No one ever would even think he would do that. At my place of work, they were devastated. When the police called me, they expressed their loss for me.

Bereavement process...

I got involved in Safe Place, a support group. I still read a lot about suicide. It has been a rough road. I think about him day and night. Following the suicide, I was very anxious and exhausted. It was hard to function.

I haven't yet come to terms with the loss one hundred percent. That is a difficult thing to do. When you think you know someone, after five years, and suicide happens it is difficult. There are a lot of questions—such as why?

Eventually, you have to come to terms with it. You have to. It is all time. It is something you learn to cope with but you never ever forget. I still have a rough time some days. It is really hard.

I have my days with a lot of different emotions. I feel anger towards him. He had the chance to reach out for help and he didn't. He chose suicide, leaving lots of people in a lot of pain and distress.

I have had a rough year with my own family. My dad passed away three months later. My life has been hard from the beginning, losing my mother when I was ten. It is the last thing I needed. This is truly the hardest thing in life to go through.

I immediately went to Safe Place. You have to be around other people who are going through the same pain. They understand it is painful. You have to talk about it. When I made my decision to go, I needed someone to talk to. I still go to support groups. They are twice a month. I do not go to counseling. Solos online is also helpful. There are also other websites.

I went to counseling only a couple of times. It takes time to talk things through. They were telling me things I already know. That is awful. I call the Samaritans hotline any time at night I am in distress. They can talk with you. It is twenty-four hour hotline.

Dreams and unusual occurrences…

I dream about my fiancé sometimes. I think he is going to come back.

Have you ever considered taking your own life?

In the beginning I wanted to be with him. I did have suicidal thoughts. But I couldn't do that to my family. You don't even know how painful this is until you experience it yourself.

Helpful coping methods…

Going to support groups. Reading about suicide. Hospice has been helpful with programs.

Advice or words of wisdom…

It isn't anyone's fault. You can't blame yourself for anyone else's actions. They are happy now and out of their pain. It takes a while to come to terms with that and you also have a guardian angel. Jerry is right in my heart, forever. Also, I believe they are in a happier place than all of us.

From the beginning, I have spent a lot of time in the library reading about suicide. I am eventually going to volunteer for the Samaritans. I want to help other people. It is a very traumatizing experience. If you can get through this, you can get through anything.

"Tina"

Age: 39

Current Occupation: Software Support Technician

Tina's husband, "Andy" completed suicide on April 10, 2005. He shot himself.

In her words...

My father was born in California. My mother was born in Virginia. They currently reside in South Carolina. We lived on both coasts growing up, but spent most of my formative years in Virginia. I have a younger brother, currently living in Virginia and a younger sister, currently living in Arizona.

Growing up in my family was typical, I guess. There were no big issues except the fact that we moved a lot (in my opinion). I was born in Washington, D.C. We moved to California shortly after my birth. We moved from California to Virginia when I was in 2nd grade. We moved again when I was in 3rd grade and again when I was in 4th grade. We finally moved again with I was in 8th grade. The older I got, the more difficult it was to make friends. I ended up hating high school as I didn't know many people. This gave me a serious case of low self-esteem, which lasted for years.

Andy was my husband, best friend, lover, and confidant. We had been together 10 years, married for six and a half. When we first met, he was so vibrant and full of life. He was such a loving and caring man. Then the depression struck. It changed him. In my estimation, he had become depressed during the last year or two, which pushed our relationship on the backburner. We were more roommates than husband and wife. Sometimes, I felt like his mother, which I hated. He was drinking too much and I was always complaining. I knew in my mind that we would never divorce. I figured we would work through our issues and come out stronger on the other side although I had no idea how that would happen.

The suicide...

I found my husband in the basement of our home on a Sunday evening. I had just returned home from being out all day. At first, I didn't grasp what had happened. Seconds later, I was screaming and trying to find the phone to call 911. I was petrified of him. He was lying there, motionless, one eye partially open, and a pool of blood around his head. The gun was lying on the floor beside him. I was afraid to touch or look at him. The police and paramedics arrived shortly after I called, and they told me that he was dead.

My husband had started talking antidepressants, which were prescribed by an Internal Medicine doctor, not a psychiatrist, in January/February 2005. Andy told me in late February that while he was taking Cymbalta, he had suicidal thoughts. He immediately stopped taking the medication and called the doctor. I found this out after the fact. When he told me this, he said he was feeling better. About one month later, after switching to a new antidepressant, I asked him if he was having suicidal thoughts again (he seemed particularly down that day) but he assured me he was not. I don't know if that was true or just what he wanted me to believe.

He was in pain from two herniated disks in his cervical spine. This had been an issue for years. He had surgery, but it only addressed one of the disks, not the other. I was just so tired of always hearing about the pain and I know that I should have been more sympathetic. His pain was in charge of our lives. I would ask him to do things with me and/or for me, but the pain always took precedence. I was irritated and tired of coming in second. I know he didn't want to be in pain and he was seeing many doctors to try to help, but nothing was changing. I feel so guilty for not being a better wife to him. I feel that had I been more cognizant of his pain, maybe he would have felt he could talk to me about his suicidal thoughts and I could have helped him overcome his problems. But I wasn't, and now he's gone.

Besides all the pain he was suffering, he was on a multitude of medications to control other issues. He had ADHD, hereditary high blood pressure, cluster headaches (the cause of which was never determined), depression, asthma and allergies. He was so tired of taking medicine! Even with all those ailments, he *never* talked about suicide until he started taking antidepressants. I completely believe the anti-depressant medication was the root cause of this tragedy.

I called close family and friends that night and told them about the suicide. Beyond the immediate family, everyone else was notified by someone other than me, so I didn't discuss the details regarding his death. If asked, I tell people the truth, although I don't discuss it with strangers.

People didn't really know how to relate to me. Some pretended everything was fine, others cried with me and still others told me they didn't know what to say, which was fine. I would rather someone acknowledge my loss, even if they don't know what to do or say, instead of pretending nothing happened. There are still people I work with who have not acknowledged my loss, which has really hurt my feelings.

The authorities treated me well. They called a police pastor and he came to my house to talk to me and pray with me. They allowed me to leave the house and go to another location while they dealt with the scene. There, I made all the necessary phone calls to family. The police came there to talk/interview me regarding my husband. They were to the point, but never nasty or mean.

Bereavement process...

At first, I was in shock. I was unable to do much of anything. Thankfully, my husband's parents were there to help me. His father selected the funeral home, the church, and the cemetery. Each decision he made, he asked for my opinion. He wanted me to be a part of the process and make the needed decisions, but since I really didn't know what to do, he would ask my opinion and if I didn't have one, he would just decide and make things happen. I couldn't have made it through the process without his parents. They were amazing to me. The shock "phase" lasted quite a while. I would guess a few months. I would think I saw him at stores, when my cell phone rang, I would immediately think it was him calling me, when I heard or read something I knew he would enjoy, I would be about to call or email him until the realization hit me. At first, I cried everyday. Now, at four months, I don't necessarily cry everyday, but the waves of loneliness and sadness can be overwhelming. I hear a song on the radio, or hear a news story or see a television show, and I am reminded of him and the fact he is no longer with me and I break down.

I made it through the first three and a half weeks without any health issues, then, just after going back to work, I got really sick. I think the added stress of having to go back to work after being off for almost one month was just one thing more than my system could handle. I've been sick three times since my husband died. The first two times, I was ill for a full two weeks each time. The first time, I was diagnosed with an upper respiratory infection, but it was viral, not bacterial, so I was not prescribed antibiotics to treat my illness. The second time I got sick, I was diagnosed with a viral sinus infection and again, no antibiotics. About two weeks ago, I started feeling sick again, so I started taking a multi-vitamin. It seems to have helped make the illness less severe than the past two, although I've still felt sick for nine days. Along with all I've had to deal with, I also had to sell my house and move, so that has only added to my stress level. I believe my ability to fight off illness has completely headed north. I've never been this sick in my life.

I do not believe I have come to terms with the loss. I am still working through my grief right now. I hope I will come to terms with my loss, but it is going to take time. It was such a senseless act that I just cannot comprehend.

Besides that, I also feel terribly responsible for my husband's choice. I'm seeing a therapist to work through this issue, but no matter how many times we discuss that it was not my fault, it doesn't seem to register.

I started attending a group meeting of Suicide Survivors about one month after my husband's death. I find it helpful to hear other people's stories and know that I am not alone. I've also attended a Widow/Widowers group meeting, but I just didn't feel welcome there. Maybe it was just my perception, but after my second meeting, I decided I didn't want to go back. I have also started attending another Suicide Survivors group in a different city. I started seeing an EAP counselor through my company, but after about four sessions, she didn't really seem to know what to do with me. I have since found a new counselor and have found the sessions to be very helpful. I am still attending both Suicide Survivor groups and seeing my counselor and plan to continue for the foreseeable future.

I felt it necessary to attend counseling, as this was such a huge loss in my life and I was afraid if I didn't attempt to get help, I would be lost in my grief and guilt forever.

I still love him, but I am very angry with him and disappointed with his choice. I have found out a few things about him that I didn't know since his passing and the information was completely unexpected and upsetting. I'm trying to attribute his lack of good judgment to the depression, but it's difficult.

Significance of the suicide...

I am now completely alone. We had no children; it was just he and I. Now it's just me and I feel so alone, lonely, sad and scared. We had just begun planning for our retirement and now that is completely gone. I barely make enough money to keep afloat. Most everyone I know is married and now I'm the poor widow. I don't like my life right now. I'm jealous of other families since they have what I don't. I get angry when I see a husband and wife bickering over something stupid.

After finding my husband that night, I never slept or lived in our house again. I have been living with my brother and his family ever since. I have sold our house and bought a new house. I haven't moved in officially yet. I've never lived alone before and I'm a bit scared. My life has changed completely—for the worst.

Dreams and unusual occurrences…

I don't recall any dreams prior to his death.

Here is a list of strange phenomena, which I believe may have been visits from Andy: 1) Andy and I purchased an attachment for a mixer back in January 2005. It was never opened or used. After Andy's death, I realized that I would never use it and since we hadn't used it at all, it didn't hold any particularly special meaning. I decided I wanted to return it and get the money back. I started looking around for the receipt and could not find it anywhere. I looked high and low.

Then, one afternoon while people were at my house helping clean and pack, I walked into the hallway upstairs and saw a piece of paper just lying on the floor that had not been there previously. I picked it up and it was the missing receipt. My sister-in-law and niece were in our home office working and I asked my sister-in-law if she knew how that paper got to be on the floor. She had no idea. Maybe my one-year old niece put it there? Strange occurrence. It's my belief that Andy knew I would not use that bowl and put the receipt there for me to find so I could return it and save the money. Normally, when receipts needed to be found, I did it. So, I think Andy was "returning" the favor.

2) Andy worked for a government contractor that required him to have a security clearance. In addition, he had security badges he wore to work, which gave him access to his office building. After Andy's death, the human resources person at his company asked that I return the badges. I looked around for them and was unable to locate them. I looked in his cabinet where he kept all his personal items, but they were nowhere to be found. After I told the human resources representative I couldn't locate them, she said that it was okay. Then, shortly after that, I had some friends over to help pack up the house and my friend cleaned out Andy's cabinet and put all the contents in a box. Later, when I looked through the box, I found the missing badges. I asked her where she found them and she said they were in the cabinet, which I had already searched. I believe that Andy wanted me to have the badges, since they had his picture and they were part of his daily work life. He made sure they weren't found until after they were no longer needed by his former employer.

3) One afternoon, I had gone to our house to meet Andy's parents for lunch. They were at my house helping get it ready to put on the market. There was much to do and they kindly offered their help with packing and fixing a few things. Before I arrived, his mother went upstairs to the kitchen and happened to notice something on the deck that was moving around. When I arrived, she asked me if I had put anything on the deck or

had expected anything to be there. I said no. I opened the door and we stepped onto the deck to check things out. What we found was a heart shaped helium balloon that looked to be brand new, completely inflated and showed no signs of being weathered. The weight attached to the ribbon on the balloon was caught between the boards on the deck, so the balloon was just floating and swaying in the wind. I had not seen it there previously and I have no idea how it got there. It was if Andy knew I would be at the house that day and sent me a message. The balloon said, "I love you."

Helpful coping methods…

Taking about my loved one is helpful. I can't forget he lived. He was such an amazing man and I refuse to act like he never existed. I also cry a lot. It helps to get it out and not hold everything inside. I also asked questions and did my own research into depression, antidepressants and suicide. I need answers. I don't know that I have any more information than I had in the beginning, but it was something I needed to do and continue to do.

Thankfully I was able to get short-term disability from my job and I was off for three and a half weeks following my husband's death. I can't imagine having to go back to work right away.

Advice or words of wisdom…

Give yourself time to grieve. Talk about your loved one with family and friends. Cry whenever you need to. Seek help—group and/or individual counseling. Understand that not everyone is going to know what to say to you and may say really stupid things. Most people just don't know how to deal with suicide survivors. You may lose friends. You may be disappointed with family and friends and how they treat you. Most people aren't trying to be ugly; they just can't possibly understand what you are going through. You can choose to take it to heart or just let it slide. Let people help when/if they offer. You may be angry—and it will come out when you are stressed. Let it out. Hit a pillow, break a dish, do what you need to (as long as you aren't going to hurt yourself or others). Don't push yourself to hard to get things done. It will all get done in time. Don't make any rash decisions. I had to sell my house as I could no longer afford it, but I wish I had not had to make that decision so soon. Don't start giving away your loved one's things too soon because you think it will help others. Take your time going through their things. There is no rush.

"Lucy"

Age: 58

Current Occupation: Elementary School Teacher

Lucy's husband completed suicide in 1992 at age 45. He shot himself.

In her words...

I have two grown children. I remarried in 2000. I am Roman Catholic but was not raised in strong religious household, except in grandmother's home, where a lot of time was spent. I am the youngest of four children known as the "baby." I have a very close relationship with my siblings. I have a big brother, who I relied upon and we all looked to him for advice. I have a big sister who I looked to for advice as well. We were very competitive and always jockeying for a place in sports, games, dinner, food, grades, although it was "known" that my big brother was the smartest and the intelligence went down the line, or so we were raised to believe. I grew up with a mother and father whose parenting skills were very poor, but not for a lack of love. My parents were not taught how to survive in the worst of times...and provide for a family. I learned survival skills from my brother. After age eight, I no longer had mother care. I was raised by my father for physical needs. I was reunited with my mother at age 21. My father stressed education, reading, music, games, and spent a great deal of time "priming my brother" to be a doctor, and my sisters to be teachers or nurses.

The suicide...

I learned about the suicide from the state police, who were searching our home and property. I felt shock, fear, numbness, embarrassment, and disbelief. I wanted to crawl into a hole and be left alone.

I had no idea my husband was anticipating the act, not a clue. I did not even think such an idea would enter his mind. His behavior was unusual at the time but I did not put the clues together to even think that this would be his alternative. But, prior to the act, his behavior was different—the only thing that came to my mind was "why is he always running out?" It was as if he did not want to meet someone or was expecting someone to come to the house. Everyday we would have to leave the house if we were home together. He would not answer the phone when he was home. I was working two days or three days or a whole week at a time, and did not put the actions together. The time period was very short between this behavior and the act. There was no time to talk things out. He was depressed at the time, but not an unusual amount. Depression happened often, due to the business and family, but it eventually passed. We discussed money problems. It seemed that he was not taking care of the family money problems, so I took over accounts for our home after a hearty discussion (not a fight). I noticed his appearance was also being neglected, but I thought it was due to the fact that he had no money to get his hair done, etc.

I don't know why he took his life…I'm guessing that he could not live with circumstances surrounding his life at the time. Maybe he could not find answers to his problems. Life must have been unbearable and he saw no way out.

I did not tell others he completed suicide. Only the family knew. I told people he died of a heart attack. I still do.

At first, my family closed in and helped. My brother offered advice, my sister came and stayed, my adult children came home and we "closed ourselves in." My son became protective. My friends were consoling in the beginning offering help, food and advice. Later, no one invited me out—to their homes or to dinner. As the weeks went by it got lonely, except for my sisters asking me out. My son stayed home with me often or invited me out.

I felt like I was treated with indifference. "When you die, you die alone, and when you survive you survive alone." Those we owed money to—some were consoling and forgave the debt, others (like American Express and Citibank) were disgraceful in their attitude and demeanor. They were real "shit heads" and could care less. I made life miserably for them, also.

The bereavement…

I had a fear of the future. I felt embarrassment, numbness, physically ill and mentally confused. I could not think clearly. Thoughts kept speeding through my head. I felt anger towards people, but not towards my husband. I did not care to live. I felt life was done, my job was done; there was no need to go on. I felt like I had no future left. I could not read a full sentence or concentrate. It was very sad and depressing seeing older couples together. I felt like a hole was in my heart. I felt as if I did not fulfill my obligations as a good wife.

I do not feel as though I will ever come to terms with loss. I will never forget. I think about my husband everyday. The first few years, all I could think about was having him come back. I would do anything to have him come back. I found no answers to the situation, so I cannot have closure. "He is on the shelf for me to see everyday." Because of the circumstances involved in the suicide (financial/business), I could not pursue the matter with police or his business associates, so I never found any answers.

I believe society still blames the living (those closest to the victim) for the actions of the deceased. It is the responsibility and the *duty* of the husband, wife, mother or father, to know what is happening in your home and do something about it. Society still places a stigma on the survivors. Why were you not there for them? I did not know! What do you mean you did not know? Where were you when this was all happening? Didn't you talk? What kind of a relationship did you really have? We carry these questions like a weight around our neck and people see us like a pariah. It haunts us terribly.

I did not seek counseling. I did not feel the need to. I come from the "old school" of fess up; be stoic, find your way in the dark, learn to survive on your own. Counseling was not going to change anything.

I miss my husband terribly. I think about him everyday. I used to visit his grave often to talk, but now only once a year because of the location. I still talk to him.

Have you ever considered suicide?

No…never…I find solutions…maybe I'm a coward.

Significance of the suicide…

His death signified the loss of family life and the loss of planned future. I felt as if I lost part of my history. I now question the relationship I thought we had.

Helpful coping methods…

Sleeping, reading, music, working-out, physical activity, working, thinking—a lot of thinking.

Advice or words of wisdom…

Don't let people convince you that you will 'forget" as time goes on. You will never forget. The memory stays with you. The hurt remains consistent. The "act" itself plays in one's head like a never-ending video. As stated before, one has a tendency to question the "whole relationship." I want to believe we did have something good. We had 27 years together. They were mostly happy and caring. We were raising a family, struggling, making a success of life. From the generation I came from, having a family and a home were important goals, and we met our goals. We knew our place in the relationship and what was expected. Thoughts of what did I do wrong? Where were the shortcomings? They prey on your mind. I don't have words of wisdom, but pay attention to your loved one's behavior. If they are out of their routine, ask questions, get help, get to the heart of the matter. Don't be demanding. That was a difficult thing for me in the past. I was stoic, demanding, extremely disciplined and expected everyone else to be the same way. Historically, suicide victims were continually punished from the townspeople they lived with; victims were buried at the entrance of the towns for all people to walk or ride over, showing great disrespect. The Catholic Church condemned their souls to hell forever. Survivors were shunned. Growing up with these so-called laws of society causes great conflict for the survivors. You become afraid people will then condemn you for the victim's actions. Maybe future generations will be more forgiving to those who have completed suicide and to the people they left behind.

Shea McFarland

Age: 37

Current Occupation: Stay at home mom and home health care

Shea's fiancé, Jerome, completed suicide two years and five months prior to the interview. He asphyxiated himself using a belt.

In her words...

I have three children, ages nine, seven, and one. Two of the children were from a previous marriage that lasted 13 years. The youngest is the child of my fiancé. I live on a farm. My mom and step-dad live across the field and my sister lives right next door. We are not wealthy, but the kids are happy for the most part.

Growing up in my family was good. We never had to worry about food or clothes. It was a very stable family. I had a wonderful mom. My biological father caused a lot of pain, but other than that, all was good.

My fiancé and I were happy—very happy. I was pregnant and he was going to be a daddy. We had not been together for long, only about six months. The relationship was different for me. I was free to be 'me' with him. He loved me in spite of myself. We were going to be married in December. He was an over the road truck driver, so we spent numerous hours on the phone. He left on a Sunday, after we had made plans to go shopping for baby items the following weekend. Everything seemed wonderful. He never came home.

The suicide...

My fiancé's best friend had his wife come tell me. It was like a nightmare. I couldn't believe it. I was in shock. I was devastated. I was numb. I was so many things all at once. After I was able to get some sleep, the next morning sometime, I remember waking up and praying that I had been dreaming.

I had no idea that Jerome was considering suicide. There were no signs given to me, not one single sign. He wore a mask with me. He was happy, secure and wonderful. He told me he was finally happy. He said I was the woman he wanted to spend his life with, that he finally had what he wanted in life, a good woman and children. He seemed so excited about the future.

I believe that Jerome was bipolar (undiagnosed). I don't think he planned it. He left one day saying he would be back in five days to go shopping for baby stuff. He even put money in the bank. I have since

108

found out that after he left he stopped at a casino along the way and wrote over a thousand dollars in checks to cover the gambling (checks that were not going to clear the bank). After running out of money and not winning he got into his truck and started to drive. He got pulled over and got a ticket for something. Then he drove some more and got pulled over again, this time they told him he couldn't drive his truck for a week. So, after not winning at the casino, knowing he had all those checks he had to cover and then getting told he couldn't drive his truck for a week I think he felt desperate. One thing I had told him from the start was that we had to be honest with each other, about everything. Before he left I asked him if he had a gambling problem, I assured him if he did that he and I would get help for it. That we would make it. But he promised me he didn't have a problem. He went on to say that he hadn't been in a casino for months, which I later found to be a lie. I didn't know he had a gambling problem, but his grandmother told me he did. I trusted his word over hers. I think he didn't want to face me after he lied to me. There was no way he could hide all the bad checks he wrote, which would lead to him gambling. He sent me a letter telling me he wasn't a man, he wasn't good enough for me or the kids. He said he was sorry, that he knew I wanted to help him with the gambling.

What did I tell others about his suicide? With the exception of my children, I told the truth. I told the kids that he got sick while he was out on the road and died. I have since told my oldest child what happened. I will do the same with the two younger ones when they are mature enough to handle it.

After the suicide, other treated me very cautiously. No one I know has ever experienced the loss of a loved one to suicide. My family and friends tried to be there, but they just didn't know what to say or do.

The authorities treated me like a nobody...I wasn't married to him so I had no rights. The coroner was good to me. They talked to me.

The bereavement...

It is an ongoing process. At first, I lost it. I cried and cried. Then I got angry, so angry at him. Then angry at his mother, then angry at me. I stayed mad at myself for a long time. I still am at times. Up until my son was born, which was five months after my fiancé died, I spent most of my time in denial. I stayed in denial until the DNA tests came back proving my fiancé was the father. After that it was like I started grieving all over again. It wasn't until my fiancé had been gone a year that I stopped crying every day. I slowly started allowing myself to remember the good times I had with him. I am not mad at him anymore. I still feel the pain. I still yearn for him. But most of all, I feel sorrow that he was alone during a time when he was so desperate. I feel sorrow that our beautiful child will grow up without his daddy.

The physical symptoms were vomiting, headaches, weight loss, and excessive tiredness. Emotionally, I cried everyday, hour upon hour. I hated myself for not knowing. I hated him for putting my children through this. I became and still am very depressed.

I have come to terms with my fiancé's death. I am not sure of when, not long ago. Perhaps three or four months ago. I don't know why. Maybe because I have no choice, I have three kids to raise.

I tried to find counseling, but my insurance company would not cover it. I ended up getting some counseling because of a program here for pregnant women. They paid for it. I did not find the counseling helpful at all. The woman was sympathetic, but she did didn't have a clue. I saw her four times. She used talk therapy I guess.

I love Jerome still. I am not mad at him, but rather feel sadness that he suffered in silence. I am not sorry I met Jerome. I am glad that he knew what it felt like to be loved before he died. I still feel that perhaps, had he not met me, he would still be alive, because he wouldn't have felt like he wasn't good enough for me. Irrational thoughts. I have a beautiful son who looks just like his daddy, and I am thankful for this.

Dreams and unusual occurrences...

No dreams prior to the suicide, but since I have had two. One was of my fiancé's friend trying to kill me. I would run away and Jerome would pick me up and carry me back to him. This happened several times in the dream, and then it was over. The other one seemed real. In the dream he and I were standing face to face. He had one hand on my head with his fingers in my hair; the other hand was caressing my cheek. That was it. I woke up and I could almost swear that I still felt the warmth of his hand on my cheek. I then realized it was a dream and burst into tears.

Have you ever considered taking your own life?

Yes, I have. When I was married I suffered from clinical depression. After having our children, the depression got really bad. I had no self-esteem. I felt totally worthless. I can remember waking up and crying because I was still alive. I eventually convinced myself that if I killed myself, my girls would be better off. They would get a new mom who would love them and be good enough for them. The only thing that kept me from doing it is the fact that I did not want them to grow up and think that they were at fault. Or that I didn't love them enough to want to live for them. My father died when I was 17. I always considered his death to be suicide because he was told that he would die if he went back to drugs. He went back to drugs and sure enough, he died. It took me having my own children to realize that he didn't love the drugs more than he loved me. But, the years of these thoughts took a toll on my self-esteem, one that seems to be permanent.

Significance of the suicide...

I know more about suicide now than I ever have. I don't trust many people. I don't know that I will ever be in another relationship with a man. I constantly fear that one of my children will die by suicide. I have no tolerance for people (adults) who whine about things that I now find childish. I am becoming very anti-social, I think.

Helpful coping methods...

The online support group was very helpful.

Advice or words of wisdom...

Reach out to others walking this path, please don't go it alone. It wasn't your fault. Time may not heal the wounds, but eventually the wounds will scab over and not be as raw.

Robin Rice Lichtig

Age: 64

Current Occupation: Playwright

Robin's ex-husband completed suicide 34 years ago. He died by asphyxiation from car exhaust.

In her words...

My parents were extremely close and loving to each other. Mom had me when she was 20. I am the oldest of four daughters. My mother was President of League of Women Voters and active in Congregational Church. My father was on the school board. Creativity was encouraged, but emotion wasn't—very proper WASP behavior. Naughty behavior was swept under the carpet.

My ex-husband was my first big love. I dropped out of college to marry him at age 21. (He was 23.) It was a highly charged relationship, very emotional. I didn't realize it when we married, but he was on the verge of full-blown schizophrenia.

After having two children and a rocky marriage, I finally left him after eight years—to protect my sanity as well as the sanity and physical wellbeing of our young children. I left him the night he beat me for the second time.

The suicide...

I found out about the suicide when the police told a co-worker and she told me. It's etched in my mind. I felt like the bottom had dropped out of the world. I sat on a flight of steps at the newspaper office where I was a reporter with the woman who had given me the news and just shook. I couldn't drive the few blocks to my apartment. She drove me there. Something inside my stomach didn't stop shaking for weeks—even after I went back to work. I finally went to a doctor. The shaking stopped when I took a tranquilizer he prescribed.

I didn't really have any idea he was considering suicide. He told me that he had almost done it a few times, but that didn't seem conceivable. He loved his children. I didn't really think it would happen.

He was in terrible shape mentally and physically. His eyes were red-rimmed. A few days before he lied to me to get me into his car, then drove around hitting me when I tried to escape. I called the police about it, but didn't get a restraining order because it seemed useless. (I called his psychia-

112

trist who said, "He has an appointment on Monday." That was four or five days away.)

I believe the emotional pain of schizophrenia, combined with me leaving him and taking the children (although I perhaps unwisely let him take them whenever he wanted, even on trips) was too much to bear.

Right away I told our six-year-old daughter that he had been in a very bad accident in his car (it was his car he died in). Our son was too young to understand. I don't think I told him anything then. I told other people the truth, including his parents and sister whom I phoned right away. (My daughter, now 39, claims that she was never told it was a suicide. I don't know how I could have not told her that. I think I must have and she repressed it or something. But I have lingering guilt over this. Maybe I didn't handle it as well as I thought I did at the time.)

The police wanted me to identify the body. I was astounded that they would ask this. I refused. Later, I remember talking to someone on the phone from his insurance company. They said I would get nothing because it was a suicide. They were very unsympathetic. My income as a reporter (supporting the kids totally—he never gave me anything) was extremely low. The damn psychiatrist whom he had been seeing and whom I had phoned just a few days prior came to the memorial service. I wanted to kill him.

My parents came to stay with me for the memorial service. (Dad went with me; Mom stayed with the kids.) Then one of my sisters took the kids to live on a commune with her for a week. Friends came from out of town. There was a lot of drinking.

The bereavement process...

I had nightmares for over a year—every night. I'd dream of him and wake up sobbing. Although I was on good terms with his parents and they were close to the children, they had been through so much we never spoke about it. They had sided with me in the divorce. I still dream about him sometimes. I don't feel guilty about what happened. I know I did everything I could. But the pain he went through was terrible.

It took me a week before I could go back to work. There was also a big release. I had been told that he had a gun and wanted to put the children "out of the misery of this life." To say I was frightened is minimizing what I was going through. Also, I knew that his pain had ended, and that was a relief.

I only regret that the psychiatrist, on whom he was so dependent, would never try medication. Only talk. Since we were divorced, I couldn't have him committed. I'm convinced that medication might have saved the day. Because of this, I haven't fully come to terms with what happened.

I don't think I ever will totally because it caused such heartache for my daughter. My son doesn't remember his father, but my daughter still struggles with the loss. It mostly seems like it happened in another lifetime to me.

I had had it with psychiatrists! No counseling for me. I blame that psychiatrist for the death more than anything else.

I still have occasional nightmares that he's looking for me to kill me. On the other hand, I occasionally have a deeply loving dream that involves him being healthy.

Dreams and unusual occurrences...

I seem to have blocked out that dream that reoccurred every night for over a year. I don't remember any visuals. Just the same overwhelming sadness that had caused me to wake up sobbing night after night.

Significance of the suicide...

The effect it had on my daughter was the major significance. It caused problems with my second husband, especially during her teen years when she idolized her dead father.

Helpful coping methods...

I guess drinking doesn't count as a good coping mechanism, but drinking and talking about him with mutual old friends and crying—that was the main method. A number of years later I wrote about it for a college class, which I remember was both painful and a release.

Advice or words of wisdom...

It is such a delicate matter. Any answer depends on the specific, individual situation.

"Kim"

Age: 36

Current Occupation: Public school teacher (7th grade special education)

Kim's lover completed suicide on July 21, 1990. He hung himself.

In her words...

My family is a very straightforward white family from rural Iowa. My mother and father are still married. They had three children. I'm the middle child; I have an older sister and a younger brother.

I have always felt odd, different, somehow misplaced. After studying so much in college, I understand that part of this is just my personality, and part of it is because I am intellectually gifted. I see things differently, and often this would lead to conflict with my family members, however mild. I was often ridiculed for saying things my own way or doing things my own way. I'm sure my family does not believe they treated me this way. I have come to terms with this feeling, as it was pervasive in my life. I often felt like "the weird girl in the corner" all during school, and for much of college. By the time I started grad school 10 years after undergrad, I had come to terms with myself.

I met "Kevin" in college. After watching a theatre performance in which he performed, I wanted to meet him. By chance, we met online about a week later. This was 1988 and just the beginning of the Internet; it wasn't even called "the Internet" yet. It was an online bulletin board system/general discussion list, which had instant messaging capabilities. I was chatting with him online, and he revealed that he was in the theatre performance I had seen.

Kevin and I were lovers. When we met, he was living with another woman. I was uncomfortable with pursuing a relationship with him while he was in a "committed" relationship. He did not break up with her right away, but continued to see me. He was into sexual role-playing games, and liked to be dominated. I was not comfortable with spanking him, which he wanted, but I would boss him around and such. One time he spent the night, and the next morning, very early, I received a phone call from a mutual friend, asking if he was there. Of course, I said he was, and then I heard in the background on the phone, his girlfriend screaming, "Did she sleep with him!" I talked with my friend on the phone for a bit, telling him that I would not divulge any of my behavior to him as it was none of his business. He understood, and simply asked to talk to Kevin. So I went to Kevin and told him who was on the phone. He said, "Tell them I'm not here!" I said, "I already told them you were here. I'm not going to lie for you." I essentially forced him to tell me the truth about his girlfriend by forcing him to talk to her on the phone in front of me.

That was not the end of our relationship, however. He was cowardly, and wanted to be with me without breaking up with his girlfriend. I told him that I wouldn't be with him if he was still with her, and he had to choose. He chose to break up with his girlfriend and be my non-exclusive lover, which was fine with me.

We would have long, philosophical conversations, during which he would ask me questions that were all designed to see "how far I would go" for a friend. For example, he would say, "Okay, you're captured by terrorist scientists, and they have you in one room and a rabbit in the other. They offer you the choice of watching them kill the rabbit, or cutting off one of your fingers. Which do you choose?" I also remember one conversation we had in which he couldn't accept my idea that a mother instinctively loves her child. He couldn't understand the concept of love. He also did not like his parents very much at all. They would send him money for shoes, but he would not spend it on shoes. He preferred to mend his shoes with duct tape. He always hated that his parents would try to buy him shoes.

The suicide...

He hanged himself in an out-of-the-way closet at his work. He handcuffed his hands behind his back, in order to ensure he wouldn't change his mind, apparently.

I was in Vienna, Austria, attending school for the summer in a language program. At the time, I was living in a dorm. It was nighttime, because I was in my nightshirt. The phone rang with a double-ring, indicating that the phone call was coming from outside the dorm. This was strange for both me and my roommate because we never got phone calls at all. She answered the phone, and gave it to me.

On the phone was a friend from college. He was a friend of Kevin's as well. I was initially very excited to talk to him, asking him how he got the number. He explained that he called my parents to get it. He then said, "Kim, Kevin killed himself."

When he told me, I sort of fell against the wall. First my head, then shoulders, then butt, and then my knees buckled and I slid to the floor. I asked my friend, "How did he do it?" He told me that he had hanged himself. He then went on to tell me when the service was going to be, etc. I was in Vienna for two more weeks, so I would miss the service. It's a bit hard to remember, but I think we made arrangements at that time for him to get me at the airport, since his family lived in Chicago, where I would be arriving. He volunteered to drive me back to Iowa City. When I met my friend at the airport, I don't think I've ever been as grateful to see a familiar face.

Over the previous Thanksgiving, he attempted suicide by taking pills, but was thwarted in his attempt by his family, who discovered him and took him to the hospital. I remember talking with him about it, incredulous that he wanted to die. His simple reply was, "That's just the point I'm at in my nihilism." As if that was something everyone had to go through.

I believe it was because he was very intelligent, and couldn't find anyone who understood him. I tried to understand him, and bore the guilt of his suicide for a long, long time. I remember thinking, "If I hadn't gone to Europe, he would still be here." As if I alone could have prevented it. I now realize this is folly.

Kevin was GREAT in bed. Amazing. He was very free sexually. I think that's one of the reasons that I felt so guilty; I often missed him for purely selfish reasons!

Kevin was a writer. He wrote plays and screenplays. When I was teaching drama in high school, I found his play that was performed in college, and I had the kids at the high school perform it. They loved it, and I was proud once again to have been Kevin's friend. His writing touched more people than I'm sure he imagined.

In college, we had an amateur theatre night. Kevin performed in it many times. It was widely known, though, that the people who ran the theatre night did not like Kevin at all. After his death, during the first amateur theatre night of the year, a friend of mine, who was Kevin's best friend, went to the theater with me. He had a script of Kevin's most loved performance at the amateur theatre, and he was going to perform it that night. I remember him leaning over to me while we were sitting in the audience, and he said to me, "If anyone tries to say ONE WORD about Kevin and how 'special' they thought he was, they are going to hear from me." I didn't say anything, knowing that my friend would be justified in it. Sure enough, they started off the show that night by someone making an "announcement," well they tried to make one, anyway. They started to say that the theatre has experienced a loss, or something like that, and my friend, very loudly, shouted, "I don't think it is appropriate for YOU to say anything about Kevin. Everybody knows that none of you liked him. So please stop talking about him. You don't deserve that honor." (I'm paraphrasing. It's been a long time.) The person who was making the announcement was embarrassed, and ran out of the theater. The show went on, and my friend performed. All of Kevin's friends were there, and were very appreciative. It's just another example of how many people were affected by him. Even the people who hated him were moved to say something, and my friend and all Kevin's friends knew that if they did, it would be a sham. I'm sure Kevin would have appreciated the whole thing. He loved interpersonal drama.

I love him. I'm sad about his choice, but that was his choice to make. I'll always love him. He taught me a lot about philosophy, and about love, even though he didn't seem to understand love.

I didn't have to tell too many others, as my circle of friends were all quite close. I told the friends I roomed with, and I told my parents. They were all as supportive as they could be, depending upon where they were in their understanding of it all.

Everyone was very kind. I don't remember anyone being anything less. However, I do remember my boyfriend at the time (he was my boyfriend before I went to Europe, too) breaking up with me because, he said "It's more like you need me than want me. Right now you're like a tree that's died away in winter. You'll be back, but right now, you're barren and dead. It's just not the right time for us." I was mad for a little while, but was soon glad he broke up with me. He was not good in bed, and never gave me an orgasm. I'm certainly being snarky about it now, though, aren't I? I guess I'm still a little mad. He broke up with me when I needed someone. It's true that he wasn't good in bed, though.

The bereavement process...

Oh, yes, I remember that I didn't sleep for three days straight after I found out. As a result of this, those three days were a bit of a blur. Actually, the last two weeks of that trip were a bit of a blur.

On the day that Kevin's service was to take place, I dressed in black, and took my Walkman, and walked to St. Stephen's Cathedral in the middle of Vienna. I didn't want to go to that one, but the smaller ones were all closed. I lit a candle for him, and sat down, and played his favorite song on my Walkman: "The Boxer," by Simon and Garfunkel. I sat there and listened and cried, in front of hundreds of people who were milling about, lighting candles, taking photos of the architecture and praying. I remember a man approaching me afterward, asking if he could buy me a drink, because I "looked so sad." I remember thinking that his words struck me as incredibly naïve. "Sadness" didn't even come close to what I was feeling. I politely declined his invitation, and walked back to my dorm.

During the next school year, when I was having a very difficult time, I called my mother. I didn't often call her for emotional help, but this time I was glad I did. She said something that helped me immensely, by simply acknowledging my feelings. I didn't realize that we had much in common, but she said, "Yes, Kim, I know exactly how you are feeling, and the feelings are real. I felt exactly the same way after my father died." Until that moment, I didn't realize that she DID know what I was feeling. I never knew her father, as he died before I was two years old. It was a great comfort to talk to my mother at that time. I remember she encouraged me to get help, saying, "If you don't have your health, you don't have anything, and that includes mental health."

During the year after Kevin died, I had a very difficult year. I remember hanging out with a friend who was "into" using an Ouija board. He came over to the house, and we sat out in the yard at night, and we were playing around with it. I remember, at one point, I tried to "contact" Kevin. When we tried this, an overwhelming feeling of heaviness and sadness came over me, literally weighing me down, and the marker on the Ouija board slid very quickly to "goodbye" and slid right off the board. I asked my friend if he felt that, and he said he did.

I remember that school year was pretty bad for me. It is hard to explain, but it was simply "difficult." I did not seek counseling, simply because I was too busy in college. I believe now that I should have sought some counseling.

Well, after 15 years, I believe I have come to terms with it. I no longer cry for Kevin. As a matter of fact, about a month ago, I was lying in bed before falling asleep, and thought about Kevin. I wondered "where he was" and "how he was." Right then, I felt a gentle touch tracing down the back of my neck. It made my hair stand on end, but then I was overcome with a feeling of extreme happiness. I believe Kevin come to terms with it, as well.

I can't say when it occurred. Maybe a month ago, when I felt his spirit happy again. I don't know. Now that I think about it, maybe I've NOT come to terms with it. Perhaps I never will. It doesn't permeate my life, filling me with sadness and torture every day, as it did that first year. I think about him....maybe several times per year now.

Dreams and unusual occurrences...

As I said before, I was awake for three days straight after hearing about it. I now remember saying to someone, "I'm afraid to sleep, because he might visit me in my dreams." Hmm. During that fall school semester, I remember reading in the living room, and feeling very strongly that Kevin was "there" in the room with me. I called my friend, and he talked me through it. He was incredibly understanding.

I guess I haven't had any dreams, per se, but dreamlike/surreal experiences.

Have you ever considered taking your own life?

It has only crossed my mind when things have been overwhelming for me, but it is only a fleeting thought. I now have a family of my own, and because of Kevin's suicide and its effect on so many people, I would never do something so irresponsible and selfish.

Significance of the suicide...

Every time I hear Simon and Garfunkel songs on the radio, I think of him. It can't be helped. One time, my husband and I were cleaning the house, and all of a sudden he said to me, "Whenever I hear Simon and Garfunkel songs, I think about your friend Kevin who killed himself. But I never knew him. Why is that?" I explained to him that it was probably just my energy affecting him. My husband is amazing that way; he can pick up on my thoughts and feelings very clearly, but at random moments.

Helpful coping methods...

I have talked with mutual friends about him, and their thoughts and feelings about it. Those who are still close with me are willing to talk about it. We don't talk as much about him anymore. It's been a long time.

Advice and/or words of wisdom...

Talk about it as much as you need to. Go into therapy even if you think you don't need it.

Deborah Darby

Age: 55

Current Occupation: Writer

Deborah's long ago love completed suicide in 1965. He shot himself.

In her words...

I grew up in a typically dysfunctional 1950s family (post-WWII, war-hero father, chronically ill mother—both alcoholic—with 2 kids). At least it looked typical to me. I've got a story about this, too! There was violence in the family, which took a huge toll on my mother and caused my brother to beat me up pretty routinely.

Monte and I were both looking for love; both drinking too much, a teenage rite of passage in West Texas.

The suicide...

My mother told me about Monte's suicide when she read about it in the newspaper. I didn't have even an inkling Monte was considering suicide. All the boys I knew (and liked) were wild and crazy like Monte, yet none of them killed themselves.

Monte was a crazy kid; lots of us were. He acted out in many ways and he had a shotgun. Looking back from an adult standpoint, I'm sure he was lonely, almost certainly abused in some ways, and called upon to be "tough".

The bereavement...

I was numb. It was my first real experience with the death of a loved one (other than pets). It didn't seem real. I was angry (at my mother) and confused and very sad. I blamed my mother for not telling me until after the funeral, so I became quite the martyr. Only one of my friends really knew Monte, though, so it wasn't all that effective to be martyred.

My long-time friend Laura and I were estranged for a while, uncomfortable speaking to each other. When we finally did speak, she told me the details of the suicide and we reconciled.

I wasn't aware that I would need to grieve. It was years later when I felt the bereavement. I did, however, feel guilty and shameful. In my family, blame was a common factor, and I was sure that something I had done or not done in my brief acquaintance with Monte had caused him to kill himself.

No counseling at the time; it wasn't offered and I was just a kid. I had lots in my 20s, dealing with the grief over Monte as well as other childhood trauma.

It wasn't long afterwards that I "fell in love" again with another wild boy, and this time I lost my virginity, which began a long career of promiscuity in my teenage years and my 20s. That behavior was probably going to happen anyway as I was desperate to be loved and knew no other way to get attention.

I think writing the story about Monte has put me at ease, plus the decades that have passed. I have spent many, many years recovering from lots and lots of childhood trauma.

I have a deep fondness for Monte. He shines in my memory.

Dreams and unusual occurrences…

This one was written down; I'm sure there were others. There were two of me—or one may have been labeled Deanne (my best friend in school) — and a child at my boyfriend's house. I had talked to the child and knew that he or she was going to shoot the gun. Then I was cleaning house when the other me yelled that the child had shot himself. The child was okay, but definitely shot in the hip. I went into kitchen where a telephone and a clock hung on the wall over the sink. I tried to call my boyfriend, who was a doctor, but I couldn't remember his number. I dialed 381-1037, and got a man with party sounds in the background; he said my boyfriend had made a phone call and left. He thought my boyfriend was at "Emily's".

Have you ever considered taking your own life?

I was strongly suicidal for almost the entirety of my first 50 years of life. Long-term (high functioning) depression and unwise choices kept me literally begging for the relief of death off and on, though I managed to have a successful career. My personal history wasn't nearly as successful, however, with many episodes of promiscuous behavior and substance abuse. I left my only child with her father and hid in affairs and self-medication for many, many years.

Even after I gave up using sex, drugs and alcohol as escape mechanisms, I still longed for death. But after September 11, 2001, in a desperate depression (though by that time I had been on medication for several years), I had my last serious urge to kill myself. A spiritual experience in the truest sense of the word caused me to, at last, re-evaluate the value of living this life to the best of my ability. Perhaps it's just the wisdom of age, but I no longer wish to die at my own hand. I do support one's right to do so, however, and am active in the right to die movement, Compassion and

Choices. And, of course, should I find myself at the end of life in pain and/or other unacceptable circumstances; I reserve the right to rescind my decision not to kill myself.

Significance of the suicide…

It was a pivotal point in my adolescence; a true moment of high drama in my relationship with my mother. It marked the transition from childhood to my "who cares, we're all going to die soon anyway" adolescence.

Helpful coping methods…

Denial, denial, denial.

Helpful advice or words of wisdom…

I now know that choosing to end one's life is a deeply personal decision. It has almost nothing to do with the ones around us. Yes, it's selfish, but only in the sense that every action we take is our way of seeking to achieve homeostasis. And for some, homeostasis is, in fact, death. I have been a fan of death all my life, and still am, for I know there are realms beyond that are more accommodating to our life spirit than this one.

Some people kill themselves actively; some passively (i.e., my mother via drugs/alcohol and obesity). Some people live long, fulfilled lives and go cheerfully into the end of life. All of us have other places to go, other lives to live, other realms to explore. This life is just a stopover on a long journey.

As a former Hospice volunteer, I've seen people for whom death is a true joy. I've seen people hang on long past the time that this life had meaning, but my favorite patient, my first, just "got it" and made the transition quickly, gracefully. Much of my life-long personal writing career revolves around death. I feel sad when a friend or loved one dies, but I also celebrate their ability to go forward into their next life, whether by illness, injury or self-immolation.

After all these years, I'm "good at" grieving. There is some evidence that those of us who have that trait are the ones who live very long lives: that being able to let go of those we love gives us some kind of constitutional edge over those who are devastated by death.

When my father died last year, I experienced a huge grief, though it was his time and we had discussed it in some detail. Being good at grieving doesn't mean I don't feel it…I feel it intensely, face it, curse it, brood over it, experience it in every way, then hit bottom and start looking up again. I take the time I need to grieve now, which very few people do. Most go back to work as soon as possible and many act as if nothing had happened. I've been there. That doesn't work for me. I believe that among my life's callings is being supportive of friends who are going through their grief processes as well as supporting those who are dying. I daresay that my early brush with death, via Monte, has had some significant impact of these leanings.

CHAPTER FIVE
Siblings

Susanne Johnson-Berns

Age: 41

Current Occupation: Accounting Dept. Manager

Susanne's brother completed suicide on May 16, 2002. He died by strangulation.

In her words...

My parents divorced when I was seven. My mother remarried when I was 13. My father did not have much contact with us. There are five children in our family—my older sister (48), an older brother (44), myself (41), my brother (who was 34 when he died) and a stepbrother (25). My mother died of ovarian cancer in 1999. My mother worked full time. I would say we had a normal upbringing. Not unlike many others my age, we faced the divorce of our parents, and adapted to my mother's new marriage. We fought as children do. I feel like my mother was sometimes preoccupied by making the new family work. She gave birth to my younger stepbrother at age 42. There was always conflict with my biological father, who did not tend to us very much. Later, as we all went to college and pursued our own lives, my deceased brother, Joerg, stayed close to home. He always lived near my mother.

When we where growing up, Joerg and I were very close. We played together; we shared a lot since we where so close in age. We became more distant when we were both married and moved away from home. After my mother died, we became much closer again and he would call me all the time. Especially when he was troubled. Looking back I truly believe that my brother's spiral with depression began when my mother passed away. He had a very difficult time with her illness. She was always there for him and during the last days of her life he had trouble visiting her in the hospital. She had lost all her hair and was disfigured and often confused and incoherent, due to the medication. He was angry and the night she died, he and I had an argument that made him storm out of the hospital. Mom died that night and he was not there. I believe today that he felt very guilty. He never recovered from the loss. We had no idea how he felt; we never discussed how he felt about it.

The suicide...

My sister in-law left me a message on my answering machine. She was screaming hysterically that my brother had hung himself. I passed out, and found my son, who was 16 at the time, kneeling over me. He too had heard the message. I walked around confused and I kept saying, "Oh, my God. Oh, my God." My son helped me make the necessary phone calls to confirm the worst. I guess until I heard someone actually say that he was dead, I could still hope that he had survived. I think I knew, but nothing could have prepared me for those words, he was gone.

Initially I was unable to breathe. I screamed out loud. I felt this unimaginable pain. I was hysterical and I sat in the floor the entire night crying. I felt completely lost and childlike. I was very confused and tried to deny what happened. This is very difficult to put into words. I felt horribly guilty. I immediately asked why, why? Mostly I could not understand why. I did not know this could happen. I felt very lost and I wanted to die myself.

He was troubled before and he had called me a few weeks before, telling me that he felt as if he was making a mess of his life. He was having some marital problems. He said he felt as if he had two choices, one he said would be for him to come see me (we lived 400 miles apart). My husband and my brother did not get along well so I knew it would be hard for me to have him come stay. I kept asking him about what the other choice was and he said, "You're a big girl, figure it out." That was about two weeks before he ended his life. I, of course, discovered a lot of things later—that he was depressed, that he had lost his job, and he had been drinking often. He often spoke about missing my mother terribly. I believe he somewhat announced his suicide and I wished today that I had never heard people say, "People do not announce their suicide." I knew in my heart something was wrong but I did not act on it because primarily I believed the statement that people do not announce their suicide.

He must have felt hopeless. I think he felt a lot of guilt about my mother's death. He was close to her but I also know that he often avoided her because of the state she was in. She has always been the caretaker and she was a strong dominant women. When she became ill and immobilized by the cancer he did not know how to cope with that.

I often lied about how he died. Only very few people knew the truth. Most people would ask me if it was an accident, and I would say yes. I did not want people to think of him as a bad person. I wanted to protect him from that. I also felt unable to discuss it. During those first weeks and months, I could barely get through the days. It has taken me three years to be able to speak about it out loud.

Many people seemed to avoid me, or at least that is what I felt. I lost some of my friends because they thought I should just be over it after a while. I was being avoided, not included anymore. Laughter would stop if I entered the room. I felt very isolated. Everyone expected me to just be the same person I always was, all put together, happy and in control.

The bereavement process…

I was unable to sleep the first three months. I had visions of his death. I became severely depressed. I became afraid that it could happen again. I was afraid it could be me. I thought a lot about death.

I tried to read a lot about suicide. I saw my physician, who put me on antidepressants. Eventually I saw a counselor and I also went to a group for survivors of suicides. I spent my nights doing arts and crafts. I have actually become a pretty decent painter. I also began to write down my feelings. I have written most of them in poems.

I went to group sessions with other survivors. It was helpful to talk about my brother. It helped being around others who understood what I was going through. It helped to have a place to cry openly. I also saw a therapist but only three times. I did not find this very helpful. I was severely depressed and at the time even thought about suicide. That may be very normal, however, the therapist did not relate to me very well. Through a friend, I meet a woman, whose son completed suicide in 1999, who lived several states away. We called each other regularly. We were each other's life-lines, so to speak. She was a savior to me.

Coming to terms with it. I am not absolutely sure what that means. I have accepted the truth that my brother ended his life by suicide. I am no longer in denial. I have no answers and the "why" will forever remain buried with him. The rawness of my pain is gone and it is now replaced with silent private moments of grief. I still miss him terribly. I still miss hearing his voice and hearing his laughter. I miss who we were before that horrible day in May that changed everything.

I believe that I have come to accept who I have become. I have stopped searching for the person I was and have began to learn to live with this new me. I guess it took about two years to get here. I believe that once I understood that life would never be the same, I began to cope better with the loss of my brother.

I feel sad about my brother, and it still makes me cry to think about him. I hurt for him deeply. When I think about the anguish he must have been in, especially on that day, it takes my breath away.

Dreams and unusual occurrences...

None that I can recall prior to, but lots afterwards. I was not there when he died but in my dreams I would witness his suicide over and over again. This is why I chose not to go to sleep for many nights. I still have those dreams sometimes. I had said once that I think I may be okay if I can cut him down from his rope, in my dream, and just hold him in my arms. So far I have not been able to.

Have you ever considered taking your own life?

I did spend a lot of time thinking of death after my brother's suicide. I felt life was too much trouble. I wanted to stop hurting. I struggled from day to day. I felt guilty for not saving my brother. I did not think I could go on. I did, however, constantly remember what I would do to my son and husband. I would pass all the pain and guilt I was carrying on to them. I would do to them what my brother did to me.

Significance of the suicide...

It has changed my entire life. It has changed how I look and act around people. I always think carefully about what I say to people. I am more fearful. The biggest impact has been in how I relate to my 19 year-old son. I am always afraid now that he could become disappointed or discouraged, or feel alone, or become depressed, and that he could contemplate suicide. I have experienced trouble disciplining him in the past because of this fear.

Helpful coping methods...

I spent a lot of time reading as much as I could in reference to grief and suicides. I began to write poetry and little essays. I spoke to other survivors and found that to be most helpful because we truly understand one another. I believe that only those who have personally been affected by suicide can understand the turmoil it causes. I also sought help from the minister at the church.

Advice or words of wisdom...

Talk about your feelings openly. Tell the people around you how you feel. Say: "I am sad," "I am having a bad day," "I want to scream," or "Please help me." Those around us who love us are not all affected by the suicide in the same way we are (my son told me that wise statement). Each of us deals with it differently. If we share how we feel, we actually allow them to help us, to understand us, to comfort us. Saying "nothing's wrong" closes the door on them.

Losing my brother was the most devastating experience of my life. I would have never expected to find myself there at that point, dealing with his death, making funeral arrangements, and standing there in front of the casket. I was unable to physically speak to anyone during those first few days. It was as if I was watching someone else's life. I felt as if a part of me had been ripped away. Life seemed to move in slow motion.

Later I felt like I had to hide my emotions, life was supposed to just go on. My own family wanted to just hide it somewhere. We just did not discuss it; no one wanted to discuss it. Everyone was waiting for me to get over it, to come back as the happy strong individual that I had been. It took a lot of courage and a lot of true honest feelings to realize that the person I was before May 16 would never return. She, too, died that day. Even my son told me about six months after my brother's death that he had never seen me fall apart before. No one had. I was always strong upbeat, cheerful, always looking on the brighter side of life. I was always helping some cause. Life took on an entirely different meaning for me. It has become unpredictable. Yes, we have always known life to be that, unpredictable. I, however, have learned that it truly is so. I have learned that you can come home and with the blink of an eye the world you knew seconds ago can change not only itself but it can change you, forever, and the more you resist the change the harder it will be to go on from here. I truly believe that we do not recover from a loved one's suicide. We can only learn to live with it, somehow.

The Why

Sitting here in silence

Whispering your name

But you are gone forever

Life will never be the same

My every waking moment
Is filled with thoughts of you
Sorrow, questions, grief and anger
I don't know what to do

I close my eyes and see your face
A smile, a word, a cry for help
Embracing now each second shared
Searching for the pain you felt

Why did you go and leave me
That I will never know
For the answer to that question
Lays deep within your soul

In memory of my brother, Hans-Joerg

"Wendy"

Age: 40

Current Occupation: System Director

Wendy's older brother completed suicide on May 13, 2004. He took an overdose of morphine and OxyContin.

In her words...

My family, in a word, is DYSFUNCTIONAL. My parents are Italian immigrants. "Tony" (my brother who died by suicide) was 20 months older than me. We also have a younger brother, who is nine years younger than me.

There was little to no affection shown as we were growing up. We were both depressed as youngsters, however, I didn't have it in me to even attempt suicide. I always hoped for a better life when I was finally able to get out of there. Tony always talked as if he didn't care and would some day end it all. Although his death was very disturbing, it was not a total surprise that he took his own life. There was some physical punishment when we were young, but mostly there was emotional abuse, which continues today.

As we were growing up, my brother and I confided in each other. We were unable to show how we cared about each other (no "I love you" or hugs, etc.) but actions spoke louder than words. We knew we cared about each other. He decided to up and move his family to Arizona, (we grew up in New York) about as far away as he could get while staying in the states, to get away from all the family bullshit. We kept in touch at first by telephone, but in more recent years, by email and instant messaging. He wrote to me once for every 10 emails I sent him. Mostly he wrote to me when he needed someone to talk to. When he separated from his wife and when he needed to vent about how bad things were with his home life.

The suicide...

My parents called me. At first when my mom said he "was gone," I hoped that meant he got on his bike and left. Then as I realized what she was talking about. I just knew it was suicide. My parents didn't know for sure right away how he died. His estranged wife found his body, but did not (and still has not) let anyone see the notes he left behind. (I know they exist because they are mentioned on the police report, however, for whatever reason, they were not taken into evidence.)

In hindsight, I guess I should have known. In his last instant message to me he spoke about how he would be working until he was dead (no retirement) and how he didn't even know why he bothered to get up in the morning. The only thing that got him up was to "take a piss." I guess I should have known, but he always talked like that. I never really wanted to believe that he'd actually follow through.

He often talked as if he would someday do that. He also left notes. His daughter told me of one of his lines from the note where he asked the wife to tell the kids "this is my destiny."

When I didn't know for sure how he died, I conveyed the line of crap his estranged wife was telling everyone—that we don't know yet—possibly a heart attack. After I found out the truth (I sent for the coroner's report, death certificate and police reports) I told everyone the truth.

My husband was very supportive. Co-workers didn't really say much. Some friends just avoided the subject while one emailed me a really off color racist "joke" about why Muslims commit suicide. When I asked her to please not send me jokes of that nature, she got very upset at me and stopped all communications with me.

My dealings with the authorities were over the phone, but they were very professional and kind. The coroner was very kind. I was upset with the police because they didn't follow protocol and didn't have any record of the notes that were left behind, but they were also nice and sympathetic.

The bereavement process…

I went online and found a book by Carla Fine (*No Time to Say Goodbye*). I found this book extremely helpful. I joined a bereavement group online (GROWW) but they didn't focus on suicide and I felt it wasn't really working for me. Finally, I found Friends and Families of Suicide (FFOS) online and that group has helped me tremendously!!! I put my brother's name on the suicide wall and my husband even created a website to honor his memory. All this was very therapeutic.

I cried at the drop of a hat for the first few weeks. Some chest pains—not like a heart attack, more like from holding in the tears—like a pressure. There was lots of stress from all the lies surrounding his death.

I did not seek counseling. I don't want to be put on any medication. I feel that the support group I joined has been extremely helpful to me and I don't need to see a therapist. I think the best people to talk to about this and to help me heal are people that have gone through it themselves.

I believe that I have come to terms with the loss. Deep down, I always knew he'd eventually do this. I tried to help him to see all the good in his life, but it didn't work. It took a while—I guess right about the one-year mark or just before that.

I miss him dearly. I understand all that he was going through and how he felt so totally helpless. I don't think any less of him because of what he did. I am grateful for the times we shared together.

Dreams and unusual occurrences...

The night I found out about his death, I had a dream where I saw a beautiful blue butterfly and a voice said, "Your brother did not die of natural causes." A few months later when I finally received some of his ashes, I had a dream that we were sitting at our dining room table talking and I asked him, "Why can't they all leave me alone?" (Referring to certain family members who were making my life a living hell.) He said to me, "You have what you need now—you have me—don't let them get to you anymore." That dream is what keeps me going and what has given me the strength to live my life as I choose—without taking any crap.

Have you ever considered taking your own life?

As a teenager I thought about it. I didn't really want to die, I just wanted to change the way my life was. One day I crossed the avenue by my house and decided I wouldn't look for any oncoming traffic. I didn't care if I got hit by a car (as a child a young girl was hit by a car while riding her bicycle and died right by our house). When a car almost hit me it was like a wake up call. I knew I didn't want to die, but I so desperately wanted to do what I had to do to get out of that house. At 17, I met the man I eventually married and he helped me to see the good that could be—and he proved to me that life could be better.

Significance of the suicide...

I have decided that I will not allow anyone to make me feel like less of a person anymore. I will not be in the same emotional position he was in. As a result, things with certain family members have been very strained, but so good for my self-esteem. I'm not taking anyone's 'shit' anymore. We allowed people to treat us poorly growing up. I will not end up the way he did.

Helpful coping methods...

I have a small container with some of his ashes. That helps me to feel close to him. I don't know if you can call this a method, but the dreams I have with him make me feel good.

Advice or words of wisdom...

Find someone sympathetic to talk to about it, preferably someone that has experienced it first hand. I like the online support group because it is always available—whenever YOU need it—day or night, 24/7.

When I was younger, a friend of my brother in law's died by suicide. He was very young. I remember how I felt about it back then. I try to remember how I felt upon hearing about it and try not to judge people that act strange around me. Unless you experience it, it's hard to know what to say or how to react. Try not to be too harsh on people who don't know how to deal with what you're going through. If you can, talk to them about how you feel. Talking really helps—try to find someone understanding and sympathetic to talk to. It may feel like you will never smile again and that the pain will never go away. Eventually you will smile and even laugh again. The pain will always be there, but you get used to it and learn to live through it.

Karen Frater

Age: 49

Current Occupation: General Manager

Karen's brother completed suicide five years prior to this interview. He hung himself.

In her words...

I am the eldest of three children. My brother, Geoff, who completed suicide, was three years younger than me. I have another brother who is three years younger than Geoff. My father is one of five boys—his brother completed suicide 20 years before Geoff. My mother is one of four children, with two elder brothers and a younger sister.

My mother was a stay-at-home Mum. She and Dad were totally committed to family. Dad worked two jobs in order for Mum to be at home with us. He was a shift-worker driving buses so we had to be quiet in the afternoon after school if he was at home sleeping.

Geoff was born eight weeks premature, which 45 years ago, was a very great cause for concern. The survival rate was not high. As a newborn, he was hospitalized for a few weeks and Mum would make the long trip by bus into the hospital to take breast milk to Geoff. When he came home, he required constant care as he was always bringing up his formula. He was quite a sick baby, but Mum and Dad looked after him around the clock.

As was the norm in my country, when a child turned four and six months, they could start school. Geoff started school when he was four and seven months, even though developmentally, he was not as far along as most of the other children. He used to cry each day to go home and there were many times I would be called out of my class to sit with him on the school steps and console him. Yet he was also a bit of a terror. He would be the one to get into trouble at school and at home. Mum would go looking for him when he was about six and he would be sitting on the peak of the roof. She would have a neighbor help bring him down as Dad was at work, and then when she went to look for him, he would be on the roof again.

Geoff also loved animals and was always bringing home every stray dog he found. He was gentle with them and they sensed he cared for them as well. As Geoff grew older, he tended to be drawn to the groups of boys who were trouble. Geoff found it difficult to keep up with his peers in his class, so he thought being the class clown would take the attention away from his scholastic ability or his inability to catch on as fast as the others.

As a result, he became the class rascal, it allowed him to not do as much schoolwork and therefore not remind himself and everyone else that he was not coping with it as well. I often felt Mum over-protected him and Dad was always there to get him out of whatever scrape he placed himself in. No matter what it was, Geoff was in it and Dad and Mum came to the rescue. As the years went on, they tried a number of high schools, getting up early to take him there and then supporting him as he went from job to unemployment to another job.

He joined the army and somehow completed two years, but not without going AWOL a number of times and the military police ended up knowing my parents on a first name basis.

He then became a truck driver due to his army experience and found work easily at first. As the years wore on, and Geoff continued to meddle with alcohol and marijuana, he became even less reliable and was continually in and out of work. Mum would still continue to go up to his flat (as they could no longer have him living at home due to his outbursts when drunk). He had assaulted both of my parents at various times, although they did not tell my other brother and I about the assaults.

Mum continued to buy Geoff cigarettes and food while he unfortunately spent his money on beer and drugs. As the years went on, the cycle sped up. Geoff would ask us and relatives for money, he would get support for a while until we all realized it wasn't helping him and eventually he had 'used up' everyone.

We also worried if he came to visit because if he drank, he would become very aggressive. One night when he stayed, I locked myself and the children down the end of the house in our section of the house as I was afraid to sleep while he was drunk. My husband ended up telling him he was not to come anymore. One day Geoff rang to say he was coming up. My husband said he was not to come to the house. I had new twin babies and Geoff phoned me from the station and asked me to pick him up. I could tell he had been drinking. I said I could not pick him up and he said he would catch a cab and I was to pay the driver when he arrived at our home. (He frequently did this to my parents and would stay at the front door with the cab driver until my mother opened the door and paid.)

My husband rang the cab company and told them that a driver was bringing someone to our house and gave the address and told them to tell the cab driver we would not be paying and apparently the cab driver turned around and took my brother back to the station.

Over the years, Geoff's drinking and marijuana use alienated him from those who loved him. We wanted to help him but realized that we were also part of the cycle as we continually rescued him. One by one, the rescuers diminished.

My father, who had been raised with alcohol being part of his daily ritual, was able to handle alcohol well. He did not seem to understand that Geoff could not handle it and underwent a personality transformation which was not rational and very violent, yet Dad would offer him beer or give him a few bottles of his home brew to take home not wanting to refuse Geoff's requests.

I thought 'helping' was giving Geoff money, flying him to visit his girlfriend who had moved away, lending him money to get his drum set transported interstate where he was living (only to find he sold the drums), talking to him about it and at the end of the conversation where he agreed with everything I said, having him asking me for just $20 or so regardless of what I said.

We did not have a close relationship—Geoff seemed wedged between my younger brother and me—both of us graduated from the university and undertook professional careers, married, bought homes and had families and are both still married to our partners of 30 years and 20 years.

The weeks before Geoff's death, I had thought about him many times and felt impressed to phone him—but I remembered the times he could be unpredictably violent and with six children and Mum saying he was hard to catch at home, I didn't follow through.

The suicide...

I received a call from my younger brother that our parents had been assaulted. Geoff had been drinking and had thrown my mother against a wall and then repeatedly punched my father in the head as he tried to protect Mum. We did not know the full extent of what happened until the next day.

When I arrived at the hospital, my younger brother was already there. I could not believe what I saw. Mum's face was swollen beyond recognition. My father looked a broken man—the bruising and cuts on his face were nothing compared to the despair on his face—it was beyond his comprehension that he was in hospital as a result of an assault by his own child.

While our parents were waiting to have the various tests and surgical procedures, my brother and I drove the short distance from the hospital to Geoff's house. He was not home. I felt that I really wanted to see him and talk to him. I left a message on his door that we were concerned about him and for him to call me on my cell phone.

We then went back to the hospital and sat with our parents until they were discharged. My mother's sister arrived and could not believe what she saw—the swollen disfigured faces were nothing like my parents.

We finally were able to take them home. We agreed that it was not safe for them to stay there, as Geoff had been released the same night after he was charged and we were not sure how he was or whether he would show up as he had so many times before in the middle of the night.

I arranged for a locksmith to change the locks on my parent's home, a glass repairer to fix the broken window, changed my parent's phone number to an unlisted number and took them to my aunt's house.

Geoff rang that night—sober and mortified. He said that he had experienced a real epiphany. He saw his life in a way he never had before. He saw that everything that had gone wrong was the result of alcohol and he did not want to have any part of it anymore.

He asked me if I would take him to rehab—I hesitated—I was still trying to work through my emotions of what I had watched my parents go through that day in the hospital. I agreed to talk to him the next day. How I wished I would have gone over to speak to him then, but I knew that my husband would not allow him to come to our house, so I left it to the next day to sort out the details.

Geoff was told by the police, and also by me, that Mum and Dad were badly injured. I believe he realized that he was getting worse and the only way to stop himself from hurting again was to take his life. He was also fearful of jail and the police had charged him with assault. My younger brother had gone to the police station that night to see him, but he was told he could not see him. We do not know why.

The next day I tried to phone Geoff, but there was no answer. I tried a number of times and phoned my brother and asked him to try as well. I asked him to try the next day as I was in exams and then phoned him that evening. He had not heard anything. I said I was going to phone on the hour until I had an answer. I was already feeling afraid of the vision I had of Geoff hanging coming true.

I decided to try again. After a number of rings, a male voice was on the end of the phone said, "Hello." I knew right away it was not Geoff's voice. Two ideas seemed to run through my mind at the same time. One was that these people were involved with drugs and had come to see or harass Geoff. The other one was that they were police or detectives and were there to check out if everything was all right. The second hunch was the correct one.

I asked the person who they were and he asked me the same question. I said, something is wrong isn't it. He asked me again who I was. I said I was Geoff's sister and that he was hanging dead, wasn't he. The detective/policeman confirmed that he was. I do not remember much. I think I gave him my name and phone number and maybe got his number. I remember putting the phone down and wondering where to run to, what to do about my parents, how not to lose control in front of my children. My younger twins were in the bath. I could not think straight. I wanted to get to my younger brother who lived about eight minutes away. I knew that I needed to tell him and it could not be on the phone. I had to be with someone to share my absolute anguish.

I half screamed at the children to get out of the bath, quickly dried and dressed them, bundled them into the car and drove as fast as I could to my brother's house. When my sister-in-law opened the door, I asked where Rob was. She said he was downstairs.

I flew down the stairs to him. He was on the phone to my aunt. I half cried "Geoff's dead" as he stood stunned holding the phone. I think we half intelligibly told my aunt and said we would phone her back. I then told my brother and his wife what had happened with the phone call I made to Geoff's home.

Next was what to do about our parents. They had gone back to their home by that stage. I phoned my aunt and told her—total disbelief— beyond comprehension. My brother and I discussed what to do about telling our parents. I know I told the police not to inform them that night, that I would, as they had just come out of hospital and were extremely fragile emotionally and physically. I assured them I would let them know the next morning when we could get down there as our father was seeing the specialist first thing and we knew he needed to for the operation. If he found out the news that night, he would be beyond seeing a surgeon the next morning and I could not see what telling them late at night would do. They were overwrought already from their experience and needed sleep. I knew it would be many nights before they would ever have that chance again.

Geoff had apparently told my mother he was going to "do a Brett." Brett was a good friend of Geoff's who had completed suicide a couple of years previously. Geoff had also told me that when he was up north in Darwin, he had a rope, or tie, or something, and was going to do 'it'. I obviously said that it would not have resolved anything and would not be a solution and would devastate everyone, particularly Mum and Dad. He agreed.

He also had a close call when he had a one and only experience with heroin and had a severe reaction and was revived by ambulance officers. He seemed to have a strong desire to live and survive.

I tell others I have a brother who has died. Depending on the circumstances, I will share that he completed suicide but do not volunteer the information as it makes others uncomfortable and does not seem to be necessary in every situation.

Some people expressed sympathy, but most people tended to not say anything after the initial expression of sympathy. At university, one of the women said that I did not know what pain was compared to her father dying. This was not told directly to me, but from one of the other students.

The detective/policeman, who was at Geoff's house the night I phoned and with his fellow officers had discovered Geoff's body, was very diplomatic and allowed me to have the information I needed even though neither of us knew each other. After confirming that I was Geoff's sister, he confirmed what I was asking. He also agreed not to inform my parents and to allow me to the next morning. That was a very sensitive decision to allow compared to what is probably normal protocol. I was grateful that he allowed his discretion to rule.

The bereavement process…

It has been a much longer process than I would have imagined. Because my brother and I were not close, I did not realize the depth of my love and emotional ties to him. The first few days were difficult but I was more concerned with what my parents were going through. After the funeral when I was alone sometimes, I would be overcome with the deepest anguish I had experienced. The feelings were overwhelming—and would pass after a few minutes. For the first few nights, we all woke at 2am exactly. None of us realized this until my parents, brother and I spoke and we were all experiencing the same thing.

I could not let my mother know the depth of my sadness. I felt it would make it even worse for her. I would speak to her a number of times through the day but every night she would phone me and my brother and my aunt and cousin for months and cry and say the same things over and over again. This was very difficult because I wanted to support my mother through it even though I was also grieving.

If I heard a particular song (such as *Every Breath You Take*), I would start crying. Even five years later, I have to turn the radio off if I hear the song as it bring such sadness with it for me. I felt that my husband and children had no idea of the depth of my pain and sorrow.

I spoke to a counselor regarding my mother and her deep depression and learned some strategies for handling her nighttime phone calls where she would be so upset. I did not have any counseling myself but read some brochures my brother brought over and I think I read a book regarding suicide. I may have gone to the library and taken out some books as well as I remember giving some to my mother. I did not know who to go to as a counselor and I also did not want to become involved in a weekly group meeting.

I feel as though I have come to terms with the death. I used to think of all the scenarios and possibilities, of what else I could have done, but now, particularly after talking so often with my mother and explaining to her that there really was not anything we could have done differently given the circumstances, I can only look forward.

It probably took three years before I could think about Geoff without crying or feeling a deep sense of loss. Now I think of him and miss him and remember the positive things about him—the smiles and his laugh and the way he loved children and animals. It was a very gradual process, not an overnight change. It was as if I came up slowly from the depths of the ocean and now I very occasionally go there but not as deep and not for long.

I miss Geoff and know that he had a chemical addiction that had such a strong hold on him that he could not be fully accountable for his actions. My younger brother is a social worker, and he said Geoff was unapproach-able—a completely different persona when he had been drinking or taking drugs. Rob can usually manage very difficult situations and used to be able to talk Geoff into a more calm state, but he had said that it became increasingly difficult to the point where he wouldn't attempt it.

Dreams and unusual occurrences...

When I went to see Geoff the day after the assault when my parents were in hospital, I said to my younger brother, I feared that we would find Geoff hanging when we went there. I was relieved when he was not there because I knew he was still alive.

The fact that my parents and my brother and I all woke up at exactly 2am every night for the next week or so was amazing as none of us knew until we shared it a week or so later.

My sister-in-law said she felt Geoff's presence and I did as well at night when I was in bed. I would speak to him in my mind and let him know I loved him. My brother also had to identify Geoff's body at the morgue and he said when he came out onto the steps outside, he felt a mist around him like a comforting blanket.

My father said he experienced the same on one of the 2am mornings when he got up and went into the dining room—he said he felt a mist around him as if it was comforting him.

Significance of the suicide…

Taking more notice of my 'gut' feelings and having the courage to follow through on them. I wanted to see Geoff the night of his suicide but did not. I have learned how deeply we love those close to us, when they are with us, we do not realize the depth that love goes.

I wish I could let him know what I appreciated about him and would have like to have taken him to the rehab that night when he asked me or sat up with him all night and got him through the darkest hours.

Helpful coping methods…

Talking with my surviving brother and sister-in-law as I felt they understood how it was for me. Reminding myself of the positive attributes of my deceased brother. Reminding myself of the things I had done that were positive surrounding the days before his death as well as over the previous years. Sending loving thoughts to Geoff and letting him know of my love for him and asking his forgiveness with not being there when he needed me most.

Advice or words of wisdom…

I believe that their spirits live on and that they know of our love for them. They are free when we love them and are grateful for the lives they lived and the good qualities they enriched our lives with go on than us forever suffering because they are no longer with us. Their pain is attached to ours. The more we hold onto it, the worse it is for everyone. Remember the good, know that love lasts forever and we did the best we could at the time.

For many days and months, I searched for my brother's face in the crowd. I would circle a street if I saw someone who resembled him—perhaps just to remember what he was like. I do not do that anymore, and as time goes on, I remember more and more of the good and the rest fades into the past with the pain.

I know he did what he felt was the answer to my parent's pain and anguish. He thought not being here would guarantee them peace. I remind myself and my parents that is what he would want and in order for his death not to be in vain, we need to enjoy the peace he wanted for them.

Andee Nydegger

Age: 32

Current Occupation: Kindergarten teacher

Andee's brother, Abel, completed suicide on July 8, 2004. He was 28. He stepped off of a building.

In her words...

There were four children in my family. I was the oldest and had three younger brothers. Abel was the second youngest, born in 1975. He had issues with hearing in early childhood, and invented invisible friends and his own language to compensate. He was often times in his own world, and would occasionally have pretty extreme temper tantrums. Our parents divorced in 1980 and we spent our time between their homes for the rest of our childhood.

I felt I had a close relationship with Abel. He was the sibling with whom I had the most in common. When he was in 3rd or 4th grade he went to live with our mom, while I stayed with our dad, so our relationship wasn't as close as it could have been. When he was 15 he was admitted to a care center for his anger and abuse of alcohol. That was when he was diagnosed bipolar. He was on medication and in therapy from that point on.

As adults we were separated by distance, and often time zones. I always felt a special connection with him, different from the bonds I had with others in our family. I felt that he was the only one with whom I could be completely honest with. He was such a good listener, and always a strong supporter. I wish I had listened more closely to him.

The suicide...

My brother "stepped off" the 36th floor of a tower that was being renovated into condos. He had tossed his shoes off first, probably watching the fall pattern. He probably waited for the sun to rise and stepped off backward while listening to music. His body landed on the 5th floor terrace, which was probably planned; I doubt Abel would have wanted to upset, or possibly hurt, an innocent bystander. He was found by the construction workers coming on around 6 am.

My mom called me at my school around 1pm. Fortunately my class was at recess and I was alone in my classroom to answer the call.

It was like the whole world shifted in a moment. He had been gone since sometime around 6am and I did not even know it. He died in Ft.

143

Worth, Texas and I live in Seattle, Washington. I was on the 2:40 flight to get to my mom and arrived that evening. We stayed in a hotel that night because Mom could not face going to her house and seeing his Jeep. Unfortunately, we were in a room on the 20th floor and all we could do was look out the window and cry. At that point, we were still dealing with the detective and medical examiner. They could not identify his body positively without fingerprints from his work, and they would not let us see the body, so there was a 1% chance that it was not him and we clung to that. Of course, it was him.

The detective handling the case was nice enough, although the way it all played out for us was very unfortunate and perhaps he could have done more to prevent those circumstances. First, as I already mentioned, Abel was not positively identified right away. There was his employee badge found in his bag found near his body. So the police had inquired at his work initially and searched his apartment before even speaking with my mom. They had found no notes, so they were treating it as a homicide. Abel died on Thursday morning.

On Friday morning we were on the phone with the detective and the medical examiner trying to figure out what happened and what to do next. We made arrangements with a mortuary, which was randomly selected from the yellow pages, but ultimately very appropriate and comforting. The detective agreed to meet us at my mom's house, which was where Abel had left his Jeep. (He had borrowed my mom's Miata to drive to the Tower.) The detective said that he needed to search the Jeep for evidence, but expected to find nothing. It was just a technicality. He sat down with us at that point and walked through the details with us, including the fact that Abel had been listening to a CD as he fell (Norah Jones, we believe probably her song "Don't Know Why.") After that he went to the Jeep and, in fact, found three suicide notes on the passenger seat along with his ATM card with a post-it note stating the date of his check deposit and his pin number. The notes were to mom, his psychiatrist, and his best friend, a wonderful girl named Casey. The officer told us there were notes but that we could not read them since they were evidence. He said he would take them to the station and make us copies.

At this point we were in a time crunch, because it was Friday at 3pm and the medical examiner's office was closing. We were planning a funeral in Texas, and a burial next to our grandmother in Utah. We were hoping to have his body released before the weekend. The detective came up with the "not so good" idea of us going to the medical examiner's office and getting Abel's belongings (such as the key to the Miata so we could move it from the parking lot across from the Tower). He planned to meet us at the Miata and give us copies of the notes around 5pm. So we rushed into Ft. Worth to pick up Abel's identification badge, the keys, his Swiss Army watch (with blood still on it and miraculously still ticking!), and rushed to The Tower itself. The building was once a Bank One Tower and had been damaged in a tornado. They were reconstructing it into condos and the new name of it was "The Tower." So there we were in the shadows of The Tower, with Abel's bent car key, waiting for the detective. The parking maid was in our face because the car had been there for two days and had only paid for one! My uncle paid her $13 and she left us alone. At this point the construction workers, who must have seen his body or at least understood what was going on, were getting off of work. It was obvious who we were, standing there looking up and weeping. They actually stood there and watched us! The detective arrived and it was at that point we were able to read the notes. He had requested to be cremated, which we had not (for some reason) anticipated.

Everything just became even more unreal at that point. Abel's standard answer to the question, "Are you feeling suicidal?" was, "Always." He had been so sad and scared of life and lonely for so long. He was on eight different medications at the time of his death. He was also in weekly therapy. We spoke to his therapist at length after his death. I believe he was overmedicated and had no support system with whom he was being honest. He told all of us bits and pieces of what he wanted us to know. Only when we (friends and family) came together at his funeral did we see a complete picture. I cannot help but think that his choice to end his life was very brave and strong. Two traits he did not think he had.

Abel was frightened of life. He was afraid of revealing himself to anyone. He had been told over and over that he was bipolar and an alcoholic. He was told that this or that medication would help. If only he stopped drinking...If only he believed in the program enough.... If only he tried harder.... In the end, I think he didn't want to be medicated and he didn't want to drink. He just wanted to be free.

I told others the truth about his death. I did not tell my children (ages 10 and 7) how he died initially, until I spoke with a counselor for advice. We told them before the funeral a week later, and firmly believe in honesty with children and others around us. My husband and I began attending an SOS group monthly and that helped us feel like we were not alone and should not feel ashamed of Abel's choice. In fact, we participated in a "Walk for Life" Suicide Prevention Day here locally this month. I feel like maybe by understanding depression and talking/listening closely, perhaps someone else's family will not have to go through this.

Everyone I worked with knew the truth, and gave me support, but they were not interested in too many details. Certainly after a period of time, it was obvious that they did not think I still needed to be talking about it. That is about when I found the survivors group.

The bereavement process…

I have gone through a lot in this past 14 months. I got married a month after Abel died, so that was bittersweet. It was the 2nd time in a month that my mom and other brothers were all together. I had a few grief counseling sessions, then school started, and life was busy. I visited his grave in November, flying to Utah to stay with my dad and deal with what I was feeling. His headstone was up and that was comforting and painful at the same time. Christmas brought my mom and one brother out to my home (the first Christmas with my mom since 5th grade or so). Somewhere around March, I became very depressed. My husband, who I am able to be very honest with, encouraged me to speak to my doctor. I was feeling not only suicidal myself, but as if it would be better to have my husband and two sons die with me, rather than have them suffer. My doctor put me on Effexor and I am feeling more level now. I still feel as though death could not be bad, but I am no longer feeling as though it's really an option.

I had four grief counseling sessions that were covered by an EAP. After that, I spoke with my family practitioner and my SOS group. All were/are helpful.

As I said above, suicide seemed reasonable to me, after Abel's death. I felt as though my heart would burst, all I wanted to do was sleep. I definitely still need more sleep than I used to. I was scared that my children would have low self-esteem and struggle with depression and I would be helpless to prevent any of it. I still worry for the boys, but I no longer think that I won't be able to help them.

I think, in a lot of ways, I have come to terms with the loss. It sounds strange, but I feel like it's almost a relief for Abel to be free of this world. I understand why he felt like it was a reasonable choice. The only thing I struggle with now is the "blame." I have a different perception of his "illness" than the rest of my family and I really think Abel's suffering could have been avoided with different circumstances in our childhood.

I understood pretty quickly his reasoning. I felt like I was able to say goodbye to his "ghost" when I visited his grave last November. On his birthday this past August (he would have been 30) we went to where he was last happy, and finally began to remember the good times.

I miss my brother so much. I love him and everything about him.

Dreams and unusual occurrences...

I have only seen Abel three or four times in my dreams since he died. The one that was the most meaningful was this: We were all in Mom's house in Texas mulling about, very clearly for Abel's memorial. No one was speaking and everyone was sad and anxious. I had opened a drawer to get something and tipped over a tray of paperclips, rubber bands, etc. I started to cry because Mom had it arranged in a specific way and I knew I would never get it back as she had it. I bent over to begin picking it all up, feeling helpless, and suddenly Abel was kneeling next to me helping me. He said, "You don't have to pick up all these pieces. It doesn't matter if it's perfect. Mom will just have to deal with it."

Have you ever considered taking your own life?

I have suicidal thoughts all the time. I know that it's my depression coming out, and I know that acting on it would be the wrong decision. I know that I need to talk to my husband when I feel that way so that it's not a secret. I would never want to put my family through what we have already gone through once.

Significance of the suicide...

Everything changed after his suicide. All perspective has shifted now. In some ways I have a greater understanding and appreciation for life. Some things are definitely darker as well.

Helpful coping methods...

Reading the literature helps. Some books are definitely more helpful than others. Poetry really helped me as well. I was enrolled in a Speech class this past quarter and I gave a five-minute speech on suicide prevention and awareness, and that really helped me. Sometimes I feel as though I could be a suicide activist and make a difference in someone else's life.

Advice or words of wisdom...

I don't feel very wise. I know that it helps to talk about your feelings. I know that I would like to be there for someone who did/does need to talk. It's comforting to speak with others who are feeling similar things.

Julie Champion

Age: 26

Current Occupation: Manager for group home for individuals with developmental disabilities

Julie's older sister, Tracy, completed suicide July 20, 2004. She hung herself in her basement.

In her words...

My parents have been married for 30 years. Tracy was the oldest, then Peter and then me. I would consider us to be a close family. The kids all lived within 20 minutes of our parents. I talked with Tracy a lot on the phone and would stop in and see her at work. My parents are wonderful people who would do anything in their power to help us kids. I always thought we were such a normal family. Tracy was always the good one. She was the first to go to college. I always thought she was perfect. Peter was the funny one and I was the youngest.

I think we were a pretty normal family. The three of us were close in age and played together a lot when we were younger. Up until we were in high school we used to eat dinner together as a family. As we got older we still got together for birthdays and holidays and sometimes just for no reason. I have fond memories of my childhood. When I was in second grade, we moved about two hours away from all of our aunts, uncles, and grandparents because of dad's job but still stayed in contact, visited, called and wrote letters.

The three of us kids got along as well as any siblings. We all played together. Tracy and I shared clothes and gossiped. She taught me how to play golf. She let me drive her car before I had my license. She bought me wine coolers when I was underage. I thought she was a great older sister.

Tracy and I were very close. Once I graduated from high school I started to work with her at the movie theatre and we joined a softball team together. We started to be friends and sisters instead of just sisters. The last several months of her life, Tracy moved back in with my parents as things were bad at her house, so I had the chance to spend a lot of time with her. We went on a lot of walks and when she was in the hospital, two times in the last six months of her life, I visited her. When I couldn't visit, I sent her cards and letters and she wrote back. It is nice that I have the letters she wrote me and the ones I wrote her. She knew exactly how I felt about her. (I thought she was a great sister and I loved her with all my heart.)

148

The suicide...

I was at work and my dad called me and said it was bad and I needed to come home.

I left work after talking to my dad and had my fiancé pick me up because I knew I should not drive. When I got to my parent's house my brother was sitting on the porch and I asked him what was going on. He told me to go in and talk to mom. I went into the house and one look at my mom and I knew that Tracy was dead. My mom was crying and she came up to me and shook my shoulders and said we did all that we could. Then she hugged me and told me she loved me. I know that I was in shock. I stayed and talked to my parents for awhile and then I just had to leave, so I went home with my fiancé. The next couple of days are kind of blurry. My mom's sisters came the next day and they helped with so much. I think they are the reason we were able to hold it all together. I will forever be grateful to them.

Tracy had a couple of prior attempts. She suffered from depression and, at the end of January 2004, she came to spend a couple of days with my parents. We knew something was wrong with her but weren't sure what. Her husband told her if she did not stay with my parents that he would stay home from work. She woke my mom up in the middle of the night and said she was thinking of different ways to kill herself. We took her to the ER and they gave her medication and told her to see her primary physician. Maybe a week or less later, in the beginning of February 2004, we went back to the emergency room and they sent her to an out-of-state hospital (because of insurance), where she stayed for 16 days. While she was there, she made two attempts on her life. The first attempt the doctors and nurses knew about and said it was not a serious attempt. The second one, she did not tell anyone until after she was home.

Tracy went into an outpatient program Monday through Friday and things seemed to be okay. Then on April 23, she took an overdose of pills and was back in the hospital for 20 days. She then did outpatient treatment for six more weeks. At the end of June, her doctor told her she could go back to work part-time but her employer said she could not work part-time as they would need to hire another person. Tracy was pretending that things were okay. She told me that she was talking to her husband and told her husband that she was talking to me. She was planning on moving home and at that point she only had therapy every two weeks. She had been spending a few days at her house (with her husband). The day she died her husband was at work, her step-kids were on vacation with their mom. Tracy was supposed to go over to my mom's house in the late afternoon to see our niece. Tracy did not show up and my mom got really nervous. She called

Tracy's house and cell phone numerous times. She drove out to Tracy's house but Tracy's car was not in the driveway, the doors and windows were locked and no one answered the door. My mom called me and asked if Tracy had told me of any plans to go anywhere. I said no and called her husband at work. He did not seem concerned but when he got off the phone with me he called his parents and they went to Tracy's house, broke in and found her in the basement and called 911. The coroner said she died in the morning sometime. She talked to her husband two times that morning and he said she seemed okay. Months later he said she was upset when he talked to her because her phone interview for unemployment did not go well. I think she planned this out because she moved her car into the garage and she knew no one would be looking for her for hours.

My sister suffered from severe depression, financial problems, a bad job and a bad marriage. I think all of these things combined were just too much for her. I think she could have taken them on one at a time but all together it must have been so overwhelming. I believe she was hurting so badly and she just wanted the pain to stop. I believe that she is at peace now.

It was so hard telling people. I was the one who called her friends and told them. I was very honest with people and told them that she suffered from depression, had money problems, a bad marriage and had gotten fired. I did not go into many details as I felt it was Tracy's private business.

The people that I least expected to be there for me were the ones who were the best. I had some close friends who were and have continued to be supportive. My extended family was wonderful. I did have some people act very strangely around me. I had a friend call me after the funeral and say she did not come because she did not want to overstep the bounds of our friendship. At first a lot of people would not make eye contact with me and would change the subject if I started to talk about Tracy.

I thought the doctors were horrible. At both hospitals we kept telling the doctors stuff and they would not listen to us. For example, while Tracy was doing outpatient treatment for the second time, my mom found a bathrobe belt under her pillow. She went to where Tracy had outpatient treatment and talked to the doctor. Tracy said having the belt under her pillow made her feel secure. The doctor did not think it was a big deal (less than two months later she was dead). My mom and I thought that if we got Tracy to the professionals, they would help her and everything would be okay. Boy, were we wrong.

The bereavement process...

I was numb at first. I just kept thinking, we have to get through the visitation and funeral. Then I cried all the time and was so angry. I was angry at Tracy for dying and I was angry at myself for not being able to help and I was angry at the doctors for not listening to us and I was mad at her husband because I believed he was a major contributing factor in Tracy's death. Then after a couple of months, I thought I was doing really good, I joined a support group, then six months hit and that was so hard for me. It seemed like it really hit home that Tracy was gone and I would never see her again. The six months fell right around my birthday and it was just so sad that she was not there. The one-year anniversary came and was very difficult. My mom and I spent the day at the cemetery and wrote messages to Tracy on balloons and released them. I think that I am doing okay at one year and one month. I can talk about Tracy without getting upset and I find myself talking about her life and not just the suicide. I think that is a good sign.

I still get sick to my stomach when I think of all that has happened to Tracy. I still feel sick to my stomach when I see her husband especially when he is with his girlfriend. For a couple of months after Tracy died I had trouble concentrating. I just could not focus on anything.

I have attended support group meetings. I plan on going to counseling but I feel that I still have issues I need to work out on my own first. I started going to the support group meetings in February. They are every other week. I have not gone to all of them. I go when I feel like I really need it. I also joined an Internet support group, which has really been helpful. I can go on there and vent anytime I need to and there is always someone who writes back and says they understand.

I believe I am on my way to coming to terms with her death. I feel this way because recently I have started having good memories of Tracy, not just ones that are associated with her death.

Given more time I will be able to come to terms with the loss of my sister. It has only been a year and I do not believe that to be a long time when you are in the grieving process. I feel I am starting to understand a lot more. I realize a lot more was going on inside of Tracy than any of us ever realized.

I miss Tracy so much. Sometimes my heart aches and I feel like it is breaking. I still love Tracy and I tell myself that she must not have thought there was any other alternative. I am not mad at her anymore. I feel that she did what she thought she had to do. I wish that things were different but they are not.

Have you ever considered taking your own life?

I have never considered this and seeing the aftermath this will *never* be an option for me. Suicide is a permanent solution to a temporary problem.

Significance of the suicide...

I find myself wanting to make my life worthwhile. Tracy's death really made me see that life is too short. I tell my family and friends that I love them on a regular basis. I try to take pleasure in the simple things in life. I drink Kool-aid and soda out of wine glasses just because I want to, I never go to bed angry, I smile everyday even when my heart is hurting over the loss of Tracy. I try to be the best person I can be.

Helpful coping methods...

I have read so many books, anything I can get my hands on. I have read everything on the Internet I can find. My mom bought me an *Angel Catcher: A Journal of Loss and Remembrance*. This has been very helpful to me as I have the irrational fear that I am going to forget my sister. So this way I have my memories written down. I also got a tattoo on my back with a daisy and Tracy's name. I had them trace her name off of a birthday card she had given me. I actually have Tracy's name in Tracy's handwriting on my back. I did this so I will always have this permanent reminder of my sister. I plan on naming my first little girl Emily Ann, which is the name Tracy always said she would name her daughter (if she had one). My mom made a website in memory of Tracy. This is helpful because it covers her whole life, not just the suicide. One of my fears is that all people will remember about her is that she killed herself.

Helpful advice or words of wisdom...

You need to do what feels right to you. I remember asking my mom if I could put something in the casket with Tracy and she said to me, "She is your sister, you can do whatever you want." That has really stuck with me.

There were so many days when I thought we would not make it. I have found that I am a much stronger person than I ever realized. I do not think there are any words that can adequately describe how much I miss my sister and how much my heart hurts. She was a good person and she touched many lives during her time on earth. Several years ago Tracy gave me a necklace that was half a heart and said little sister and she had one that said big sister. I now wear both halves and when I am having a bad day I reach up and touch my necklace and know that she is nearby.

Rachael Emmitt

Age: 25

Current Occupation: Studying

Rachael's brother completed suicide on August 12, 2000. He jumped from a bridge.

In her words...

My family consists of myself, my mother and my father. I like to think we had a relatively normal upbringing. We were raised by both parents, who are still together today. We attended school and hung out with our friends. We always had a pretty open relationship with our parents. We were allowed to smoke and drink from a young age as long as our parents knew where we were and who we were with, and we could always call them at any time if we ever found ourselves in trouble.

I suppose my relationship with my brother was your typical brother-sister relationship. We fought over petty little things but were there for each other when it mattered. We hung out with the same circle of friends, so we spent a lot of time together. He was not just my brother; he was one of my friends.

The suicide...

I will try to explain the events as best I can. I had been out clubbing on a Saturday night with a few girlfriends, and as we were coming home at around six in the morning, we noticed an army of police cars on the side of the road and a body bag. Being still half drunk we kind of looked on in fascination and perhaps even laughed a little at what we saw as we drove on home. My friend and I got dropped off at her place to get some sleep. The next morning my friend's phone rang. She answered it and talked for a little while. When she got off the phone, she was acting really weird. When I asked her what was wrong, she told me that the phone call was from a mutual friend of ours and that she had told her that she had heard a rumor that my brother had died.

I am not really sure what was said after that. I do remember sitting with my friend saying, "No, it couldn't be him. My mum would have rang me by now." Also saying how tomorrow, my brother and I would be sitting down laughing about the rumors. I tried to ring home but there was no answer. I started to get a sick feeling in my stomach but was still convinced that this was all some kind of mistake. Then a car pulled up in my friend's driveway and my aunty and one of her friends hopped out and walked to the door. It was then I new that this was not just some silly rumor.

My first reaction when my aunty said the words "Mick's gone" was total shock and disbelief. I went numb, and wanted to see my mum right away. I remember driving to my house and sitting in the back seat of the car not knowing whether to laugh or cry. I did not understand what was happening. I thought that this is the kind of thing that happens to other people, not to me. The thing that surprises me the most looking back now is the lack of sadness that was felt initially, that did not come straight away, but came later.

The hardest thing for me to understand is that there were no signs. Even looking back now with a clearer mind, I still cannot find one single comment or action that may have given me an inclination he was thinking of suicide.

My brother had taken an Ecstasy pill that night so who knows what his thought process was. Maybe it was just that one bad pill that led to what happened, or maybe it was something he had been considering for a while. I do not think I will ever know the answer to that question.

My friends were my brother's friends and vice versa so we all went through it together, I guess. I did not really have to tell anyone. It seemed everyone already knew. Even now, I do not really mention it unless it's brought up and I am quick to change the topic.

People were very careful with what they said. People I did not know wanted to talk to me and told me how sorry they were. Even people who I considered foes wanted to make peace with me. I felt a lot of false friendships that died off pretty quickly.

Our local doctor, who had been treating the family for as long as I can remember, was an excellent source of help. If we ever wanted to see him we could go straight in without having to sit in waiting rooms and he was very comforting. The detective in charge of the case was as nice and professional as he could have been. I spoke to him on numerous occasions and he was always very honest when talking with me.

The bereavement process…

The bereavement process is a hard one to explain. I cried a lot. I got angry a lot. I even laughed a lot. The emotions that I felt were all so extreme and I still feel them even to this very day. The process is not over for me yet and I am not sure it ever will be. It does get easier but it never goes away. You have your good days and your bad days and learn to cope the best you can.

I think I felt every emotion possible—anger, sadness, guilt, even envy, which is a hard thing to understand and deal with.

I had one session with a grief counselor but I found it hard to talk to a stranger and decided to try and deal with it on my own. Thinking back now, I think I should have sought more help. I still keep a lot to myself and find it hard to deal with things. Perhaps that is why, even to this day, I still feel a very raw sense of grief.

I do not think it is possible for me to come to terms with the death. There are still so many questions I need and want answered. I do not think there will ever be a time that I have totally come terms with it, although I do accept he is gone. I still feel haunted by it every single day. Sometimes I miss my brother like crazy, other times I am angry at him. He was my brother and I will always love him. He will be in my heart forever.

Dreams and unusual occurrences...

In my dreams following the suicide everything is as it was before the death. My brother is always alive and happy and I wake up saddened that it was all just a dream.

Have you ever considered taking your own life?

To a certain extent, yes, however, having been through what I have been through I could never put that grief on to my family and friends. There are times when I have thought it would be easier to just follow my brother's lead and end it all, but my conscience would never allow it to become more than thoughts.

Significance of the suicide...

Having to rebuild a life, seeing my parents have their hearts ripped out and watching them deal with that and rebuild a life for themselves without their son, has showed me how strong they are. I could never express how much I love them and admire them. I lost a part of myself that I can never get back but I have also learned how important family is, and the importance of compassion and understanding.

Advice or words of wisdom...

The most important piece of advice I could offer would be to remember that you are not alone. There are people out there who can and will help you. There are so many groups and organizations that have gone through exactly what you are going through and would like nothing more that to give you comfort and advice. I only wish that I knew about these groups and sought help when I could after dealing with suicide myself. Instead I decided to go through it all on my own and did not cope very well.

Another thing I think is very important to note is that all the emotions you are feeling are okay, be it sadness, guilt and even happiness. There were times when I would just laugh my head off and people thought I was crazy and had no compassion but that was not the case at all. People deal with things in different ways, so do not expect everyone around you to be feeling the exact same way as you. It's just as okay to laugh as it is to cry. And do not be afraid to ask for help.

Laren Bright

Age: 61

Current Occupation: Writer (advertising/marketing/websites, etc.)

Laren's brother completed suicide in 1989. He overdosed on medication.

In his words...

I have a pretty close knit, very loving and supportive family. We are good friends as well as being family. Growing up in my family was great. My parents were very young minded, progressive and supportive of my brother and me, despite some choices we made that must have challenged them.

As I reached around nine or ten, and my brother was maybe five, we became best friends.

The suicide...

I had not heard from my brother for a couple days and assumed he might have gone out of town. I got a call one morning from a good friend of his who had been called by my brother's cleaning lady saying my brother was dead (in those exact words—he called me at work and when I answered he blurted it out).

I had several reactions. One was shock. Another was awareness of a conversation I had with my brother that, in hindsight, was his telling me he might (or was going to?) do this. Then was a sadness because I thought he must have been very sad to have done himself in—until I realized he was very loved and did have plenty of fun in his life. I experienced grief over his not being around and, simultaneously, happiness for him that he had moved along.

He had mentioned he considered suicide an option from time to time. The last time I saw him, he made some comment about his will and where it was.

He saw how the world could be a more loving place and he did not know how to make that happen. Another way of saying that is that he could not control the environment, became frustrated, and that produced depression. When he got depressed enough, and felt he could not get out of it—even though there were medications available to him that he had not yet tried—he chose suicide as a solution.

I told others what I knew, which was that he apparently had completed suicide. Others related to me no differently than before. The police who came to his home were respectful of me and my brother's friend as we waited while they did their work.

The bereavement process...

Because of my personal spiritual beliefs (and some experiences I had and have had) my bereavement process was fairly short. While I miss my brother (him having been an integral part of my life on pretty much a daily basis for the better part of seven years after I moved to Los Angeles) and think about him often, I have a trust that his suicide was somehow right and proper for him and that what he needed for his life was more important for him than my need to have him around (despite that I do not agree with suicide as a solution to life's challenges).

I experienced sadness, some grief and a sense of concern that if I had been more attentive to him he might not have made that choice. (The intensity of that concern was short-lived, though the idea shows up still, every once in a while.)

I was in counseling with my wife at the time so we worked with the counselor on this as well as the other issues we were seeing her for. As I was fairly at peace with my brother's death, we did not spend a lot of time on it— maybe a few sessions.

I have definitely come to terms with the loss. I still miss him. I would say I came to terms with the loss within a few days of his death—pretty much after the shock subsided.

I feel no differently toward him than I felt when he was alive—except that I miss being able to spend time with him.

Dreams and unusual occurrences...

I had a very profound dream of a deeply spiritual nature on the night before the morning I learned of his death. I see my brother from time to time in my dreams, though I usually don't view this as literally seeing my brother.

Have you ever considered taking your own life?

I have never seriously considered taking my life. I have briefly looked at it, however, I believe this is not an acceptable way to progress spiritually, and, in fact, has spiritual consequences that do not support my vision of what I think I want.

Significance of the suicide...

It altered the dynamic of my daily activities. There were also some financial consequences—including my brother leaving his IRA to my daughter, which pretty much covered her college tuition ten years later.

Helpful coping methods...

Just my own personal spiritual pursuits.

Advice or words of wisdom...

This was their choice. It had nothing to do with me (or you). There was not likely anything you could have done to change it. You are not in any way responsible for their choice.

Erika R. Barber

Age: 37

Current Occupation: Supervisor for Teamster Benefits Company (and currently pursuing an MAT in Elementary Education)

Erika's sister completed suicide December 17, 1983. She died of carbon monoxide poisoning.

In her words...

My sister, Andrea, was four and a half years older than me, and so she functioned in the role of co-parent as well as sister and best friend. My mother is native-born from Germany; my father is from Chicago. Both of my parents have histories of depression. My father sought treatment for his; my mother received forced treatment within inpatient settings against which she rebelled, and so has not consistently accepted or benefited from assistance. Nine years (too long) after my sister's death, my parents finally divorced.

Growing up in my family was chaotic. My mother was a stay-at-home parent whose depression only worsened with her isolation at home. Once she started working, when I was in junior high, her emotional state balanced somewhat. Yet, my parents' consistent arguments often provoked anxiety within my sister and me. We would frequently listen at the door or window outside for any brewing arguments before entering the house. Twice, while I was in grammar school, my mother experienced what doctors then termed "nervous breakdowns," wherein she became physically and verbally violent. She was hospitalized for several weeks on both occasions. Concurrently, my father encountered electric shock treatments for his depression. During these anxiety-ridden periods, my sister and I lived with a neighbor, which introduced us to our first experience with a sense of family "normalcy."

My sister and I had a typical sibling-type relationship. There was an odd balance of physical and verbal confrontations ("Mom! She's wearing my sweater again!" "Dad! She's looking at me funny!") and survivor-like bonding as we endured familial turmoil and inconsistencies. Andrea's friend told me that my sister had once described me as "a pain in the ass most times", but that we had endured so much together, that I was her best friend. Of course, we would never admit we loved each other or considered one another mutual best friends...until after she died.

160

The suicide...

It was about 10:30 on a Saturday morning on December 17, 1983. I was with my mother at her employer's home office when my dad called. My mother spoke with my dad and it was relayed to me that Andrea had been taken to the hospital by ambulance; that she had tried to kill herself again. (This was my sister's third attempt.) Although no one was told that Andrea died at that point, I recall the panicked feeling I had in the pit of my stomach as we were driven home. The typical twenty-minute journey seemed to take an unusually long time that morning. Once we arrived, my parents followed the ambulance to the hospital, and I stayed at home with one of my friends and the older next-door neighbor. Even before the neighbor answered my parent's phone call form the hospital, even before the phone rang, I knew Andrea had died. It was the neighbor who confirmed that for me.

Andrea had been home alone, supposedly preparing to go to a counseling session that day. My dad had left his car for her use, and he took a train to work that day. He called home to check on her, and when she didn't answer, he called a neighbor to check on her. The neighbor found Andrea unconscious in the closed garage, sitting in my dad's running car.

It was surreal. I remember repeating, "This isn't supposed to happen to my family." Although the December air stung my face as I stepped outside to go to the hospital, I remember feeling abnormally cold and unable to warm up, even in the heat of the neighbor's car. I could not fathom the concept that I would no longer have my big sister, my best friend, my mentor, my protector in my world any longer. I felt abandoned. My sister's friend told me she could see how lost I felt on the day of the funeral. At low points in my life, I still feel that overwhelming sense of aloneness in the world.

She had tried suicide twice before: once by cutting her wrists with a razor blade and another time by overdosing on some form of medication. Both of the previous times, Andrea called 911 herself and checked herself into a treatment facility. Maybe that's why I truly never thought she would complete it, even with such blatant demonstrations of her pain. We learned later that Andrea had begun giving away her personal possessions. Her friends received "good-bye" letters days after she died. There were also separate letters written to my mom, dad and me, which Andrea had placed beside her in the car. Her plans even included buying us all Christmas presents, which were neatly wrapped beneath the tree.

Contrary to popular belief that those who end their own lives do so as a result of "selfishness or cowardly resolution" (explanations with which well-intentioned people tried to console me), I truly believe Andrea chose to die in order to end what she perceived was incurable pain. I used to feel angry at Andrea for lying to me, saying she would never attempt to die again, and then committing the ultimate lie. I now understand that Andrea's choice was not her final punishment to me or my family, but rather her only resolution to stop her emotional hopelessness. I think my own experience with depression's effects has helped me better conceive of the desperation that is so linked with the choice to die. Even in my lowest points, there was always something that prevented me from attempting suicide; that illustrates, for me, the intensity of my sister's pain.

I usually told the truth to most people. There have been occasions when I denied having siblings when asked within casual conversation. It just seemed less complicated and offered some degree of self-protection.

I think my close friends felt afraid. They had known Andrea well also, and seeing the devastating effects of Andrea's death on me, I believe frightened them. There were many times I feel they didn't know quite what to say or do with or for me. Since I was in high school at the time, I'm sure I was the topic of some gossip in the hallways that accompanied the students' stares as I passed by. My teachers attempted to offer support, but due to my anger over Andrea's death, my desire not to be different from my classmates, especially in such a manner, and typical teenage angst, I refused to accept most of their support, preferring to maintain isolation with myself or a few select instructors and friends.

I particularly remember feeling as if the medical staff and all of the patients in the waiting area at the emergency room were laughing at me as I choked and sobbed past them on my way to view Andrea's body. I'm sure they weren't, in retrospect, but that was my perception at that time. I also recall a priest, who had come to offer support at my house, calling me by my sister's name in error. I felt outraged at him for what I perceived was a disregard for my own unique and evidently less important identity. By association, I also felt angry with God.

The bereavement process…

Lifelong! I've done a lot of grief work since Andrea died, and especially through the major life events (graduation, marriage, divorce) that have occurred. I opted to go to therapy with various one-to-one counselors regularly throughout my life and only after rejecting my mom's opinion that to seek therapy, you are admitting to being mentally ill and in need of institutionalization. As a consequence of my own experience with sibling death as well as exposure to the death of children while working as a child life coordinator in a pediatric unit, I conducted extensive research on the topic and published a book, in memory of Andrea, to assist other sibling survivors as they cope with the death of a brother or sister.

As I mentioned above, I sought out many counselors at various "needy" points in my life. Some were better than others, and I gradually became more assertive in securing an optimal "fit" between me and the chosen counselor. Consultations lasted anywhere from a few visits, for those I did not feel were the best choice, to several months. The most beneficial therapists were those who did not take notes while I spoke (note-taking only made me feel like I was under a scientist's microscope), and yet they still seemed to remember all of the details from the previous week's session. I also welcomed "homework" assignments, in which I was asked to do or practice an activity at home (relaxation techniques, grief expression work, etc.)

Shortly after Andrea's death, I was diagnosed with temporomandibular joint (TMJ), a jaw disorder that results from unconsciously grinding your teeth while sleeping. I remember the doctor asked me if I had any stress in my life, and I truthfully answered, "No." It never occurred to me that Andrea's death could affect me in such a profound way.

As a young adult, I have been treated for depression and "traumatic stress disorder," particularly during transitional periods in my life. Since I no longer had my sister's influence and advice to help me make my life altering (and less important decisions), I often felt insecure and vulnerable.

I believe I have come to terms with the suicide. Especially since the publication of my book, I feel that the stigma associated with suicide has, within my personal realms, been breached and that Andrea's death has the potential of having a positive effect for others as they too cope with sibling death. Not that Andrea's death has gotten easier to live with; it never will. It's just that I feel more able now to use my experiences and growth to assist others, who are experiencing the rawness of suicide, with the trials of surviving.

I don't think there has been certain point where I felt I had come to terms or had been "healed." Assimilating Andrea's death into my life has been a gradual and on-going process; one that's had many adjustments as new facets and life experiences have presented themselves. Yet, I feel as though there is definitely a jagged separation between my life as a sister and my life as an "only-child survivor."

Andrea will always be my big sister. No matter how old I get, she'll be timeless—exactly 20 years old, always youthful, though older and wiser. I feel so fortunate and proud to have known her for 15 years, to have shared laughter and tears and to have had her loving guidance and protection, especially when my parents were unable to provide that. Her presence will always be a large part of who I am.

Dreams and unusual occurrences…

I've had a recurring dream since Andrea's death, where I am talking to her about her suicide, and she looks at me as if I'm crazy and reassures me that it never happened. When I first had this dream, I would wake up in a sense of shock, in recognition of the reality of her death. I would, in a sense, re-experience the grief stages for a brief time.

When I have the dream now and wake up, I feel a sense of comfort, having "spent some time" with my sister. I clearly carry her image with me the following day, and it reassures me that I'm not forgetting her or her special features.

Significance of the suicide…

Immense emotional and spiritual growth. Coping with Andrea's death and constantly readjusting its meaning within my life has helped me evolve as a person. Her death has, I strongly feel, made me a better, stronger and more secure person.

Have you ever considered taking your own life?

Prior or Andrea's death, as a pre-teen, I think I had thoughts of punishing my parent's for a perceived misdeed by killing myself, but I never envisioned a plan. Since Andrea's death, I've focused on surviving and helping others to do the same. I do think that, despite the similarity of many life events Andrea and I shared as a result of being part of the same family, we had different intrinsic qualities that affected our coping strategies during difficulties. I was always the child who would seek assistance from other adults when I felt afraid or anxious; my sister internalized most of those feelings.

Helpful coping methods…

Creative expression, especially writing poetry. I have several poems related to Andrea's death in a journal I keep. Writing the book was extremely therapeutic as well, as I conducted so much research and was exposed to so many people's personal experiences with sibling death.

One of the therapists recommended that I write a "good-bye" letter to Andrea. That was very powerful as well.

Exercise has also been helpful; especially activities that involve running, where all concentration is strictly on breathing and no self-wallowing can penetrate that, at least for the duration of the activity!

Advice or words of wisdom...

Go slowly. Give yourself a lifetime to heal and survive this. Realize that asking for and seeking help does not constitute weakness. Seek all avenues of assistance: group and individual counseling, supportive books, and organizations, etc. Find the best "fit" for you.

Finally, get involved in living again. Isolation only breeds depression and negativity.

Recently, there have been two experiences that have impressed me: One relates to a class, "Death in the Classroom," that I took for my degree; the other pertains to The Out of the Darkness suicide walk in which I participated. What I found completely amazing is the global impact that suicide has had. While fundraising for the walk, there were people I've known for years, who finally felt comfortable telling me about their association to suicide and its personal impact on them.

Talking freely about a death that still carries so much stigma has opened doors of support to so many—even me. I was amazed that, despite the amount of personal grief work I've done, how emotionally affected I was while surrounded by thousands of other survivor walkers. One woman donated monies "secretly" from her husband, and refused my offer to write the name of her nephew beside Andrea's name on my walk t-shirt, stating that her husband wouldn't want the publicity of others knowing about the boy's suicide. Several days later, she asked that his name be added to the shirt, stating that she did tell her husband, and he wanted to recognize his nephew's life in such a way. I felt honored to walk for both of them.

Judith McGill

Age: 46

Current Occupation: Writer/Coordinator of a family-governed organization serving adults with developmental disabilities/Animator for Alternative Theatre Productions

Judith's brother completed suicide on June 24, 2005. He was 44 years old. He snorted crushed cocaine and blew up his heart.

In her words…

As we were growing up, my family was working and we didn't have a lot of money. Food was always fairly meager; however, they were always able to make ends meet somehow. My parents are very disciplined with their money and can stretch a dollar. They do not spend money on themselves. Their first vacation together was on their 25th wedding anniversary. That was the first time either of them had flown. They met very early as young adults and married within a few years. My father worked as a lithographer and ran four color printing presses. He worked at the same company for almost fifty years from age 16 to age 55. He walked out of high school after an altercation with a teacher and started to apprentice right away. Both my parents lost their fathers at the age of five, both work related accidents. Dad's mom got a company pension and Mom's mom did not, due to the accident happening with the volunteer firefighters. My father went to work so young to help support his mother.

My father ran a very patriarchal home. He was the sole income earner. My mother stayed home full time. I always had the feeling that she was not happy being home. At sixteen I got my mom a job in an ice cream shop with me. This was a terrible blow to my father's identity having his wife working since none of the other women in our neighborhood left home to work. My mother loved it and kept working for another 20 years at part-time retail and waitressing. She did have and still has a strong network of women in the neighborhood, who were stay at home moms that she hung around with. They have aged together. There has been very little movement of families on the street. Most of the families are still original homeowners. My parents have lived in the same house for 51 years. They bought the house for $11,000 and paid it off after 25 years paying around $33,000 in total. Their house is now a major source of equity in their retirement.

Growing up in my family was not easy. I experienced my father as highly critical and unrelenting in his perfectionism. I never felt seen by him. I always felt inadequate. My mother was depressed a lot and not happy with

166

her life. For me there was the experience of incest by my step-grandfather. I am not sure if this was true for my brother or sister. However, my brother knew about my experience and did not tell me whether he had had a similar experience.

I believe my brother was bothered by the fact that he had not gotten enough support for his learning disability. Academics seemed to have become difficult for him in high school. He felt like he had not accomplished what he could have.

In the early years, my father was dedicated to my brother since he was a talented all-around athlete and a charismatic boy. My father coached his hockey and baseball teams. As a family, we went to all the hockey and baseball games of my brother.

When my brother was 12 years old, my youngest brother was born. It was clear within the first few months that he had a disability. He had several operations for hip dislocation as a young child. At 18 months we realized he needed casts on his legs. At three years of age we realized he had cerebral palsy.

We decided to do all of his physiotherapy and exercises at home. This meant that the attention that my brother had from my father and the rest of us as the central figure in the home was lost. This was during his preteen and early teen years and it seemed to have a horrible affect on his identity. He felt abandoned to a large extent. He became very distressed. My parents tried to get him help through counseling. He quit sports and got kicked out of high school. There was lots of attention-getting things like trouble with shop lifting and doing drugs. At eighteen, he slit his wrist. This was his first attempt at suicide. Shortly after this attempt he moved out to Calgary with a friend and his girlfriend and began working. He was out there for about six years. When that relationship broke up he returned home to begin dating his high school sweetheart. She was dating a kick boxer, who was not happy to hear that she had begun seeing my brother again. He beat my brother up when he found out. This was the beginning of the end for him since his back was injured during the assault. He already had trouble with his back from his hotdog skiing in Banff.

My brother and his girlfriend married and had two kids. His back worsened and he had two back surgeries three years apart to fuse the vertebrae. This made it difficult to move and carry on with his work. He was at home with the kids caring for them while recovering from the surgeries. He became addicted to morphine and Percocet during that time. He also began to deal with serious depression. He tried to kill himself three more times while living with his kids and his wife. She found this unbearable and ended the marriage. He then began living on his own and dating various women. His addiction continued and so did the depression. He tried at least three more times to kill himself by overdosing. Three years ago we almost lost him through an overdose in the bathtub and slitting his wrists. Finally in 2003, his employer said that he would have to go into drug rehabilitation to get off his morphine addiction. He went into a program and had a number of breakthroughs with his health and his emotional pain. He started taking anti-inflammatory drugs that helped with his arthritis. He began Narcotics Anonymous and was "clean" for two years, right up until he killed himself in June. I think they played a major role in assisting him in facing a lot of his pain.

I had a fairly close relationship with him as we were growing up although not without our tensions. He teased me a lot and felt that I (a conservative, goody-goody type) was a lot different than him. He would come to me when he was in trouble during high school. He had a wilder youth than I did however I don't know if he knew my youth as he thought he did. His friends tell me he respected me although it was never spoken. I did feel loved by him in a tender quiet sort of way. I admired his ease with social situations his popularity and his sense of humor. I appreciated his good looks and his concern for the world. We drifted apart a lot as adults. He spoke very little to any of us at family get-togethers. He did not return my calls and while I tried to reach out especially during his attempts I felt rebuffed a lot. He kept telling me that he couldn't do the emotional work although I think that changed a bit with Narcotics Anonymous.

The suicide…

I had a strange experience whenever he was suicidal. My body would get really out of balance suddenly and I would feel a kind of unknown dread. For days I would be searching my heart to figure out what was wrong with me and then I would get a call that he had tried to kill himself and that he was now being resuscitated in the hospital. This time, ten days before he died, my lower back went out and I could barely sit or walk. I was going to my chiropractor on the morning he died to see if I could get an adjustment in hopes that I could manage a three-hour car ride to a cottage the next day. I waited in the office for 45 minutes. I got into the examining room and got on the table. After a ten-minute wait to see the chiropractor, I was so irritated that I got up and said I was leaving—that I had to go. The receptionist said he would be right with me but I just said I was leaving. I felt totally irrational but I felt I had to get home right away. I walked into my house, put the clothes into the dryer and then hobbled directly to the phone and it rang. I picked it up and it was the call that I had been anticipating for the last 12 years, the dreaded call, the "we have lost him" call. My parents were on the line and they told me to take the phone off the speaker. I dropped to the floor wailing, knowing that it must be my brother, the fatal call once and for all. It was devastating. My 16 year-old daughter came in when she heard me wailing and held me as I was given the rest of the news. They told me that the police had come to the house to say they had found him at six in the morning downtown laid out on a picnic table and that he must have had a heart attack. I didn't believe it for a minute. I had been told on Mother's Day in May that he had lost his job in December and that his employers wanted him to go on long-term disability. My parents had kept this information from me because they knew I would be very concerned about how he would manage being out of work. The one thing he had always managed to do was to stay employed thanks to the hospital employee benefit plan.

While attending university, I went to work in Calgary for four months and went to visit my brother. He seemed very estranged to me and distant. He told me that before he moved there he had tried to kill himself. He said that I was the only family member that knew. I felt overwhelmed with this. I was immediately angry at my father and wanted to blame him and spoke about how he had been so cruel. My brother went on to tell me I had it all wrong, that my father had done a fantastic job of raising us. I told him he should not idolize him, that he had been hurt by him. He seemed to be in either denial or forgiveness, which was a different place entirely than where I was at the time. I wanted to tell my family when I retuned home that he had tried to kill himself as a teenager. I didn't tell them until he tried to kill himself again when the children were young and his back pain was so serious.

There were many other attempts to kill himself over the years and so I went through different emotions and reactions. One time I had a sinking sense that there was no way that he could leave me behind. His decision to leave had implications for me somehow. I had made an unspoken pact with him that we would somehow get through our childhood that it would all turn out okay. I was in shock to think that he was not going to do what was required to stay through thick and thin. To leave the game early and to walk out on me was a huge betrayal and I had to work with the mounting pressure inwardly to be willing to survive him and that if he goes, he will have to go alone. I still had my own destiny to fulfill.

On his attempt three years ago, he was determined to leave and was found at the last minute and resuscitated. I felt only remorse. I felt that he may have died not knowing he was not alone. I felt that I had been an imposter of a sister to him—the perfect, successful sister that had accomplished something in her life. I felt guilty that I had until that point kept my emotional turmoil away from my family and not told them about my incest experience. I had been working for ten years struggling to survive my own horrors, flash backs and recovery. I had not told him anything about it. I felt like he was convinced that I had my house in order, that I was the successful one, and that he was the only wounded one; the rest of us had come through childhood unscathed. I went to the psychiatric ward and spoke honestly about my post-traumatic stress so that he would know that it was possible to be honest and vulnerable to one another. Although he was more loving than usual he told me he couldn't manage to hear anything about my experience. I offered to speak about it whenever he was ready and that he could decide if he wanted to hear about it. He chose never to mention it again.

After his final attempt I felt a deep sorrow that life turned out this way for him. I also felt a deep respect for everything he was and had become.

I felt closer to him and felt his tenderness in death. I realized that some are not able to face the next phases of their lives—they not only resist them they actually say no to them. I realized that he had a different sense of our temporal nature that he wanted and needed to control the endings of life. I also had a deep longing to know him better—to know more about his pain and about his life. I felt "iced out" of his life and wanted to know more. It made me frightened about the depressions that I get into and wonder about how much further a depression can go until it comes to this.

I can only postulate what drove him to finally complete suicide. It is like putting a morose puzzle together with only your intuition and mental images to work with, all of which can be projections of our own fears and thoughts. However, I think that he had finally reached his limit. He was so strongly attached to his attractive appearance and his vitality he was not prepared to suffer any further humiliation of his disabling condition. I believe he felt that the children were now adults and didn't need him as much any more; that they had gone on with their lives. I believe he felt abandoned by those he had become close to at work and was no longer going to see on a daily basis. I don't think he could picture his life with no work. He was fed up trying to make ends meet on his meager salary.

In his last few days he was crawling up the stairs due to the pain in his back. He was free of narcotics and the pain was intense. The pain was ruling his life. He had done all he could to find alternatives to his pain syndrome. He was no longer hopeful. He refused to be put in a wheelchair, which was what the surgeon told him would happen. I know he could not tolerate becoming what he considered an "invalid" or disabled.

Prior to his suicide, he left work and was considering going on long term disability. He would not have even considered that before. On the surface, he was really happy, not having the pressure of work, and was enjoying the moment—the little things. He seemed less depressed. I wonder now whether this upbeat period may have been because he was so clear about his decision and he knew his pain was coming to an end. Other clues, he made a lot of financial plans and gave gifts. He kept bringing flowers to my mom.

I told people who asked about how he died that he had killed himself and how he killed himself. I had an incredibly supportive network of people that came around me. I received 30 cards and many emails. Lots of people have been willing to talk it through with me.

The day he died, we had a police trauma counselor come and help us tell the little six-year old he lived with that he killed himself. The counselor was fantastic, a good calm listener. She helped us talk to the child and gave us an idea of how she might need support in the days and weeks to come. She also helped us talk to my brother's ex-wife about the importance of telling his 16 and 18 year-old son and daughter how he died. Telling her children was an extremely difficult process and it took a number of months before the truth finally came to the surface.

The bereavement process...

At first, I was insistent to know the truth. It felt so much like an unfolding murder mystery—surreal—unreal. I felt that he would have wanted us to care about what he had gone through at the end. His suicide letter to us was very helpful, however, for a number of reasons it did not materialize for 30 hours after his death. We were left second-guessing. Most of the family wanted to believe that he died a natural death from a heart attack while I wanted to know the truth. They were angry and hostile that I kept insisting in finding out how he died and looking for the note. I wanted to ensure that his life was honored at the funeral and so I invested all of my initial energy into ensuring that people took time to figure out what he had contributed and how he had made a difference. After the initial four days, I was left with a huge gaping silence and time to reflect on his pain and his relationship to the family as a whole. It was raw to hear my parents wail and to see my father become so angry and so bereft. I felt I was at a terrible loss, with no direction and no sense of what was next.

After all the visitors were gone, I was left with the truth of my inability to stand by my brother, even when he pushed me away. I was constantly rebuffed and left to be the sister who moved away from home and was not very close. It made me realize that while you spend your early life with a sibling there is no guarantee that the bond will be significant enough to carry you into the adult years. He had a tenuous connection to life and he liked it that way—sort of living on the edge that way—knowing that at any time he could toss it all away. His relationships were the same way.

From the moment I heard he had died, I had a phenomenally wonderful physical sensation of having my hearing become supersensitive and almost acute. This lasted for almost two weeks. I could hear everything and it was all so crisp and pointed. I felt wide-awake, especially to the sounds of birds.

The first few weeks, it felt like I had been kicked in the stomach, like the wind had been taken out of me. I wanted people to leave me alone and stop putting demands on me. I needed to be alone a lot. I could concentrate for only short periods of time. After one hour of concentration I needed to be left alone. I felt so isolated and misunderstood. I had a huge gaping hole inside that was filled with sorrow. After only two months, I am still in this feeling of sadness. I have not felt grief, which I have come to link with loss although it feels like grief is now on the edges of the sorrow. I sometimes feel regret and loss when I think of him. Where has he gone? Why did he leave so early?

There was also an emotional feeling of what's it all about anyway? Work lost its meaning. I wondered, why am I doing this? I have not yet come to terms with the loss. We haven't gotten together again as a family and I am not looking forward to that. There will be a deadening silence and sense of someone missing. I know there is a lot more work to do to let go of the sense that if things had gone differently he wouldn't have felt so convinced it was time to go.

Over the last twelve years I have done a lot of counseling that included his suicide attempts. I may over time have more counseling to deal with it. For now the solace of my friends and my own journaling is enough. I feel my brother is a lot freer in death than he was. I feel a deep sorrow for him and for his children.

Dreams and usual occurrences…

My brother appeared in his 16 year-old daughter's dream just hours, or even minutes, after his death. She dreamt that someone came to tell her that her father had died and so they went with her to the high school to help her tell her friends.

While we were greeting friends the day after his death, we noticed something unusual. As we were in the driveway, we noticed that there was a robin that kept perching above our heads and chirping very loudly. It chirped loudly enough to be heard over the tears and sobs of the loved ones. When the family was gathered in the funeral home to discuss the order of the service and what to expect, there was a robin that threw itself against the windowpane three times in an unusual effort to get our attention or maybe join us. We now believe that robins are connected to his spirit and have a special place in our memory of him.

Significance of suicide...

It reminds me that life is a gift—that families are complex—that relationships are central to your life. Our life's accomplishments get summed up not by what we did but who we were.

Helpful coping methods...

Two weeks after he died a friend organized a very elaborate eight-hour Tibetan prayer vigil with a highly regarded Rimpoche. The ceremony was dedicated exclusively to helping his spirit find its way onto a spiritual plane that was peaceful and where he was free. After this tremendously involved and significant experience, there was a noticeable lifting of my fear and trepidation about the state he was in and a sense that he was doing well in his transition. This was a breakthrough event in my grief experience as I had a tangible experience of his presence and warmth during the vigil and a sense of well-being.

I have written a song about his suicide and am spending a lot of time with a composer putting it into music. This has been healing and has given me a sense that others may be healed by his life and this song.

Advice or words of wisdom...

Try not to judge the act as wrong or weak or unjustified or anything other than his or her last act.

Not all of us have the desire for life that is necessary in this fast paced life today where meaning if harder and harder to find. Pursue your spiritual questions and find some kind of imagination for why you are here and what you are meant to offer the world then do it.

This is the eulogy I wrote for my brother:

He was a man with a heart of gold. A son, a brother, a father, a nephew, an uncle, a grandson, a cousin and most of all a friend to all of us.

He was an amazing and loyal friend. Relationships were everything to him. Just look around at each other to witness how much he invested in his relationships.

If you knew him at all, you knew that he had a kind, compassionate, listening heart. He was there for you. Even in his silent gestures—his hugs and his quiet looks. His grade one and two teacher understood this and loved him deeply. She kept in touch and wrote to him often. In her first letter she wrote:

> *Although he appears to be lively and carefree, he has a real heart of gold and was very respectful. He certainly never was discouraged easily. He has added so much to the development of the class and my teaching.*

Life was not easy for him. He was given many trials to overcome. Some he overcame with tremendous discipline and tenacity. Others wore heavily on him. Much of what he carried, he carried alone. As a family we admire his willingness and ability through the years to wake up to another day and to carry on against adversity.

In many ways he was an enigmatic character. He was charismatic and, at the same time, solitary. He was the centre of the party with his easy smile and sense of humor. People wanted to be around him. At other times he was quiet and alone. He loved intimate encounters and talking about what really matters, however, he reserved this for only a few. J. S. was one of his closest and dearest friends. They cared for one another like brothers. They shared many adventures and steak dinners together.

He was generous and loved to give whatever he could. He was meticulous about his gift giving making sure it was the perfect gift. He was also meticulously clean and neat with a dedication to details.

As a teenager, he was a popular kid. He lived life full out and played by his own rules. Sure he would come in for curfew—no problem. Then once our parents would go to bed he would leave and come back home through his window and my parents didn't need to know. I am sure there is plenty that my parents didn't know.

As a teenager, he was just plain short. But that did not stop him. When he was fourteen he had the kind of chutzpa to go out with a girlfriend, Nancy, who was almost twice his height.

He was adventuresome, athletic and always ready for a good time. He had a natural ability when it came to sports. I will never forget how beautiful it was to watch him run and skate- it was effortless. He was a hotdog alpine skier, talented gymnast, baseball player and hockey player. In fact, he loved playing games of all kinds, spent hours playing cribbage, Uno, Yahtzee, euchre. Games were a way for him to connect.

He was mischievous and loved to play pranks on other people to get a rise out of them. He could bring a great deal of levity to a situation, espe-

174

cially at work. One of his coworkers fondly reminisced how he would have them in stitches at work with his irreverent sense of humor.

He was an impeccable dresser with a flare for style. He was attractive or should I say he was "hot." He always kept his body in shape. He grew more beautiful everyday.

He was deeply connected to what was happening in the world. He railed against injustices of all kinds. He stood for the underdog. He was committed to his work with the hospital union and made a difference in many situations. He was a no-nonsense kind of a guy. If it was on his mind you were likely to hear about it. He did not have much time for stupidity or arrogance.

He had an abiding love and respect for his parents. Over the past few years he made space in his life to visit with them on a weekly basis coming for dinner and playing cards. He admired their discipline and their commitment to family. He knew that they were always there for him. Let this be an example for all of us.

He lived for his kids. They meant the world to him. He was alive with their accomplishments and was proud of who they had become. He was always there for them with a ready ear and an open embrace. This love, and our family's love of them, will live on into the future.

He was a sun worshipper. He loved the sun shining down on him and warming his body. I am sure he will be there in the light shining down on all of us.

I would be remiss if I didn't speak about my brother without speaking about his eyes. He had the kind of eyes that could embrace you, make you feel that you had been hugged, that you were loved and understood. Soft eyes. Eyes that looked right into the bottom of your soul and back again. Eyes whose torment sometimes lingered long in your heart, whose joy acted as a blessing to you. Even when he wasn't up to speaking, his eyes spoke to us of love.

It is this love that we will remember him for. His ability to give love—to offer solace—to care about the world. Let his life be a testament to the strength of the human spirit against adversity.

Jessica L. Eckman

Age: 37

Current Occupation: Retail Sales Customer Service

Jessica's brother completed suicide 11 years prior to this interview. He shot himself.

In her words...

My family was a mother, brother and four sisters. We were close and have grown closer. Growing up in my family, there was never a dull moment. As children, my brother and I were close. As adults, we grew apart slightly because we ran with two different crowds.

The suicide...

I found out about the suicide when I received a phone call at 6am. I was shocked, but not really disbelieving. I knew it had been coming for quite sometime. I also knew my family would be going through a horrible time. He made comments such as dead men don't pay bills, things like that.

I told others that he took his life. Others seemed almost afraid of me or not sure what to say to me.

The bereavement process...

It has been a long steady process. For the first year, I felt as though I was walking around but nothing much else. I don't recall much of the first year. Now my sadness is more of an underlying current that crops up on holidays, birthdays, the anniversary of his death and when I hear of another suicide.

I have epilepsy, which has gotten worse since his death. I cannot deal with stress the way I could 11 years ago. I have panic attacks and am on medication for that.

I did not seek counseling. I tried to deal with it all on my own in my own way. I felt I could get through it on my own. I had tried counseling before and it hadn't benefited me at all.

I believe I have come to terms with the loss. I believe I have because it has helped me to help others go through this grieving process. I don't really know when exactly it was I just realized one day it was okay to smile, to live my life.

I feel sadness. I do love him and wish he wasn't missing out on all the wonderful things he's missing out on.

Dreams and unusual occurrences...

Right after his death, before the phone rang, I dreamt I was standing with a friend in an all white room and I said, "Why don't they just call? I wish they'd just call and tell me. I know something has happened to Chris." Just then the phone rang, my friend woke me up, and I got the news.

Every night after Chris died I dreamt about him. One night, about a year after his death, I dreamt I was standing at his grave and he walked up and said, "Jess, get outta here!" I said, "Chris, I love you. I miss you." He repeated, "Jess, get outta here!!" I think that was his way of telling me it was time to move on.

Have you ever considered taking your own life?

Yes, I did once, after a serious breakup with someone I had been with for 10 years. I was diagnosed with depression, lost 30 pounds in one month, and the medication I was taking made me want to end it all. I eventually took myself off the medication (something I don't advocate doing) and eventually felt better. That was seven years ago.

Significance of the suicide...

It has changed me greatly. I have a desire to work with others who have gone through this and to guide them as I needed guidance after his suicide.

Advice or words of wisdom...

Accept help and guidance especially from those who have been where you are right now. Do not go through the grieving process alone. Counseling is not a bad thing.

Alexandra Hischen-Dombroski

Age: 32

Current Occupation: Mama and Homemaker

Alexandra's brother, Falko, completed suicide on February 14, 2001. He hung himself.

In her words...

I grew up in northern Germany, in a suburb of Hanover, with a lot of nature around us. My brother was born when I was six years old and I had longed for a brother for a long time. When we were younger, I had my friends and he had his. We always played together with neighborhood kids (kids of all ages living in the condo complex). My mother began working again when my brother started pre-school at four. Sometimes I had to pick him up and liked to play big sister. My mom did a lot of artsy things with us. My dad showed us nature and took us into the neighborhood forests. We had a great childhood. When I was 11 my parents started to build a house, which put a lot of stress on their marriage. My dad was doing many things in the house by himself after work and relieved his stress by drinking, sometimes too much. There were fights that scared me. My mom was more the decision maker. My dad stayed in the background. When I reached puberty, my brother sometimes got on my nerves. He always wanted to be part of everything. I had my first boyfriend and he wanted to be right there in the middle. My parents did not discourage him from annoying us. When my brother turned 13, we started to relate more to each other. I introduced him to some fun music, we had the same political views and our characters were very similar. We became friends.

Growing up in my family was mostly fun. We did not miss anything. Even though there were times when a special fashion was in, my mother put her foot down and said she was not spending $100 on a sweater. Back then, I was mad. Today, I think it taught us a lesson. There was always something to do. On the weekends we went on day trips, explored nature. We took vacations. Both of us learned to play instruments.

My mother was definitely the one who was more involved with our lives. She knew about our teachers and friends, while my dad stayed more in the background. Our parents gave us boundaries but also tried to help us explore the world. My parents always wanted us to succeed, which we did in our own terms. There was not a lot of praising, some recognition. But if the success was in a field that was not so mainstream, it was not really that appreciated. Our parents are very straightforward people: you do this then this happens. If you do it another way it is not that great. But for some reason, my brother and I both did not choose to go the straight way and that threw them off a bit.

Until age 13, my brother was just my younger brother who lived with me under one roof. But then something happened. I guess he looked up to me and I understood him more in what he was—an individual. We shared interests and worldviews. He became more mature. When my brother was 14, I left Germany to be an au pair in the United States for one year. We wrote letters to each other and became quite attached. He visited me the following year in 1994. I extended my stay in the United States with brief visits home. But my brother and I stayed in close contact and he became my friend and acquaintance. He knew well before my parents that I had found the love of my life and that I would most likely stay in the United States, which was probably not very easy for him to handle.

I adored my brother for all the talent he had and for voicing his opinions, even if it meant swimming against the stream. After my brother's first stay in a psychiatric clinic in 1997, he withdrew a bit and I was not as informed about his life. But I figured he was growing up and busy with his own life: studies, girlfriend, etc.

The suicide...

When my mom called me, it was really late to receive a call form Germany. I was a bit worried when I picked up the phone. Her words: Alex, your brother did it. I knew immediately. I just started screaming: Noooooooooooooooooo.

I was devastated and could not believe it. It literally tore my heart out. But, on the other hand, I was also very organized. I rebooked my flight. (I had planned to arrive in Germany exactly a week after my brother took his life. He knew about the trip.) I went to work and made sure everything would go smoothly without me: all business. At home, I researched suicide and reasons via the Internet and a whole new world opened up for me. I purchased literature on suicide and mourning. I wanted to be prepared when I had to face my family.

I felt guilty that I was not physically there for my brother and maybe could have intervened. I was mad that he did not wait until we saw each other. I had not seen him in two years. I was studying and did not have the money to fly home. I regretted ever leaving for America and leaving him behind. I wanted to be strong for my parents. I hated him, I loved him and I missed him already so much. I thought I was in a bad dream and would wake up, hopefully, very soon. It was a nightmare.

My brother had his first psychosis in 1997. I was the one he came to with suicide thoughts and I took action because I was there that summer. He went through therapy and was doing great. He got back to his life and continued towards his goals. Christmas Eve 2000, my parents were expecting him but he did not show up until some friends dropped him off and said that he was very confused. My brother experimented with drugs: Ecstasy and who knows what else. His entire circle of friends did also, but he was the one who ticked off and they loaded him on my parents. He had another psychosis where he was not himself. He became violent, which was so out of his nature, and my parents were afraid for their lives. The police had to take him away. I was not there. This is what my mom told me. We thought he received the help he needed in the clinic. When they let him go to an outpatient program, we thought he would come out of it. I did not think he would have taken his life. After he was released, I talked to him and he was anticipating my visit and he was so excited to show me his new apartment. I was convinced he was doing okay and that he was on the path of healing. He had me convinced but he had already made his decision.

I wish I knew why he decided to take his life. I assume his pain and the thoughts in his head had just gotten too heavy and big and he could not turn the whirlwind off. He probably just wanted to have peace and quiet. The medications were not working. Therefore, he may have thought death was the only escape.

I told others the truth about his death. I was amazed to learn how many of my friends suffer from depression and that it only comes up if something drastic happens. I mostly had positive reactions and support. My mom said that the authorities were very understanding and giving of their time.

The bereavement process…

While I was in Germany for my brother's funeral, I tried to be very strong for my parents and made sure they received the help they needed. Once I got back to Chicago, it became very difficult. I felt alone, even though my husband tried to be there for me. Sometimes I just needed to be sad, so I listened to the recordings of my brother's music. It was hard going back to work and doing banal things like nothing ever happened. I joined Loving Outreach Survivors of Suicide (LOSS), a local support group, which helped me a lot. I became pregnant shortly after my brother's death. I needed to create life.

I first had a sad phase; sometimes I was angry at my brother. Today, I just want to be active and try to change how people think about suicide and to help others in the same situation as my brother. For this reason, I decided to participate in the "Out of Darkness Overnight." I also had my brother's music exhibited, along with other art from artists who completed suicide, in the "unNOTiced" exhibit.

After the suicide, I hurt inside. It felt like my innards were twisted by some outer force, heart pain and longing. I also started to have major sciatica problems, which today always visit me when I am under high stress.

I went to a support group for about nine months. Yes, it was very helpful. It gave me more insight into suicides and made me aware that there are so many people out there with the same experience.

I believe that I have come to terms with my loss. I assume the reason for this is that I received help and support. I educated myself on suicide and I tried to see my brother's sickness from his side. I believe that I accepted my loss after my son was born, a year and four days after my brother's death. (My due date actually was my brother's anniversary.) It felt like a re-incarnation.

My brother, Falko, always loved life. He made people laugh and his enthusiasm was contagious. He always had great ideas on how to change the world to make it a better place. He had tons of friends and was a popular and loving person. He was also very good looking and a great poet.

I love my brother. I miss him so much. I am not really angry, just sad that he can not share in my life, see my children, his nephews, grow and that I got robbed of the same experience: having nephews and nieces and taking part in my brother's life, sharing worries about my parents and sharing their attention.

Dreams and unusual occurrences...

Prior dreams, I really cannot remember. But occasionally, I dream that I am looking for my brother, I find him and can see him but he is unreachable and cannot hear me, I lose him again in a crowd or some other place, but the dreams are always a bit different. Nonetheless, he is always unreachable, at least physically.

Have you ever considered taking your own life?

Really seriously: No. I have contemplated: what if I jump out this window, etc. But those were just thoughts.

Significance of the suicide...

I do not trust people as easily as I used to. I built a bit of a wall around myself. Sometimes it is hard for me to love without boundaries, even my children. I am afraid that I will get too attached and then suddenly the person is gone. I have grown cold towards other people's destinies and trage-dies.

Helpful coping methods...

Talking about my brother over and over again. Making a memory al-bum with photographs and memories of our times together. Crying with my mom, being able to call her any time of day. Remembering my brother on special days. Having friends who listened. Helping in organizing an ex-hibit that included his music. Walking the "Out of Darkness Overnight." Creating life.

Advice or words of wisdom...

Get help! Talk about your loved one and your feelings. Speak their names. Allow yourself to be angry and mad at the person. Cry. Grieve. It will get better. You will learn to live with the loss over the years. Read, in-form yourself about suicide. Remember the good times you had together. Make a shrine or memory place. Do not let yourself be influenced by peo-ple who condemn your loved one because of the way he/she died. Those people are not your friends.

I am very glad that I decided to take part in the "Out of Darkness Overnight." Fundraising and participating in it gave me strength and made me feel that I could do something in honor of my brother and to help oth-ers suffering from depression.

The following is my experience of the walk:

I did it—20 miles of empowerment! It was an amazing experience! I arrived at Soldier Field at 5:30pm. The site was bustling with people wear-ing the overnight T-shirt, adorned with pictures of their loved ones. I spent some time at the unNOTiced tent and talked to people about the exhibit. Before the opening ceremony, I listened to Falko's music to give me strength and to remind me why I was doing this walk.

We were sent out at 7:30pm after hearing stories that were so similar to mine. Two people with torches lead the crowd through the museum campus around the Shedd Aquarium into the dusk. It was an unbelievable sight.

The first pit stop was reached fast. The pit stops were located every two to three miles. We kept walking along the lakefront and made our way up north.

At the unNOTiced tent, I met a young woman, Jen, with whom I connected and ended up walking the entire time. We walked at the same pace and kept each other company.

The first 10 miles were a breeze and brought us to Foster and the lake-front. We fueled up on a late night dinner and made our way back down south. The crowd had grown much quieter by now and more spread out. We kept setting one foot in front of the other. The first pit stop after the 10-mile stop had not even opened up yet. So we passed that one up.

About one mile before North Avenue Beach, I definitely could feel my legs growing heavier. We kept going mechanically, yearning for the end. We reached Navy Pier, the last stop before the finish line. Here we wrote messages on paper bags and put luminaries in them to place them on the path two miles from our destination: Lighting the way. I started reading the messages as I walked the path. There were too many—I gave up.

The last stretch was the toughest. Exhaustion set in and my legs felt very heavy. Rounding the Shedd Aquarium, I could see Soldier Field. I just kept focusing on that not paying attention to my legs.

I reached the site at 4:00am. I was greeted and cheered on by the support crew who was amazing and gave us strength to make it until the end. Since we arrived so early, we did not come "Out of the Darkness" but the sun came up not long after the arrival. Jen and I hugged each other and, at that moment, I felt very emotional, weak and empowered at the same time. My journey for Falko took eight and a half hours.

I did miss the closing ceremony. I felt nauseous and ended up at the medical tent. My blood pressure was very low and I felt light headed. But after two bags of IV fluids and some rest, I was doing fine and took a cab home. (Thanks to the medical team. They were very caring.)

It was an amazing journey full of emotions, sadness, tears and laughter, but absolutely empowering and encouraging. I pushed my body to a place of limits it has never been.

Falko, it was for you. You will be forever in my heart and in my memories.

Nancy Sessions

Age: 50

Current Occupation: Education specialist for college counselors, visual artist and poet

Nancy's brother completed suicide 12 years prior to this interview. He shot himself.

In her words...

My family is fun-loving and very outgoing; however, we are "moody" jocks and artist types. We are highly intelligent, very creative, kind, loving and sincere.

I felt always very close to my brother. We share the same birthmark.

The suicide...

I first heard about the suicide over the phone, from my dad, at my job. I felt disbelief and numb, like I was lost in worry about him.

He used his own gun, a 45 revolver. He had a collection, and hunted. He had gone bankrupt and his wife left him.

When he came to my Christmas party, 21 days before he died, he was not "himself." He was very withdrawn and kept to himself, which was not his nature. A sort of huge apathy, sadness, had taken him over. I thought it strange. It worried me a great deal.

I told others that he killed himself. Others treated me with care, and great concern about my own mental health.

The "shrink" my bother was seeing seemed very remorseful and acted guilty.

The bereavement process...

I seemed to cry forever. I "hid" as much as I could from the world. I quit my job four months later. I did not seek counseling because I have strong faith in God.

I do not feel I have come to terms with the loss because he was my dear brother. It was a huge loss to me. I do not feel I will ever come to terms with the loss. Only time helps somewhat.

I still feel sad. I miss him so much!

Dreams and unusual occurrences…

I know I saw him in a dream a month after he died.

Have you ever considered taking your own life?

No! Never! I am an artist. I want to live to honor his life and create!

Significance of the suicide…

It is hard for me not to stay depressed because of it.

Helpful coping methods…

Praying. My faith as a Christian. I know I will see him in Heaven.

Advice or words of wisdom…

Time will help. Talk about it with others. Pray.

Do not take anyone you love for granted. If a loved one is not him/herself, do not let it be. Talk to them. Be with them. Don't leave them alone. It only takes a moment for someone to take the life. You can help make a huge difference by giving of yourself.

"Angela"

Age: 47

Current Occupation: Author/Speaker

Angela's younger brother completed suicide March 31, 2005. He suffocated himself.

In her words...

My mother was a single parent. She worked as a waitress to support the family. My biological father was estranged from our family since I was five years old. My mother remarried when I was 10; my brother was seven. My stepfather died when I was 16; my brother was 13. I also have a sister five years younger than me.

My mother was gone much of the time during our younger years since she had to work. She was short tempered. My stepfather traveled during the week (Monday through Friday) for his sales job.

I was very close to my brother during the teen and college years. After a few years of marriage he put up a wall between us. I attribute this to the onset of bipolar disorder. My brother attempted suicide at least three times before he was successful.

The suicide...

My mother's friend called to tell me my mother had found my brother dead in her basement, where he had been living for six months.

I was not surprised; I was very concerned for my mother. I also had a little anger because my mother had told him he had to find his own place to live. He was in such financial straits that it wasn't possible. It seemed selfish of her since she had the room but she didn't want the bother of another person living in the house. She also refused to seek involuntary commitment so he could get help for his depression. She refused to acknowledge he had a mental illness.

My brother told us the most compassionate thing he could do for his children and ex-wife was to complete suicide. He was very despondent. I believe he took his own life due to mental illness and desperation resulting from his financial circumstances.

Those who I didn't know well, I said he died suddenly. I told close friends he took his own life. Others treated me with sympathy. Some, especially older relatives, were uncomfortable talking about it. I was not present since I lived in another city but my mother said the police were very callous when questioning her.

The bereavement process…

I grieved the relationship my brother and I had when we were younger, before his bipolar disorder. As an older sister, I've always been protective and wished I could have done something to prevent his suicide. For a couple of weeks, I found it hard to leave the house; I slept a lot. I lacked motivation for self-care, work, etc. I also had to deal with anger at my mother, for asking him to leave her home, without confronting her. I know rationally it was not her fault, and could never confront her, but the feelings were still there. I just pushed it aside knowing that bringing it up would only cause hurt and not change the situation. I often see men who resemble my brother and a lump rises in my throat.

I did not seek counseling because I was not ready to talk about it. The pain was too fresh. In fact, this interview is more painful than I expected. The old "lump" is back in my throat.

I believe I have come to terms with the loss but I still miss my brother and grieve our relationship before his illness. My brother was a Christian, and trusted in Christ for his salvation, so I look forward to seeing him again in heaven. I realize my brother was living in such a torturous state as a result of his mental illness. He is now made whole in heaven and doesn't suffer with a mental illness.

I love and miss my brother. I wish I could have helped him.

Dreams and unusual occurrences…

I have had a dream where I am at the funeral home with my brother and I keep wandering from room to room. Then I have to keep coming back for more funerals because more loved ones died, my college-aged son being one of them.

Have you ever considered taking your own life?

Not really. Just briefly when I was a child and angry at my mother.

Significance of the suicide…

I am more alert for signs of depression in my children. I manage my own depression through medication and listening to family members when I start to "sink" and need to adjust my medication, exercise or get out of the house. I have given them signs to watch for, not that they really needed it.

Helpful coping methods...

Getting back to normal activities. Being busy. Not very healthy, hmmm?

Advice or words of wisdom...

Take some time to be still and allow God to comfort you. Cry when you need to. Let go of guilt. Realize that you can't control the choices of another. Do your best to make sure mental illness does not go untreated. Hold your ground with family members who refuse to acknowledge that a mental illness exists.

Pamela K. Cabrera

Age: 44

Current Occupation: Disabled

Pamela's brother, David, completed suicide on August 25, 2001. He took sleeping pills and alcohol.

In her words...

I am the oldest of four children, Pamela, Donald, David and Angela. Our parents are deceased. Both our father and stepfather were alcoholics. I believe our father was also bipolar, but undiagnosed. Donald was, as they called it back then, hyperactive. Our real father was abusive. Our stepfather was mouthy but not physical. We were raised by our mother and stepfather.

I think my brother and I had a normal relationship growing up. When David turned about 17, he started trying to kill himself. He never felt he was loved. When we were around each other it was good, but he disappeared for eight years before he died. During that time, our mother passed away.

The suicide...

I was in Nashville, Tennessee and my daughter called me and told me, "Uncle David killed himself last night." I was in shock. I felt numb, even though deep down inside I knew it would happen someday. I did not have any idea he was considering suicide this time. David was living in Boonville, Missouri at the time. He didn't call any of us. David was a very emotional guy took things very seriously and he didn't feel he was worth loving.

I told others the truth about my brother's death. I didn't care what other people thought. I knew David had mental problems and I tried to get him to seek help. At the beginning, others were helpful. Then it was like, he's gone, go on with your life.

The bereavement process...

I have had ups and downs through the past four years. But I do realize that there were a lot of factors that contributed to the suicide.

I felt depressed, sad, and guilty. My blood pressure went up and I gained weight.

To a point, I have come to terms with the loss. But I still miss him and wish he was still here. I think it went a little further than what he really wanted it to go or he changed his mind at the last minute. I'm not sure which one. But I had a reading done and it said that he waited too long before he asked for help. Being bipolar myself, I understand, but I wish I could have had the chance to talk to him before he tried this step.

I did not seek counseling. I looked for an online support group instead and found it to be great for me.

I still love my brother and miss him terribly. I don't want him to be forgotten. He was a person and had problems. I know one day we will be together again. Until then, Mom is taking care of him.

Dreams and unusual occurrences...

Recently, I have had dreams of David going to Hawaii with me. I leave August 1st for 10 days.

Significance of the suicide...

I am more aware of the symptoms and causes and I watch for them all the time. Maybe I can help someone else so their family doesn't have to go through this.

Helpful coping methods...

I do a Memory Tree every year around Christmas time in memory of David and others lost to suicide.

Advice or words of wisdom...

No matter how often someone says they are going to kill themselves, listen because you never know if it will be this time or not.

Debra Egan

Age: 43

Current Occupation: Homemaker

Debra's brother, Darrin, completed suicide on Thanksgiving, November 25, 2004. He was 39 years old. He hung himself.

In her words...

My family is basically average—my mother, father, brother and I. We were lucky to have both sets of grandparents live very close to us, so we grew up with them in our lives. Early on, my family was pretty normal. Our parents divorced when I was 14 and, my brother was 11 or 12. It was an ugly divorce.

My brother and I were very close as adults.

The suicide...

My husband came home from work and told me. I lost all control. I just started screaming, "No." I went into complete shock and denial. I was physically as well as mentally in pain.

I had no idea at all that he was considering suicide. I had talked with Darrin on the phone four or five days before and we had talked about Christmas plans. He was coming to Orlando to spend Christmas with me and my family. We discussed what to get our mother and what my children wanted. I knew he was under a lot of stress and was tired but he gave no indication that he was considering suicide.

I don't know why he decided to take his life. I know he suffered from depression but I do as well. I have a very difficult time accepting that he wanted to die.

When anyone asked how my brother died, I told him or her that he completed suicide. Friends and acquaintances of my brother were very supportive. My friends did not give me a great deal of support.

When I asked questions of the police, they were very unhelpful. The employees of both funeral homes in California and North Carolina were wonderful.

The bereavement process...

I experienced feelings of helplessness and being alone. I truly and literally felt like my heart was breaking. There were endless tears. It was extremely painful.

I did not sleep or eat. I did not want to be away from my children. I craved a connection to Darrin's friends and his partner.

I went to counseling for a while but eventually stopped because of finances. I really felt comfortable with my counselor so it was hard to stop seeing her. She was helpful.

I have not come to terms with the loss. I still cannot accept it and have so many unanswered questions. I don't know that I can ever come to terms with the loss of my brother. I just cannot let him go.

I miss him so desperately. I physically ache for him and still just cannot accept it.

Have you ever considered taking your own life?

Yes, in my late 20s because of a great deal of upheaval in my life. But it was not a conscious decision I later felt. After my brother's death, I thought about suicide. I just didn't want to feel the pain of the loss of my brother. I felt so desperately alone and hopeless. I truly felt that the responsibility I feel toward my children was the only thing that kept me sane and from possibly taking my own life.

The significance of the suicide...

I want to surround myself with anything that was my brother's and be close to his partner's family.

Helpful coping methods...

Attending a local support group and constant communication with my mother.

Advice or words of wisdom...

Find people who are dealing with the same situation and talk. Just get your feelings out. Do not keep them bottled up.

CHAPTER SIX
Other Relatives and Friends

Gina Rusche

Age: 47

Current Occupation: Third Grade Elementary School Teacher

Gina's nephew completed suicide on August 16, 2003. He hung himself.

In her words...

I lost my brother-in-law and my nephew to suicide. For this interview, I discussed my nephew, Eric.

I am the eldest of three children raised in a strict Catholic, yet dysfunctional family. My parents divorced when I was 19 after being married for 20 years. I have been married for the past 21 years to a wonderful man. I have three sons, Alec, age 16, and Brett and Collin, age 10 (twins).

Growing up, times were either decent or awful. My parents were young and got married because my mother was pregnant with me when she was only 16. They stayed together for the children. In my teen years, my mother became an alcoholic. She has been recovered for almost 20 years. She quit drinking when her first grandson, Eric, was born. He is now deceased.

Eric was my sister's son. My sister is three years younger than me and married prior to my marriage. When Eric was born, I was elated. I was so ready for a child of my own at that time and he filled me up in a big way. I am his Godmother. He was among the most special relationships I have had the privilege of having. When he was nine months old, he and his parents moved to Northern Wisconsin. The distance never got in the way of my adoring him, knowing him and loving him.

The suicide...

My sister phoned me at 3:37am on Saturday, August 16th. I experienced momentary disbelief. I was overwhelmed. I broke into a cold sweat. I became physically ill. I had to get off the phone as I needed to vomit.

I did not have any idea my nephew was considering suicide. Eric hated, hated, hated, suicide. His own life had been so negatively touched by it. His cousin, Jason, completed suicide and then his father, Ron, did so as well. He especially hated that his father had succumbed to something so "stupid and cowardly." Those were Eric's words. He was not one to speak much about his father's death, and he remained very successful as a senior in high school. Eric had won a partial scholarship to college as he was elected to receive the state of Wisconsin's Herb Kohl Good Character Award. He was sad and missed his father terribly, but he had outlets, like guitar playing and writing. Everyone believed he was coping. He was very excited to be going away to college, but that was never to be.

Who really knows why he chose to take his own life? I believe fully that it came down to one irrational moment in time. The Eric I knew embraced life, and was successful, popular, handsome, smart, and looking toward a bright future. Something snapped in him that night. I believe that the break-up with his girlfriend (and in no way does anyone hold her accountable) as he was leaving for college and she wanted to date others, made him emotionally fueled. I believe there were triggers left from the job that his father had done. I believe Eric looked like he was on top of the world but was insecure and perhaps depressed. In the end, it really doesn't matter as all trying to figure it out does is drive you crazy. When one tries to apply logical thought processes to an irrational situation, it is a recipe for insanity.

If I hardly know someone, I say there was a tragedy and my nephew died. If they inquire further, I have no problem telling them that he completed suicide. For those I know well, I never said anything but the bitter truth. My twins were only eight then and I did not tell them the complete truth at the time. Rather, I stated that Eric "fell off a ladder" in his garage, which was partially true. I omitted the part that he intentionally fell off the ladder. I was so concerned about putting this on their radar.

I attended Eric's funeral alone. I did not bring my husband or my sons. I knew it would be a huge circus. Eric was "everyone's son." To this day people write him letters and leave them at his graveside. I wanted my boys to remember Eric as he was last they saw him. I did not see what good could come out of exposing them to the raw emotion that I knew would be paramount. Also, I did not want to rub the fact that my sons are alive and well in my sister's face. It felt cruel.

Almost all others were wonderful, kind and supportive. Some were stupid. Not out of malice, but rather out of ignorance. I remember two things that were said that I struggled with: "I'm not going to open any more email from you as it is too hard to read sometimes" (referring to the email that I sent just stating that my nephew had died of suicide).

A lifelong friend of mine never called me or dropped a card and I knew she knew. A year later I thought this is ridiculous, so I called just to say hello to her. She brought up the situation right away, stating, "I know I have not called you. I just could not deal with the news. It was too sad." I felt like saying, thanks a lot. How do you think it feels on this end? But, it seems like there was no point in doing so.

My father, being the devote (hypocritical) Catholic, spent the hours after Eric's death announcing to people that we all needed to pray as Eric had committed a sin, self-murder, and the fate of his soul was at risk. I told him to be quiet and that my God that I worship is far more forgiving than his God. By the way, I am still Catholic myself, but I view the religion much differently than he does.

I was treated fine. My sister on the other hand was given hell for "disturbing the crime scene." She is an intensive care nurse. Her instincts told her to cut him down and give him mouth to mouth, and all the while, she, too, was physically sick. When the police arrived, they were livid. She donated what she could to organ donation. She was unprepared for the intensive interview that came later on the day of his death. The interview was an hour and a half long. She said she would not have done it had she realized that fact. I know that now though she is happy that she did.

The bereavement process...

One thing I noted was significant fatigue. Grief is tiring. I needed more rest than ever before as it was so much work to make it through a regular day, trying to appear normal, when in reality I felt like I was in hell. That has passed somewhat.

I work at feeding my soul and fortifying myself spiritually. I have read many books on death, grief and suicide. I know it is a process. I know that it is a one step forward, one step back kind of thing. I forgive myself if I have a hard day. It's part of it. I deliberately seek people who enrich me, support me, and do not judge me or my experiences. I am quiet about it as I find that overall this is not a subject that people *want* to discuss. However, if someone wants to, I have no problem talking about it.

I have learned a lot about life through Eric's death. It is a pain like no other that I carry but the days I choose to be at war with this truth are very long. On the days I elect to coexist with the truth, I feel more peace.

I am a believer in counseling, but I did not seek it with the exception of talking to my priest (whose best friend/brother-in-law completed suicide around the same time that Eric did). I felt I was coping okay and I always knew that I would embrace the idea of counseling if I felt myself not moving forward.

For sometime I attended a LOSS (Loving Outreach for Suicide Survivors) group. I no longer do, but if I feel I need to, I would not hesitate.

Learning/reading about suicide has been a healthy thing for me. I try to make choices that will help me not bring myself down. Since Eric's death, many things in life that used to be commonplace are now deliberate. I remember right after he died, waking up, brushing my teeth and showering seemed to be choices I was making as opposed to being routine.

For as odd as it sounds, the truth is no longer surreal. I now know for sure that this is true. Initially, it was hard to really believe it. As time goes on and Eric is not here and I experience life without him, I no longer unconscientiously look for him to physically be there.

I believe that loss is a journey. Loss is a very important part of life. Without loss, there is no learning. Authentic learning (in my opinion) comes from living and learning and reflecting on one's experiences. I do believe that loss via suicide is unlike any other kind of loss other than perhaps, murder. That too would be really hard to put one's arms around.

For me, dealing with Eric's death is a job of sorts. I devote time to dealing with it daily. The time I now spend is less than it was initially. I spend time thinking of him and who he is to me. I believe the love he felt for me is still here, but it is in a different form than what I am accustomed to.

I love that boy. He will always be my buddy. But I do believe that his last act was really foolish and that he knew better. He knew what suicide does, firsthand. He chose that same road in spite of his experience, or perhaps because of it. Eric will always be a part of me. I just have to continue to learn how to have a "relationship" with him that is not tangible physically. That's work. And some days I hate it more than others.

I hope that my nephew is being nurtured in Heaven in a way that he could not feel here. I believe strongly, based on who he was, that Eric will not be able to rest peacefully if his loved ones are still feeling tormented. In his honor, I work at carrying myself in a way that I believe would make him proud. And, in spite of his last worldly "choice", he left a legacy that I am proud of. I have no reason not to be.

Dreams and unusual occurrences...

I have dreamt of Eric. On one occasion, within hours of his death, I had a very strong dream about him. I felt warmth all over my body. My mother says that Eric was coming to kiss me goodbye on his way to Heaven.

Have you ever considered taking your own life?

I guess so. I know I have felt desperation in my life and sincere sadness. Since Eric's death, I do not in any way flirt with such a thing. I know the ripple effect it leaves and the lives it ruins. The pain they had remains here and now everyone carries it.

Significance of suicide...

This has been huge in my life. Although I will never say that Eric's death has made me better as a person, I know deep down that that is true. Each day it is important to continue to make forward progress and not to get caught up in the downward spiral of the sadness in all of this. It has affected my parenting. I love my boys more than ever and I know fully how fragile life is, especially for a teenager who has not yet carved a niche for himself and who is full of questions with no answers.

Helpful coping methods...

Working at remembering the good things about the person. Celebrating that person's life, in spite of the way he died. Savoring the gifts that he left. Talking to friends, or not. Realizing that life is precious and can be short and above all, it's fragile. Making whatever choice I need to, to get me through the moment, the hour, or the day, depending, and choosing not to feel guilty about it.

Advice or words of wisdom...

It is futile to assign or to feel to blame; if it were only that easy to explain. He died because of me, or because of you, that would sure simplify things, wouldn't it? I wish at times that I could point my finger and blame someone or something. It is far more complicated than that. I think, as I stated earlier, that a big mistake is to believe that the suicide was a logical choice. I do not think suicide is based on sound thinking, rather skewed, immediate thinking.

Accept that this is a journey. Learning to live with this truth without hindering one's self takes time, effort and energy. Living in denial takes those things too. I make the choice, deliberately, to have a good day. The journey cannot be rushed. And, it will take a lifetime.

Shirley Bahlmann

Age: 47

Current Occupation: Writer

Shirley's uncle completed suicide seven years prior to this interview. He hung himself.

In her words...

The Uncle Joe of my youth was handsome, outgoing and cheerful. He was a church and family man, and although we lived in different states when I was a child, I saw him about once a year and looked forward to each visit.

When my husband and I were newly married, we rented the basement of Uncle Joe's dental office. Even at that stage in his life, he was upbeat and cracked jokes often. He also enjoyed hunting trips with my husband and swapped stories at family get-togethers. We were both fond of Uncle Joe and his family.

I don't know what began the change in him. Someone in the family told me that my grandfather, Joe's dad, suffered from depression. I've seen evidence of at least one other close relative to Joe and me who expresses delusions and paranoia, yet refuses to recognize it as a problem or take any steps to remedy it. So maybe it's something that runs in the family.

As to my background, I'm the fourth of eight children. For most of my childhood, my father had a traveling job that only brought him home on weekends. When I was in grade school, my mother, (Joe's sister), had a nervous breakdown. On one memorable Mother's Day, she ran away from home and sat at the bus stop for a few hours. She finally came home when it got dark.

She laughs when she recalls the time she walked into the dirty kitchen and felt something inside her snap. She picked up dirty dishes one right after the other and threw them over her shoulder, smashing them against the far wall until there were no more to throw. Then she turned around and saw all her children's faces peeking around the corner with worried eyes as big as half-dollars. Most of the time, I could get out of the house and play outside without ever being missed.

I saw visits to extended family, like Uncle Joe, as islands of sanity.

I can't pinpoint the exact moment when he started to change, but I was unsettled when he divorced his wife of more than twenty years. He remarried, but that union was short lived and he divorced a second time.

The last time I saw him alive was at a place called Willow Park, which housed wild animals. My husband and I came across Uncle Joe sitting in his truck in the parking lot, staring at the elk pen. Although he smiled when I greeted him with words of delight and an enthusiastic hug, I sensed a sadness about him that tore at my heart. I asked how he was doing, and my husband exchanged a few words with him, too. Then we had to go. We left him there, still sitting in his car, staring at the elk.

He died a couple of months later.

I wished I could go back in time and slide into the seat beside him and hold his hand and say, "I love you, Uncle Joe. I love you a lot, and I always will. I care about you so much that I want you to always be around. Always! You can come and live with us if you want to. Let's find a way for you to get happy again." But that didn't happen, and it was too late now. It wouldn't have changed things anyway.

He'd attempted suicide a couple of times before, but I was not given any details.

This time he finished the job. His younger brother found him and called my mother. My mother called all of her children. A heavy weight plunked itself down on my heart, and I cried, wishing I could have somehow let him know that I loved him enough that he wouldn't have wanted to kill himself.

I told my teenage children how Uncle Joe had died. If it came up in other conversations, I just said he died. The exception was my friend who was crying in church one day. I found out her uncle had just completed suicide that morning. This was just a year ago, but we ended up clinging to each other and weeping, and I told her that my uncle had killed himself, too, and how much it hurt because I loved him. As far as I know, anyone who knows the true story behind my uncle's death treats me just the same as they did before. I don't really put much stock in what people think of me anyway. I have people in my life who love me no matter what, and if anyone decides they don't, well, then they weren't really my friend in the first place.

The suicide…

My mother told me the day it happened. Her younger brother had found him and called her. She then called all of her children. A heavy weight plunked itself down on my heart, and I cried, wishing I could have somehow let him know that I loved him enough that he didn't have to kill himself.

My husband and I didn't live in the same town as my uncle did when he died, but we were visiting the area and were at a place called Willow Park, which houses a few wild animals, most indigenous to Utah. We happened upon Uncle Joe in the parking lot, sitting in his car, looking at the cage with elk in it. I could sense a sadness about him that tore at my heart. I hurried over to him, all smiles, and greeted him and hugged him and told him how delighted I was to see him again. I asked him how he was doing, and my husband and he exchanged some remarks. Then we had to go, and we left him there, still sitting in his car, staring at the elk. He died just a couple of months after that. I wished I could go back in time and slide into the seat beside him and hold his hand and say, "I love you, Uncle Joe. I love you a lot, and I always will. I care about you so much, that I want you to always be around! Always! You can come and live with us if you want to. Let's find a way for you to get happy again." But that didn't happen, and it was too late now. It wouldn't have changed things anyway.

He'd attempted suicide a couple of times before, but I was not given any details, and it was downplayed quite a bit. He was depressed. I don't know for sure if there was a heredity-type depression in him already, but he did feel badly about his two failed marriages, and his business that wasn't working very well any more.

The bereavement process…

I cried a lot, I had an ache in my heart for quite awhile. One talk at the funeral helped me feel better, when the speaker said that in God's eyes, if a person kills himself while his mind is chemically imbalanced, then God will take that into account on Judgment Day. Even though I don't think of it often anymore, some situations can bring back all the tears and the hollow, aching loss, like last year when my friend went through a terrible time of losing her uncle.

I did not seek counseling. Just prayer. I am pretty much a take-life-as-it-comes person. Overall, I've quit worrying, because it never changed a thing. All it did was make me tense. I was content with prayer for my therapy.

I believe I have come to terms with the loss because I believe in God. I turn hard things like this over to Him. Then my heart is lighter, and I can go on living. Coming to terms with the death probably started at the funeral when the speaker gave his words of comfort. It wasn't too long after that when I stopped getting misty-eyed every time I thought of Uncle Joe.

I still love him, I hope he's found happiness in Heaven, and I look forward to seeing him when I die. Then I can hug him (okay, now, I'm crying here!) and tell him how much I love him.

Have you ever considered taking your own life?

I once had a bout of severe depression where I was sure my family would be better off without me, but my plan was to run away to Arizona and work as a waitress under a fake name. That's not the same thing, is it? I finally decided I wanted to crawl out of my depression hole when my husband put his arm around me when I was crying and sniveling and said, "Shirley, I love you, and I want to live with you, but I don't know how to make it better." I decided that if he could say he loved me when I was in that condition, then he must really mean it. I wanted to get well so I could be a better wife to him. I started praying regularly and reading the scriptures, and bit by bit, I pulled out of that debilitating "I'm-worthless-the-family-would-be-better-off-without-me" depression.

Significance of suicide…

I never want to do that to anyone. You're supposed to live until it's your time to die, and only God should decide that.

Helpful coping methods…

Prayer, talking to family, the support of my son and his thoughtfulness. When we were at the funeral and I didn't want to view the body, my son said he'd stay at my side, and I went with him to see Uncle Joe's corpse. I couldn't see for the tears, but then my vision cleared and I laid my hand on Joe's still chest. "I love you, Uncle Joe," I whispered. Then I turned away and my son walked me back to my seat.

Helpful advice or words of wisdom…

Turn it over to God. He loves all of us more than we love ourselves (well, sometimes that's not so hard!) or even more than we love each other, including the person(s) we love most in the world. God will take the burden if you give it to Him, and he will take care of the loved one who is gone, no matter who he or she is. He loves us all.

If someone kills himself, it's not your fault. Having dealt with depression first hand, I know that words of love and appreciation tend to bounce off the brain of a person who feels worthless. Even if you mean them with all your heart, they won't sink in if the person you're addressing feels like a rotten banana peel in disguise. They figure that if you could only see the *real* them, you'd say the cruddy things they're thinking about themselves out loud. Maybe they nod or stop crying just to get you off their back. But you haven't made a difference at all. They have to want to change, as I decided to do when I finally let myself believe that my husband loved me, because he told me *yet again* when I was at my worst, and it finally broke a chink in my rusted-from-so-much-crying armor. You can't get through to them unless they open up and let you. You can treat them kindly, be patient, say you love them, offer to help, but that's all I know. They still make the ultimate decision. Don't blame yourself.

Everett Despirito

Age: 34

Current Occupation: Food service and recreation leader

Everett's best friend completed suicide on April 15, 2005. He was hit by a train.

In his words...

I have two siblings. My mother has a mental illness and my father died on a heart attack.

I could never measure up. I was verbally abused. There was not much closeness but it was not all bad. It was a Christian home.

Greg and I were best friends. We were closer than brothers. We had a very special bond. He was my brother in Christ. We worked together, talked together, encouraged each other. We were there for each other as we struggled with depression. I miss Greg!

The suicide...

Greg drove his car onto train tracks. A train hit him and he died instantly.

I found out from our boss. Greg killed himself on a Friday. The Monday I found out was horrible! My world stopped. I felt like someone had stabbed me. I felt incredible sadness, pain and anguish. I got physically sick and depressed.

Greg was bipolar. He had been hospitalized for depression a week before he completed suicide. He talked about going on "his journey." I think it was mostly from bipolar disorder. Greg was sick. His depression and feelings of despair led to his suicide.

I told others Greg completed suicide. I tell them he was bipolar. I have lost three friends and some others have alienated me. Some people avoid me. But some befriended and supported me.

The bereavement process...

Loss of appetite, crying, horrible nightmares, anger, depression, low self esteem, shock, blame, sadness, guilt, insomnia.

I attend survivor support groups monthly. I journal and write poetry. I talk and talk some more. I take "baby steps." I also have an art therapist who I see weekly because I do not want my clinical depression to get worse.

I think my counseling will be for several years as it is helping me cope and live.

I have not yet come to terms with the loss. If by coming to terms you mean accept as fact then I have. I am healing but I am still grieving. I have forgiven Greg. I really miss him. I get angry that life got so hard and unbearable that suicide happened. I love Greg as a brother.

Dreams and unusual occurrences…

I see Greg killing himself. I see his messed up body after the suicide. I get hugs from him before he kills himself.

Have you ever considered taking your own life?

Yes—when life gets overwhelming and I feel trapped by my circumstances, or when my depression gets severe and I feel overwhelmed and trapped by my pain. Even though suicide may seem like a solution, it is not! It is a permanent way out of a temporary problem.

Significance of the suicide…

It was a major traumatic event. The worst thing I have ever gone though. It was life changing.

Helpful coping methods…

Talking and remembering the good times Greg and I had. Allowing myself to grieve.

Advice or words of wisdom…

Allow yourself to grieve. Feel what you feel. Take baby steps. Do what is right for you. Stay healthy.

I am in my own struggle with clinical depression and I may be bipolar. I understand that to live is a choice. It may be hard but living is worth it. I am a survivor and I will get through this. Now I do what I can to prevent other suicides from happening. I participated in an Out of the Darkness walk to raise awareness about suicide and to raise funds to help in the prevention of suicide. Greg is dead but his memory goes on forever. I will always have him in my heart.

Terri Rimmer

Age: 39

Current Occupation: Freelance Writer

Terri's friend completed suicide in June 2004. He hung himself.

In her words...

We were middle-class, suburban, with an abusive dad and alcoholic mom growing up. It was chaotic, loud and unpredictable.

He was my friend's husband and I had known him since 1998. I had seen him sober for several years then relapse and not be able to get sobriety back. He always had a smile on his face so you never knew what was really going on but he would do anything for anyone and had many friends.

The suicide...

I first heard about the suicide from a mutual friend. I was shocked, sad and depressed. I immediately called his widow and called my other friends who may not have known. I looked up his obituary in the paper and remembered all the times and memories we had together. I believe he was high on cocaine and didn't know what he was doing.

I told others the truth. The ones who didn't know him didn't know what to say and didn't want to talk about it.

Bereavement process...

I was tired, morose and depressed. I wrote about his death, prayed about it, talked to others and dreamed about it. I am still sad and shocked by it.

I was already in counseling. I have not come to terms with the loss because I can't make sense of it. I don't know if I will come to terms with it because I have known others who have completed suicide, too.

Today I am still sad and angry.

Dreams and unusual occurrences...

After the suicide I dreamed about him a few times. He was telling me not to complete suicide.

Have you ever considered taking your own life?

Yes. I suffered from depression since age 12. I didn't do it because I didn't want to hurt my sister or daughter.

Significance of the suicide...

It made me realize how much we are loved and don't know it.

Helpful coping methods...

Writing, talking to others.

Advice or words or wisdom...

You can get through it but you have to reach out to others.

A writer needs material and I had it before the age of ten. The material of life continues to inspire me, though now I am a bit wiser to its meaning.

"Jocelyn"

Age: 63

Current Occupation: Writer/Publisher

Jocelyn's ex-daughter-in-law completed suicide four years prior to this interview. She shot herself.

In her words...

She was my daughter-in-law. She and my son had divorced about one year before her suicide.

I have a husband and two sons. I have three grandsons by my other son and his wife. We're pretty low-key. We all get along well, all really like people. We're pretty average all the way around.

I was one of three children. My parents were wonderful. Our children grew up in the suburbs, had a normal life and attended parochial schools through high school.

When she married our son, she had been married twice before. We knew she had problems but we loved her dearly. She was a sweet, friendly person, with lots of energy but she had an incredibly low self-image. She came from a troubled family—lots of fighting, antagonism and a very controlling mother. Her father was not in the picture, but she had a stepfather she loved. She would be part of our family—then withdraw completely and not be involved in anything. Our son always related it to her depression and medication.

The suicide...

I learned about the suicide by a phone call. It was the morning of September 11. All that horror paled in comparison to the news about her death. I couldn't believe it at first. My immediate reaction was to protect my son. He didn't know yet, and I didn't want him to be alone when he heard. He was still very much in love with her. I called my other son to go be with him and tell him. They both live a couple of hundred miles from me. My husband and I then got ready to drive up.

There were clues I missed. She did editing work for me, and she hadn't been getting her work done. That was not at all like her. Her work was excellent and timely. Other than that, I knew she was troubled and things were not going well. She had asked our son for a divorce, but she still had a strong connection with him. They were having major financial problems. She felt like a total failure—her third divorce. She also avoided us as much as possible—feeling like we wouldn't like her anymore. She would clam up when we told her she would always be part of us and welcome in our family. She was crazy about our grandkids—her nephews by marriage. She babysat a lot before the divorce. She and our son were supposed to have dinner a couple of nights before her death, but she cancelled at the last minute. He later said that was a definite sign something was wrong.

We found several notes. She thought the world would be better off without her—particularly her son and ours. She stated over and over in her notes that she just wanted to know peace.

Our elderly family members and the kids, we told them she died but not about the suicide. Others, we told the truth. No one who knew her could believe it. Everyone thought she was so lovely.

Most people avoided talking about it or mentioning her name. We have several friends who have experienced suicide in their families. They understood but they didn't want to talk about it either.

The bereavement process...

It started with disbelief and a week of pain. She had a son by her first marriage. He was in his early 20s and was totally devastated. Most of my time was spent with him and helping plan her funeral. Our son retreated into disbelief and was incapable of making decisions, except for his involvement in the funeral.

There was nothing dramatic—just the pain of loss. I did find it hard to concentrate and get back to my normal work. I still find it hard to work sometimes. This interview is very painful. It will be hard to get past it today.

Following the first couple of weeks, I became very angry with her. She let so many people down. She had no idea how well loved she was and how many grieved for her. Of course, had she felt worthy of that love, she probably would never have done it.

I actively grieved for her for the first couple of years. I find a suicide so much more difficult than a natural death. It's so senseless and such a waste. She was such a wonderful person, and everyone saw it but her.

My heart still aches when I think of her. Every time I see something she would have liked—she collected pigs and loved her home—I think of the loss—hers and ours.

I miss her in a spiritual and psychological way. I didn't see her that much the last few months of her life, although I talked to her about once a week. But I miss her potential, her love of life and pretty things and her artistic nature. And I still grieve for my son. He can talk about her now—

her, not her suicide. We both feel guilty that we didn't do something to prevent her death.

It was a horrible waste. She messed up her medications frequently to save money. Then she became very despondent. I don't think one can ever come to terms with suicide. I think I have come to terms with her being gone. It took about three years for that. I love her, but sometimes I'm still angry and hurt, that all of us who loved her weren't worth living for.

Have you ever considered taking your own life?

No. There were times when I thought no one would care if I died, but I learned that is far from the truth.

Significance of the suicide...

It has totally changed the way I look at my family and friends. I try to be more aware of where they are.

Helpful coping methods...

I think the fact that I had to plan the funeral helped me. It held other emotions at bay for a few days until the shock was lessened a little.

Advice or words of wisdom...

You can't blame yourself and you finally have to accept that you weren't responsible for your loved one's pain. That was an overwhelming part of my grief—that I should have done something to change things. I know I couldn't have but there are still times when I think about it.

Let people know the value they have and how much you care.

Karen M. Spring

Age: 33

Current Occupation: Professional Writer and Stay-At-Home Mom

Karen's friend completed suicide on September 27, 1994. He jumped in front of a train.

In her words...

I am married and have toddler twin boys. I had a normal "Beaver Cleaver" type of family growing up. Dad worked outside of the home while Mom stayed home with me and my younger brother. Growing up in my family was pretty normal. My parents really put the needs of me and my brother first and truly loved us.

Jeff was a guy I knew in college. He was a member of a fraternity that I was friendly with and he always seemed to be around when I was out socializing. He and I dated briefly but he seemed a little too intense for me and I broke off the relationship quickly. He did a few things that scared me, too and I didn't feel comfortable with him.

The suicide...

I was at work and friends of mine were calling my house all day. When I got home from work, my mom sat me down and said that someone named Jeff had completed suicide.

I got really upset and started to shake. I remember having to go and lie down. I couldn't believe he'd done this but in a way, I wasn't really surprised since something about him had always seemed wrong and I just could never figure out what it was.

I didn't have any idea. But he seemed to be a loner in a respect. He was involved in a lot of school activities and had friends, but after Jeff died, I realized that he had always seemed to be on the outside of things. He couldn't really get too close to anyone.

I think he felt a lot of pressure about his senior year of college and getting a job. Also, I think he was feeling that he didn't have anyone whom he could truly confide in, even though he had friends.

I told people he'd died and how upsetting it was. Friends of mine banded together to be supportive of me. We had all known Jeff but I'd dated him and I think they were worried about me.

The bereavement process...

The viewing was very rough for me. It made it all so real. I met Jeff's mom and dad and they were so devastated. I couldn't imagine losing a child this way. But it made me think back to when I was 13 and had contemplated suicide. I began to see how this would have affected my family. I was in denial for a while. I kept thinking, "Maybe it was an accident. Maybe he hadn't meant to jump on the tracks." But my best friend was at school when it happened and she heard the witnesses describing the incident to the police. They all said that Jeff's actions were no accident. That he'd deliberately gotten down on the tracks. That was so hard.

I felt anger, frustration, and extreme sadness. I was angry with myself that I had not reached out to him more.

I do not feel I have come to terms with the loss. I suppose I see his death as such a loss, such a waste. And I feel very guilty even though it's been a long time. I'm not sure that I'll ever come to terms with this. I had treated Jeff badly when we were together and I never had the chance to apologize. I suppose I'm still sad about that.

I feel sad that he has missed out on the finer things in life like having a family, children and a home.

Dreams and unusual occurrences...

I've dreamed about Jeff, but nothing really sticks out to me. I've had thoughts that he was suffering in the afterlife. As if that commandment "Thou shalt not kill" was hanging over him because he killed himself. I wonder if wherever he is if he is happy or if he is still crying out in sadness.

Have you ever considered taking your own life?

I was 13 and in 8th grade. I'd hated my school and I had begged my parents for years to put me in public school. (I was in a Catholic school.) They refused. I think I complained a lot about things for so long that they didn't hear me anymore. By the time I was 13, I had had enough and I decided that death might be the answer. I started examining the knives in the kitchen to see which one could do the job. I really was going to do it. Then, I went out shopping one evening with my aunt and I was acting like a brat. She and I had a huge fight in the parking lot of the mall and she asked me what was wrong and I started screaming about how I wanted to die. My aunt started crying about how she had lost both her parents to cancer when she was young and how she couldn't deal with losing any more of her loved ones. We had a good cry. Afterwards, I assumed she'd told my parents what happened because they suddenly seemed more intuitive of things and being more available for me emotionally. There was no mention of the suicide

212

thing until Jeff died. Then I mentioned it to my mom—how I wanted to die, how I'd fought with Aunt Sue at the mall, how I was examining the knives. My mother nearly had a heart attack! She'd had no idea the whole time.

Significance of the suicide...

I am more in tune with mental illness nowadays and I have more compassion for depression and issues like this.

Helpful coping methods...

Talking things out with my family and friends.

Helpful advice or words of wisdom...

Prayer is helpful. Also counseling is a must for those very close to the situation.

"Martina"

Age: 58

Profession: Freelance Writer

Barb's next-door neighbor completed suicide in the late 1970s or early 1980s. She died of hypothermia.

In her words...

She was my next-door neighbor as I was growing up. I was very close to her. She took off her hat and gloves and went to sleep with the temperatures hovering around freezing.

I'm the second youngest of three sisters. There is an age span of 15 years between the older two and me and my younger sister and as I grew up I saw very little of them. My family was upper-middle class and was very materialistic. My father owned his own business, and both my mother and father subscribed to the mindset of "keeping up with the Jones's." By 16, I had my first car, and our family had all the latest amenities. My father was quite a fisher/hunter, loved the outdoors and loved people. When I was younger, my father took me everywhere with him. I was the apple of his eye. As time went on, he spent most of his time with his friends, and was absent from the home much of the time. My sister and I were happy about that since he had started to drink heavily and was verbally abusive. My mother was very stoic and formal. She never encouraged us to talk about our feelings.

I felt very different from the rest of my family. I didn't feel comfortable sharing any feelings with my mother or father. Consequently, I resolved problems on my own or with the help of people I looked to as being in the role of mother or father. I didn't subscribe to their values and have grown up being very anti-materialistic. An example of how my family never talked about anything; I found out that my father had been arrested for drunk driving when I was his name on the front page of the newspaper.

The woman I call Smitty lived next door. I adopted her and her husband when I was very young. He was a doctor and had delivered me. She was an operating room nurse. Both of them were mentors and advocated for me when I needed therapy. I remember very vividly overhearing both her and her husband. They felt I should go to the Child Guidance Center. Of course, I didn't because of my parent's strong belief in stoicism and trying to keep up with the Jones's. Up to my teenage years, I think I was over at their house more than I was at my own.

The suicide...

214

She didn't suicide for about a month after she told me. My best friend told me he read about her death in the obituaries. Since I knew she was going to suicide, I wasn't shocked; however, I do remember feeling surprise that she actually killed herself and sadness at having lost a good friend.

There were clues. She suffered many losses and she gave away her personal possessions. I think having been a nurse, she knew she would be dependent on others to take care of her because of her chronic health problems and she was a very independent person.

I told others the truth about her death. There was no difference in the way they related to me.

The bereavement process...

I remember going to her memorial. At that time, I was volunteering on a suicide prevention hotline so I was around a lot of counselors, and processed my feelings with them. Also, writing about the experience helped.

My reaction occurred when she told me. I felt like I was listening to someone else say they were going to kill themselves. I couldn't believe the words were coming from her mouth.

I came to terms with her death when she told me what she was going to do. The fact that she killed herself is very surprising because it is not consistent with the person I knew. However, I think her suicide has further emphasized the fact that people have the right to make that decision.

Significance of the suicide...

I still think about it but do not feel guilty about my decision not to tell.

Helpful coping methods...

Talking to friends, writing about it.

Advice or words of wisdom...

Behavioral clues are often hard to pick up, even for trained professionals. For example, I've been a volunteer counselor on a suicide prevention hotline for over 16 years plus I am trained as a psychotherapist. Recently a caller completed suicide. I assessed the caller as having low lethality because I felt he did not meet the criteria for high risk. A few days later he completed suicide. When I spoke with the supervisor, she said a lot of counselors he had talked with placed him at low risk level. Also, if a person wants to kill himself or herself badly enough, they are going to do it regardless of what you say or do, you can't stop them. All you can do is to do your best and try to let them know they are in control and there are other options besides suicide.

Gunilla S Hodkin

Age: 40

Current Occupation: Writer

In her words...

One of my best friend's husband completed suicide 14 years ago, when their twins were only 14 months old. He died of carbon monoxide poisoning. My best friend from elementary school also took her own life six years ago. She jumped off a bridge. Recently, less than two months ago, my ex-husband's cousin and dear friend of mine completed suicide by jumping off a bridge.

I spent most of my life (about two decades) being suicidal. I wrote about it in my book *Return of a Runaway Spirit* (www.windwhisper-magic.com).

I do not have many family members remaining. They were dysfunctional for many years. My brother died early due to severe neglect by Catholic nuns. We all suffered the consequences for many years. I was more or less estranged from my family for several decades. Today I have a great relationship with my mother but not my sister. My father is dead and other relatives are dead.

It was hard growing up in my family. I had to find my own way of functioning—and did. Life today is great. All the hard work of finding my own style and fighting for it has been worth it.

The suicides...

I found out about the suicides through our friends or from their relatives. I experienced shock, nausea and wanting to throw up. I wished I could shake the suicidees.

I believe the suicides were the result of despair, pain and seeing no way out.

I was on the other side of the world so I did not have any clues.

I told others the truth about the suicides. Most of my friends can relate; they know somebody who completed suicide. Some even had someone close to them suicide.

The bereavement process…

I allowed it to flood through me. There were lots of tears and wishing I could have "saved" them. There was lots of sadness knowing how much pain they had to have suffered through to commit the act.

I did not seek counseling when coping with my friends' departure, but I did when trying to find the reason for my own suicidal tendencies many years ago. It was helpful in the way that I discovered the underlying causes for my wishes. My book describes this intimately.

I believe I have come to terms with the losses shortly after. I've worked on my spiritual side for years. I guess it is paying off. I manage to swiftly move through stages. The show must go on.

I love them all.

Have you ever considered taking your own life?

I tried twice and continued to live a very destructive lifestyle for years. I was seriously depressed and wounded. I suffered from post-traumatic-stress-disorder for decades. I learned a lot from the connection with my spiritual self and am now living a very fulfilling life.

Significance of suicides…

Well, I have already come to the conclusion of not taking my own life (we can't really die or disappear anyway—we just change form) and don't struggle with suicidal issues anymore. Suicide does not have more stigma to me personally but I know it does in society at large (partly why I wrote my book). So there has not been any particular significance to their actions as such. However, I want more than ever to help educate people about suicide and assist them in alleviating pain, coming out of depression, finding joy in their hearts and assisting them in learning to enjoy life and living. Because I know it is possible. Suicides can be prevented—I have no doubt about that. Having said that; souls choose their form of departure and have the right to do so. I respect their decision—I just wish they had been clearer in their thinking. Most people who complete suicide are depressed or under the influence of some kind of drugs.

Helpful coping methods…

Spiritual and emotional growth and maturity.

Helpful advice or words of wisdom…

Don't hide in shame. Talk about it. Educate people. Educate yourself. Don't allow it to continue being a taboo subject—lets bring it out of the closet!

I believe a lot of suicides are due to the illusion of "losing face" (look at people in the stock market for instance, and other "successful" individuals). People fear not being able to cope, not facing the world, not facing themselves. If we believe we cannot live up to the image of ourselves— some choose to "check out." I believe a lot of people complete suicide because they are afraid of facing the future, growing old, changing and not being able to live up to the image of themselves. Let's embrace instead!

CHAPTER SEVEN
Stories, Essays and Poems

I HATE SYLVIA PLATH

Sandra Perlman

My mother, Betty, completed suicide last year at 86—pills. The first attempt that I witnessed was when I was eight and I saved her life by calling my father home from a late night meeting. My mother told me later our family doctor pumped her stomach in our 1950s Philadelphia kitchen. Though I don't remember this, I am sure I knew something was happening and it wasn't muffins. Then it was against the law and would have been in the newspaper that she had attempted suicide and probably would have been admitted to the psych ward, which in retrospect may have been the best thing that could have happened. But then hindsight is so much better close up than from afar.

My mom continued to tell me she was killing herself for the next 50 years whenever she was sad or lonely, which was often. Or if I wasn't living the life she had fantasized for me, which was more often. Or when she just had too much to drink and too many pills. Interestingly enough, her last phone call four days before her death was the best one we had since my childhood. My remark to my husband was, "If that was the last conversation with my mother it would be all right." And it was. Of course it is never completely all right. But at least this time she had not told me she was going to do it <u>and</u> it was my fault—her mantra for the last 40 years since I left home. Interestingly enough, her father, my grandfather, completed his suicide by swallowing poison when she was eight years old. But that's another story—or perhaps it isn't. Her father's suicidal "love" note left for her

219

definitely warped my mother's ideas of love, parenting and death. I have spent a lifetime trying to create new definitions. My poem, *I Hate Sylvia Plath*, is one more response as a woman, wife, mother and always—a writer.

I Hate Sylvia Plath

Hate her dead, head in the oven.

I long to be mother, wife, and writer.

After checking the mail for yet another rejection

I search the mirror for signs of madness.

In return for the smallest success I seduce my husband

Bake cookies for my daughter and buy an electric range.

SMITTY

"Martina"

Little did I know when I accepted Smitty's invitation for lunch I would be faced with one of the hardest decisions of my life.

Smitty got up from the blue overstuffed chair he was sitting in as soon as he saw me walk through the door of the reception area.

"I'm glad you came," he said hugging me. "At last I'll be able to have a normal conversation. The people here either talk about things that make sense only to them or their aches and pains."

His words puzzled me. They didn't sound like the Smitty I knew. I met him thirty years ago when I was five. I was playing ball in front of his house. The ball slipped out of my hands and rolled into his garden. He picked up the ball, smiled, and said, "Is this yours?" I liked the way he treated me. He didn't yell like most adults do when a kid makes a mistake.

We became instant friends. I went over to visit daily. Smitty always had time to talk. If he was busy, he'd give me small jobs to do, like bringing him plants or sanding a piece of lumber. Then we'd have our time together.

When I started school Smitty volunteered to tutor me. He made learning fun. When I was studying fractions, Smitty took a pie his wife had baked and had me cut it into pieces equal to different fractions. When I was studying astronomy, he let me look through his telescope.

As years went by, Smitty developed rheumatoid arthritis. It was difficult for him to go downstairs to his workshop or kneel in the garden. When Smitty's wife died, he decided to sell his house and move into a retirement home.

While we were having lunch, I noticed Smitty wasn't his usual bubbly self. When he spoke, he seemed downhearted and low-key. When people passed our table, Smitty invited them to stop by his room. He told them he was giving things away and wanted them to choose what they wanted.

When I heard his invitation, I was puzzled. I knew he was generous but why was he doing this when I was here? Something wasn't right. Smitty had lost his wife of 60 years, his health and home all within the past year. He was depressed and giving his possessions away. Both my instincts and my training as a suicide prevention counselor were telling me something I didn't want to hear—Smitty may be having suicidal thoughts.

I must be wrong, I thought. I *have* to be wrong. This couldn't be Smitty, the man I had always looked to for advice. He was the poster boy of mental health, the person who always saw the glass half full instead of half empty. Maybe I was just being melodramatic and imagining he was suicidal. I had to ask him so I could be certain and quit speculating.

When we went back to his apartment books, pictures and bric-a-brac were lying in neat piles on his bed. Larger items like lamps, plants and a television stood in the middle of the floor.

I hope this doesn't ruin our relationship, I thought taking a deep breath. I turned, looked Smitty in the eye and asked the question I wasn't sure I wanted to hear the answer to the question, "Are you thinking of killing yourself?"

"Yes, I've decided it's time for my life to end," Smitty said in a-matter-of-fact tone. "I wrote to the Hemlock Society and told them my health was failing and I wanted to die with dignity while I was still able to function. They advised me to take some time, think about my decision then call back. I thought about it for several weeks, then called. They talked with me about why I wanted to kill myself. When they were convinced I could make a rational decision they told me about some methods."

As soon as I heard "Yes" I felt like I was in a dream. A stranger was telling me this, not Smitty. Reality proved different. I heard correctly. I couldn't wish it away. I wondered what I should do. Should I tell someone in authority like I'm supposed to? Or should I hold what Smitty told me in confidence?

I wanted a reprieve from the present situation so I might get a clear perspective, so I did some mental time travel. I thought about Smitty in his home with his wife. I remembered how he loved puttering around the house and taking a vacation whenever he and his wife saw fit. Then I thought about Smitty now; his health failing, no family and very little independence. I thought about the many times I confided in Smitty. I knew I could trust him not to tell my parents. Now he was putting his trust in me. What was I going to do? Was I trying to help Smitty by telling the administrator or hurting him by restraining him only adding to his sense of being out of control? I needed to let go, and honor Smitty's decision.

After a few minutes, I returned to Smitty's room to face the situation at hand. I walked over to Smitty. Putting my hand on his shoulder, I said, "I'm not totally convinced about the morality of suicide, but that is between you and God. I'd much prefer you wouldn't go through with your plan because I'll miss you a lot. But, this is your life. I know you've given a lot of thought to this and haven't arrived at it lightly. I won't tell anyone and promise to keep this as our secret."

Smitty smiled at me, "I had a long talk with God. Afterwards I felt a peace I haven't felt for a long time. I know in my heart it is okay with Him."

I left the retirement home that night emotionally drained but confident I had made the right choice.

After that momentous day, I made it a point to go to the care facility three or four times a week. I tried not to dwell on the fact that Smitty would not be around much longer and to focus on the remaining time we did have together instead. We went on car rides, out to eat, and spent time enjoying one another's company.

One morning, several months later, I was looking through the newspaper when I came across Smitty's obituary. As I read the words tears welled in my eyes. It was a bittersweet moment. I was sad he would never be in my life again. At the same time, I was honored he trusted me enough to take me into his confidence giving me the opportunity to pay him back for the love and respect he had given me all these years.

WILDFLOWERS FOR DAD

(Oswald Rigodanzo - October 17, 1924 - August 1, 2004)

Terese Rigodanzo-Adom

The wildflowers this year were abundant. In the several road trips made this summer, I had the opportunity to view them frequently. With all the beauty, joy and comfort they provided to anyone looking, I should have embraced them more deeply.

Not even sure of each one's name, I felt they graced the landscape like good friends offering cheer. Their multi-colored hues delighted the eye offering kind messages a companion might speak; each one unique reminding us of the Master Hand that created them and painted them the colors of heaven's rainbow.

As your spirit, dear Dad, takes wing and soars

On this earthly plane with us no more

Wildflowers remind us of your presence

Keeping close to nature was your essence.

You had such kind and gentlemanly ways;

Family and neighbors never to betray.

My friends all wished they'd had a dad like you.

People say, I'm just like you what will I do?

I will honor the God whose pallet true

Painted these wildflowers for us to view.

And remember you, Dad, with awesome love

Just like the Creator does from above.

JOHN (CHRIS) ECKMAN
Pennsylvania
June 13, 1969 - May 15, 1994
Gunshot to the head

Jesse Eckman

The last time I saw Chris was the day before he died. I was worried because of two things: one, he was bringing things home he said he didn't need; and two, he had a big smile on his face. This was unusual for Chris because he rarely seemed to smile. At this time I had very little knowledge of suicide. However, these two things brought up red flags in my mind. I remember wondering why he was doing this. I got a bigger hint that night when I dreamt about him and the answer when my mother called me the next morning to tell me Chris was dead. I knew when my mom called and told me Chris was dead that my family and I would be going through hell. My mother shouldn't have lost her only son one week before Mother's day. My grandmother shouldn't have lost her only grandson the day before her birthday, but they did.

When Chris died, I remembered feeling stunned and angry. I thought, who the hell do you think you are? Later we found Chris's diaries. He had the whole thing planned—the how, why and where. He even left his leather jacket on my mom's front porch with what reminded me of a to-do list, though it only had one item on it. It read: "Ask Mom (mommy) if I can wear my leather jacket at my funeral." Even though we were told by the county coroner that it would need to be a closed casket, Chris wore his leather jacket. We dressed him just the way he would have dressed in life and even played his favorite music at his memorial service. Some people weren't very happy with this but we felt that this is what Chris would have wanted. When we finally did purchase a tombstone for his gravesite, my mother felt that my sisters and I should be involved. We chose one together and had Chris's favorite thing, his car, carved into it.

The night Chris died he talked my mother into driving him to his house almost 40 miles away. She agreed but only if he gave her his gun when they arrived. He agreed. When they arrived, he said he searched and couldn't find it. He said he would be okay because a friend of his was there. He said, "Mom, nothing will happen to me." He lied. Chris was in his bedroom. His friend was in the living room. His friend said he heard a noise and thought Chris dropped his soda can. When he didn't hear anything else he checked on Chris and realized what really happened. Chris ended his life with a gun.

225

After Chris died I was depressed for a year. I had panic attacks daily but told no one so I wouldn't have to bother with going to see a therapist or taking drugs. My youngest sister was fifteen years old when Chris died. It was extremely difficult for her. She tried to complete suicide twice just so she could be with her big brother. At the funeral home and later the cemetery, her father had to pull her off of Chris's casket when we were leaving. It just broke my heart to see my mother and sister in so much pain. It hurt me more than I can say.

I mourn for anyone who has lost a brother, like me and my sisters. We will no longer hear his voice. Even though we did argue a lot, I would love to hear his voice and be able to argue with him again.

I wish I could listen to his favorite songs without getting that sinking feeling in the pit of my stomach. I wish I could have done something to stop Chris from completing suicide. Deep down I know if it hadn't happened then, eventually it would have happened. Don't let anyone ever tell you, "You will get over it." There is no such thing as "getting over it." You will get through it the best you can but you will never get over it. There is no such thing. Eventually what replaces the pain is memories.

Chris's death changed me in a lot of ways. It is now almost ten years since his death and my mother, sisters, and I talk about him a lot. After Chris died, it was difficult to hear his favorite songs without crying. Once, shortly after he died, I was shopping in a crafts store when Chris's favorite song began to play, I became panicked and wanted to run out of the store and never go back again. Instead I just stood there the whole time the song played shaking with tears streaming down my face.

Now when I think of Chris I think of a little man with a devilish grin and a great sense of humor. He had a sweet, gentle side of himself he rarely seemed to show.

Chris felt that by ending his life he was doing his family a favor. He was so very wrong. I think of him nearly every day, especially on holidays, his birthday and the anniversary of his death.

I will always love and miss my little brother. When I get sad, I try to think of my favorite religious saying: "In my Father's house there are many rooms." I can picture Chris and my grandparents walking around in Heaven together. They are buried near each other. I have never told anyone this but there is a very small part of me that is glad Chris didn't live after the gunshot because my handsome little brother would have been disfigured. Also I somehow sensed that if he wouldn't have completed suicide then, he would have continued to try until he would have completed suicide.

The day after Chris died I went to back to work. Work after suicide was difficult enough. After work, I ended up going to the doctor's office for some very sudden laryngitis. The doctor was stunned when I told him about Chris.

Chris and his best friend were volunteer firefighters. After Chris died his best friend said, "How will I ever find another best friend?" At the funeral his best friend got out his volunteer firefighter blues uniform and stood at Chris's casket during the entire service. At the end of the service he turned around and saluted Chris's casket. It is something that, even now almost 10 years later, brings me to tears.

Things Chris said before he died:
1) Dead men don't pay bills.
2) I'll be dead by the time I'm 40.

The first time I heard about Survivors of Suicide was the day Chris died. Ironically, there was an article in the newspaper about a family that attended the group. My mother and I decided to go to the next meeting. It was the first Thursday in June 1994. I remember walking into the room stunned at the number of people there. For the first time in my life I was speechless. Everyone went around in a circle saying their name, the loved one who completed suicide, how long it had been since the suicide, and how their day was. I attended the group for weeks. Every time they asked if I had anything to say, the only word I could say was no. It still helped enormously to be around people who had been through the same thing I was going through.

I remember going home after the first meeting and saying to my mother, "I feel better." My mother's words were, "I don't but if it helps you we'll keep going back." Ironically, my mom went to the meetings longer than I did. When I did go to the meetings, I remember having so much hate and anger at Chris in my system. Whenever I went to a Survivors of Suicide meeting, my heart would beat very fast until more people came. Only then did I feel safe.

Prologue

Eleven years have gone by and now I am helping others through the same situation I went through. It feels good to help others, however, it always breaks my heart to hear about another suicide. I often say if I could show my little brother and others what life is like without them, they might reconsider suicide, very much like the movie, *It's a Wonderful Life.*

227

My life has changed in many ways; so has my mother's and sisters' lives. My extended family is growing. My eldest sister is now a grandmother of four children. My second eldest sister now has a daughter-in-law. My youngest sister is engaged and recently gave birth to a beautiful baby girl.

My grandmother passed away. When I look at my great-nieces and nephews and my new niece, I visualize my brother and think how much he would have loved it! In my daily life, I no longer have a lot of sadness, it is more a mellowness. I often feel Chris here with me, especially when I play his favorite songs. I feel like I have a sixth sense about things and that at times of great crisis in life I have an angel looking after me. That angel's name is Chris.

He was born June 13, 1969.

He was the only son in a family of women.

His father walked out on him when he was young

Male influences in his life were few and far between.

Growing up was tough for him,

He loved his mother and sisters but was never sure how to show it.

No matter what he did all his life, his mother and sisters loved him back.

As he was growing up, life was hard. He had trouble with girlfriends, money, and drugs and alcohol. His father was an alcoholic.

Even though he had problems he was a very caring, sensitive, loving brother with a great sense of humor.

He had two loves in his life: one was his music, the other was his car.

He was almost twenty- five when he took his life with a gun. The day he died was a beautiful day in May. The flowers were blooming. The birds were singing. The sun was shining.

But that evening in a little house in Maytown, Pennsylvania, my brother lost all hope.

He died as he lived, loved by everyone who knew him.

MONTE

Deborah Darby

Right after we'd given each other hickeys, he told me that his pickup truck was stuck on the railroad tracks. High centered, he said. Monte Crowe. A lean and handsome 16-year-old: cowboy, rodeo rider, drinker, small-town West Texas macho. Tough. Proving it by getting drunk and doing stupid, stupid things, and being proud of it.

From the moment my friend Laura introduced us, just a couple of hours earlier, I was totally attracted to him. At 15, I couldn't believe that somebody as cool as he was wanted to kiss me, for I was young, and not yet able to understand what gifts I had for men.

My friend Laura, with whom I was spending the weekend, and her boyfriend, Mike, left me with Monte to go parking; a time-honored tradition of boys and girls who need a little time alone to explore life's mysteries. For me it was a rare, unsupervised evening and I wanted to participate fully. I was even drinking some of Monte's beer, another forbidden but tantalizing activity.

Monte and I made out heavily in his pickup truck. He had driven out into the dry, desert pasture, turning down a winding dirt road and, inexplicably, driving up on a railroad track. I was from another small town 50 miles away, so I didn't know the rules of his realm. For all I knew, he was the king of Big Lake, Texas. He liked that about me.

The truck surged and fell back as Monte tried to dislodge it from the tracks. There was no train in sight, but he had turned on his outside running lights and spotlight so that "…if a train comes, they might see us in time…"

"Monte! Get us off the tracks!! I'm getting scared!"

"I'm tryin' Honey. But we're stuck."

"Well, let's get out and walk to town," I said, clinging to his arm, but taking another swig of the beer.

"No, no, I can get us out of this." His earnest young face was illuminated by the dashboard lights and the bizarre set of outside lights a cowboy's pickup had to be equipped with in that more innocent, but less resource-minded era.

The engine of the truck revved way up. I looked at the lights as they bounced around, reflecting off the creosote and mesquite bushes that surrounded the slightly elevated railroad track.

"I'm getting out," I said, handing him the empty beer bottle.

"No, no…Honey, no, wait." He stopped trying to move the truck but left it running, lights ablaze, and turned toward me, reaching for my face. His hand touched my cheek. He worked weekends on a ranch, so his hand was rough. But the touch was gentle. Then he leaned across me and tossed the beer bottle out the open window, as I smiled, gazing into his slightly glazed eyes.

"Whut?" I said. He said it almost simultaneously. "Whut?"

Laughing, he pulled my face toward his. I hesitated only a moment, my heart pounding almost through my sweater.

I looked up, hoping to see myself reflected in his sweet, intensely green eyes. They were closed. "Hey, Monte."

His eyes flashed open. He looked a little dazed, but he smiled.

"Whut?'

"Who are you kissing?"

"Oh...you…Honey. You're my honey." He moved his hand down to the back of my neck. He tugged my face toward his, eyes closing. "You're my honey…" he murmured as he began to kiss me gently on the lips. My lips responded. My body was young, undereducated. I got lost in his kisses.

He was smooth, but at that moment with my mother's admonition that "boys only want one thing" ringing in my head, I made every woman's valiant effort to maintain what was left of my virginity.

"Monte, no," I mumbled when he moved his hand toward my breast. "Nuhn uhn." But I never really stopped kissing him. Instead I wiggled, attempting to deflect his grasp. He liked the wiggling and held me tighter, twirling his cowboy-slim hips as well, turning his body toward me, kissing me more intently.

I was bewitched, giving in to his dexterity again. I felt my body being spun around, mirroring his movements. Then, without realizing the extent of the posture change, I was laying on top of him. We continued to kiss, and he couldn't keep himself from writhing under me. I pretended not to notice, not wanting the kissing to stop. Finally, though, the intensity of his thrusting was too much. "Monte..no…" I attempted to raise my body off him, half-heartedly.

"No, no, no, Honey, no, don't stop." He was pleading, not quite desperate, but deeply interested in continuing. I pushed up off him, my chest away from his. He instantly and expertly attached one hand to my breast, fumbling only a split second to get under my sweater. His other hand was trying to pull me back down.

"Honey, please. Please don't stop." He looked at me imploringly. I let him bring me back down to his chest. His kisses were astonishing, passionate in ways I had not encountered. Massaging my breast vigorously, he abandoned himself to the moment.

I went with him as far as a 15-year-old semi-virgin could, but the rapid beating of my heart was more from fear than sexual excitement. I began to twist out of his grasp, firmly that time. He held me for a moment, trying to focus his eyes, then relented. "OK," was all he said.

I pushed myself off him, moving to the other side of the seat, patting my hair and rearranging my bra discreetly, almost formally. He swung his long bowlegs off the seat of the truck, glaring out the window; stretching, rearranging, well, I was afraid to think of what he had to rearrange.

"Monte...I'm sorry, but I just can't do that." It was a discussion I'd had with several other boys in my young, but overly curious lifetime. I slid back toward him, leaning into right side, laying my head on his shoulder.

"I'm gettin' this goddamn truck off the tracks!" was his heated reply. He nudged me away, reaching for the gearshift.

The truck was miraculously able to drive right off the tracks once it became clear that I wasn't going to put out.

After that, Monte, who had already been drinking pretty steadily all night, tossed back beer after beer. His drinking was the behavior I grew up around in the wilds of West Texas with alcoholic adults in my life and lots of young, drunk friends, so it didn't disturb me. What was unusual, however, was that though I had hardly ever had anything alcoholic to drink before that night, I was trying to keep up with him. Watching how the grown-ups in my life handled alcohol had prepared me to attempt that self-destructive trick, but it was a maneuver that almost killed me.

I sat beside Monte, holding his beer, matching him drink for drink, my head spinning with the lust and lushness of youth. I never even knew I was drunk. I was just in another Universe. And that Universe spun precipitously. Approaching headlights blurred together and then exploded in my eyes as we drove back toward town. My tongue was thick. "Monte, I think I'm going to be sick..."

"Okay. Okay, Honey." Although he had hardly spoken a word to me since we'd driven off the railroad track, a seasoned drinker like him knew when to be solicitous to a fellow drunk. He pulled the truck over to the shoulder of the road.

I barely made it out of the cab of the truck, unsteady on my feet, lurching forward and throwing up in one movement, catching myself with my arms. Monte waited in the pickup, then gave me his beer to "wash it down with."

I drank deeply and kept drinking.

When we met back up with Laura and Mike, the evening went hazy, misty, backlit with a strange kind of surreal motif. We were all talking and somebody suggested that we have a drinking contest. I can still hear the words in my memory, but I don't recognize the voice. I know it wasn't Laura, though, because she refused to take part in the contest. It was just me and the boys.

The other guy had an almost full bottle of Old Crow whiskey. We got our cups out of the car; cups that had earlier held our Dairy Queen cokes. The guys filled the cups and we chugalugged them. They were amazed that I finished first.

It's the very last thing I remember about the evening.

What I later heard was that Laura and I had gone home then, back to her house, sneaking in because we were late and drunk. There are flashes of this memory in my head, but nothing clear; something about the room spinning. The next morning I was critically ill.

I stumbled into the bathroom, seeking to throw up again, but fainted on the tile floor. Fortunately I was kneeling over the toilet when I passed out, so it wasn't far to fall. I lay there for awhile. I don't know how long, until Laura came in and picked me up and made me wash my face. I had not been able to throw up. I was poisoned and it was already in my system. Despite my youth and lack of experience, I knew I might die. I longed for it, almost, feeling so bad in this life and so incredibly near the next.

Struggling to maintain so her parents wouldn't know how desperately sick I was, I went with Laura to the local meat locker to pick up something for lunch. The people who owned the meat locker lived in a small apartment, attached to the locker. They sat drinking their morning coffee. Laura suggested that coffee might help me. I refused. I had never had coffee and I knew that drinking strange things was what had gotten me in this predicament. I did eat some scrambled eggs, though, longing for the normality they suggested.

232

Stumbling a little, I followed Laura into the meat locker and the cold closed around me. I leaned against the rough plank wall and took a shuddering breath. I relished the coldness, wrapped myself in it, staying in the locker for almost 20 minutes before they made me come out. The intensity of the cold sobered me up and brought me back to this universe. My body still ached, but youth would save me this time. My head cleared.

A couple of weeks later on a Sunday morning, my mother didn't come in to wake me for church. She knew I liked to sleep late and would sometimes let me get by with it on summer mornings.

I awoke when a friend called to ask me if I wanted to go get a coke. I never turned down an opportunity to get out of my house, to drive up and down the main drag in my little town, so I dressed quickly and ran into my mother's room to tell her where I was going. She was in bed. She had a life-long history of migraine headaches and spent most of her time in bed, day and night.

"Mom, I'm going with Bonnie to the Dairy Queen," I said.

"Well, then bring me back a sour lime," she said, not raising her pain-filled head from the pillow. "Get your daddy to give you some money."

Daddy was in the other room watching football on television and handed me two dollars without even glancing up. "Get your mother a sour lime," he said. "She likes those."

Bonnie honked the horn and I ran out. She was full of talk. She and her boyfriend were planning to run away and get married soon. In those days, many of us were still looking for our knights in shining armor and we mistakenly thought our first loves were riding white horses.

I talked to her about Monte, the love of my life. Although he had not contacted me directly since our evening in the boonies, I knew without a doubt that he loved me and was thinking about me. Laura had written me that one day in home room Monte had told her to tell me that he really liked me, or at least that's what she said. My parents didn't really let me date yet, so they knew I had met a boy named Monte Crowe, but they didn't know anything else about him.

Bonnie and I had our lemon cokes, drove up and down the streets a couple of times, drove past the popular guys' houses for no reason, honked the horn when we saw somebody we knew or wanted to know, and laughed as only innocent adolescents girls can laugh.

When I got home, I glanced in her room and thought my mother was asleep. I had gone back in my room after putting her sour lime in the freezer, but then she was standing at my doorway. She looked strange.

"There is something I've got to tell you," she said. Now she looked really strange, upset. She was holding the Sunday newspaper in her hand. She handed me the paper, open to the obituary page. There in column one was a school photo of a familiar face. "Monte Crowe, age 16" was the caption. Though our tiny towns were miles apart, his death, so young, so tragic, had rated an obit in the area Sunday edition.

I read the obituary silently, my universe shifting. The words didn't make sense to me: "...apparently from a self-inflicted wound...services were held Saturday at the First Baptist Church in Big Lake ..." Looking up at her, I said, "What does this mean?"

"He killed himself," she said, answering the unanswerable question. "I didn't want to tell you, but I was afraid that you'd find out from your friends," she said, the pain of her migraine and my reflected anguish on her face.

I screamed at her, "Get out of my room! Get out!" I was devastated, inconsolable. The boy I was in love with had blown his brains out, without a word to me. No call. No note. Nothing. I sobbed. I rocked myself in a desperate attempt at comfort. I was utterly alone. My sense of shame was palpable. In some twisted way, I felt certain that this was probably my fault. All my fault. How could I ever face Laura again?

Although I had barely known Monte, I had loved him with a 15-year-old certainty: absolutely. My God, he had touched my breast! His tongue had been in my mouth. I called Bonnie and poured out the story. Finally I went to sleep, tossing and turning until the next morning.

We never spoke of Monte again at my house.

At the end of that same summer in which I had met and lost Monte, I saw Laura parked in her mother's station wagon on the main drag in my town. I hadn't talked to her since Monte had died. She hadn't called me either. Finally, after we had driven past her car several times, I had Bonnie stop. I walked up to her car.

"Hi Laura," I said, as if nothing had happened, my phoniness masking my pounding heart.

"Hey, where have you been?" she sounded just as cheerful as I did.

After we had talked for about half an hour, someone brought up Monte's death. I don't remember which one of us it was.

"Yeah," said Laura "they said that he put the shotgun in his mouth and pulled the trigger with his toe." Her eyes were large behind her sunglasses. "How did you find out?"

"It was in the newspaper," I said. "I was really pissed at my mother. She made sure I didn't know until it was too late to go to the funeral." As if I would have been able to, anyway. For a 15-year-old girl in West Texas in the 1960s, getting a ride to a town 50 miles away was almost like visiting another planet. But that declaration sounded much more dramatic than, "I didn't find out until it was all over."

Laura and I eventually re-established our friendship. I even made another trip to visit her the next year during spring break. She fixed me up with another boy, who managed to get his truck stuck on the very same railroad tracks, but other than some horrendous hickeys that I had to cover up on Easter Sunday, I didn't have an evening to remember with him.

Whereas Monte, I will never, ever forget.

TIM

Terri Rimmer

You, always ready with a smile, helping hand, laughter, jokes.

No one, not even your wife, best friend knew of the pain within.

Everyone thought you were doing so great. You seemed to be, they say. You'd lost weight, repaired your marriage, strengthened your friendships.

Or so it seemed.

But one day before one of your son's birthdays, you headed home from work like any other day, stopping off for a detour that would change your life forever and inflict such pain in the hearts of your loved ones still in shock.

You told her, "You need to come get the truck" after calling the police, telling them someone was after you.

You must have had it planned for months, or so your doctor said.

What went through your mind as you drove that road, off the interstate headed for trees? Did you have second thoughts? Did you think what if? Did you think of anyone else?

You pulled your truck up under a tree, got out, ended it all. One of your sons with his friend found your body on the ground, your belt used as a weapon to say goodbye at 45.

The crowd was magnificent at your service, standing room only in the back. So many people left behind, the numerous lives you touched. Your company shut down the whole building as your co-workers told you goodbye.

A friend cried beside me and later said, "I just didn't want him to die."

One of your sons spoke at your funeral and said, "Don't let his life go to waste. Let's finish the good work he started together."

His speech was met with tears and audible signs of grief.

They played religious music, though you were not religious, the minister preached on virtue and hope and how drugs had led you down the wrong path bringing you there today. Hymns were sung, prayers read, people spoke, heads bowed. I touched you lightly on the arm, looked at your face one last time as we said goodbye amidst flowers, wreaths and rain.

236

We stood outside and waited for the journey, people talking, smoking and contemplating.

And now a family of ducks follows us toward water where you're to be buried. Rain is threatening overhead and bagpipes play for you. Some drove, some walked to your burial site, some didn't go at all. Some had to be helped there, some were seated, and some were there in spirit.

The floodwaters came the day before and I missed your viewing.

But now as the music played above and a final prayer was said, the crowd dispersed to eat awhile and wonder aloud at the day.

You are the third statistic I've seen, an utter tragedy, not counting the passive ones who just let things take over.

Hard to believe that just last year I attended a female's funeral just like yours, one who ended her life in much the same way, only hers not such a shock.

Ironically I have known many times how you felt that fateful June. And now that you are gone I reflect on my past selfish plans.

Strangely enough after so many dreams, you walking in my sleep, I have a sense of calm and yet am aware of this fragile life, this weird journey we all take, everyone scarred in some way.

Who knows to what lengths one person will go to when the other shies away?

And who can say who has a God and which Higher Power that is? Be it money, lust, things, or greed, what drives a person's success, saying "No more for me. This was my life. And I am ready to flee?"

THE STORY OF EUGENE MY BROTHER

Mar. 30, 1967 - July 26, 1995

Sister Mary Fides

Ten years ago I assisted as the doctor turned off the machine that kept my brother breathing. I can still vividly remember the look of pain on his face as the nurse covered him with a white sheet. I was just standing in a corner. Dazed. Not crying. Feeling like I was floating in the air. I wasn't even praying. I was devastated, shocked beyond words. Yet I wanted to present a self that is able to cope well. I wasn't ready yet at that time to face the truth.

As I walked in the garden this morning I knew things were settling down within me. There was growth in hope, in assurance that life is beautiful, still. My brother is dead and I have accepted that. He didn't just die, he killed himself and I have learned to accept that now too.

There is now a glimmer of acceptance in me. Was he right or wrong? There is no answer. There never will be. It was too dark for my brother to see, he was in too deep a pit to reach out to all those who wanted to clasp his trembling hands. I believe my brother struggled deeply but his gentle fragile little spirit was already shattered to pieces and never had the chance to get healed in this world. He fought hard and hurt us immensely in the process because he needed us to have a glimpse of his pains and the horrendous howling within. In his death I came to know his abyss of pain and sorrow.

A battle he could not win

Broken glasses, broken hearts…we were afraid of him, of his violence. He, on his part, was intensely afraid of life that kept wounding him. Maybe Eugene battled with an undiagnosed mental illness. Maybe he had a bipolar problem aggravated by his chemical dependence. Maybe he was destroyed by our painful family life beginning with the fatal shooting of our policeman father when he was only 11. Maybe life was just plain cruel to him.

Beneath all those rages was a little boy left whimpering in a corner, so scared, so unloved and so wounded. Nobody seemed to care because his violence was his only way of coping. His only way to relate was through his maddening anger.

I, the sister to next to him, saw a little boy who turned into an old tired man. He wrestled with life's complexities alone as he alienated himself more and more. Eugene took refuge in alcohol and drugs to maybe numb himself and pretend that nothing was wrong. But instead of silencing the noise, it allowed him to scream out the demons in his mind and invited more wounding experiences that pulled him deeper into the danger zones of this life. It trapped him in a long filthy tunnel where no light could reach him. It was the beginning of his many deaths within and the darkest times of our life as a family.

A series of major losses, including the sudden death of his infant first-born son, his separation from his wife, his difficulty in finishing his studies, my entering the convent and finally the news that his wife was already living with another man, took a heavy toll on what was left in his desire to survive life. The horrendous howling within him was too much for him to bear. He went to see a psychiatrist but it was too late. It was time to take off the heavy armor as the warrior chose to quit and walked away filled with deep sorrow for the battles he knew he could not win.

On July 25, 1995, the tired old man of 28, closed the window beside his bed, stood on a stool, took a nylon cord and hung himself in our house. No letter, no goodbye. For many years I was in extreme anguish as to why he killed himself. I blamed so many people including myself. Then I began blaming him and God too. Memories still cut so deep, gnawing pains that could not be named. I hated myself for leaving him as I opted for a life of my own when I thought he was on his way to healing.

I remember when I would visit him in the rehabilitation center. He looked happy and filled with hope. I was there every week. I forced myself not to cry as I saw him going out of the building with his shaved head and exhausted look. But he had gained weight and was smiling. I thought that was the beginning of a new life. Sadly, people failed to support him when he tried his best to start anew. They forgot to remove the old label they had put on him and continued to relate with him the way they used to.

I do not adhere to suicide as an option but I now accept that my brother had to do it. This is actually the most hurting part—that my brother *had* to do it. Was it a choice on his part? I believe that Eugene was ill, that he was emotionally crippled to choose life.

Journey towards acceptance

I now accept his death. I stand before him holding the nylon cord and I bow my head in utter acceptance and surrender, in honoring him as my brother. In honoring his life, the battles he fought all by himself and the endless tears he shed that he tried so hard to hide. I bow my head in gratitude to God for giving him to me as my brother. Eugene will always be a part of my life. No matter how dark, no matter how everything sounds so depressing. In my heart he remained the brother I knew before the darkness in his mind took over. The problem was not just his chemical dependency but the very huge hole in his heart.

A great part of my brother's short life allowed me to penetrate the depth of sorrow a human heart can experience. It made me dwell in a land of darkness where I never dared imagine I could enter. When I was able to finally feel my feelings deeply, I confronted God. The anger was the last to be acknowledged because of my old notion that it was not right to be angry with a dead brother and with God. Yes, I was so angry with God for not taking care of my brother, but later I had to accept the truth that He cannot take away the free will He has given each one of us. This sort of coming to terms with my raw feelings, which took a long time, came as I learned to let go of my old notion that God would take it against me or punish me for being "irreverent." Talking to God in the simplest way I could, with none of the usual trappings, led me to believe in faith that He is still with us despite of his seeming absence. It was then that a gradual settling down within me started. I came face to face with the reality that there will be no answer, no matter how I search for it. I had to let go of my obsession to figure out where God was the day Eugene died and to let go of my own guilt for not having been there for him when he needed me most. I have forgiven myself for not having been able to shield my brother in the many bruises he had to go through in his short life.

I also need to honor that we, his family, tried to reach out, and that we did the best we could with the inner resources that we had at that time. We each grappled with our own fears and confusions. The myth that "it could have been prevented if we had done more, been more attentive, and been there at the right time" tormented me immensely but the acceptance of the many paradoxes of life and the possibility of my brother having a bipolar syndrome are gradually setting me free. I have accepted that I could not be and will never be the "savior-sister" I wish I was for him.

Life is so complex and the many ambiguities of this life will always leave us with our unanswered questions. The need to understand, the need to have all the answers had to go gradually before the little piece of light allowed me to hope and firmly believe that there is still life after the death of a loved one through suicide.

Yes, I now accept his death. I now accept that he wanted and he needed to end his pain. Eugene was then in an ocean of despair. I would have talked to him that day and plead for him to change his mind. He would have changed his mind or delayed his plan but the anguish in his heart that is something we cannot fathom nor take away from him. No one in this life is doomed to kill him/herself so long as there is a glimpse of hope and love. But s/he fails to see rightly because of a clouded mind and a huge pile of life's bruises and ugliness. No one "freely" chooses suicide. My brother was free to choose life but he did not maybe because he was already dead long before he killed himself.

Family and friends of suicide

As years went on there were friends in and outside my religious community who held my hands as I courageously began sharing my brother's story. Journaling helped me a lot too. Finding the group Family and Friends of Suicide Survivor on the Internet was a landmark in my healing. I began corresponding with people who are journeying in the same path as I am. We are ordinary men and women from all over the world bonded by the death of a loved one through suicide. We reach out to one another for support and healing. Because of my being in a monastery, I could not actively participate regularly but the group was an immense help most especially when I was just beginning to come to grips with the reality of Eugene's death five years after he hanged himself. The group was a part of my being empowered to revisit the "sacred ruins" of my life. I learned through the story of each one in the group that there is no one special way to grieve or process this kind of deep wound. I learned concretely that the million ghosts within us will haunt us endlessly unless we face this very sad part of our lives.

There is so much pain in remembering. It is easier to shut off and move on with life, seemingly unfettered by life's painful past. It took a long time but I know I am in a better place now than before. There is healing in remembering. So very gently we will feel our own readiness to own the truths of our story. It is a long turbulent process that we do not force upon ourselves.

Gems in the rubble

There are unexpected gems in the rubbles too as out of my pain I was able to realize that I had with me an archaic belief of a God out there with whom I need to prove my worth. The nun-in-me with such a paradigm eventually had to go. The Light within me revealed Himself as a mother, a father, a Friend. More than anything else H/She is a loving, merciful companion who accept and loves us without condition. He is not an authority figure with whom I need to prove myself to gain a little piece of Heaven after I die. All along he has been and will always be, walking with me and all of us, in all our sorrows and joys.

Why did God allow Eugene to end his life?

I cannot claim I have found a clear answer to this. I didn't find an answer actually. I was led not to a rational sort of understanding but to a Person, to the One who accompanied me and is still accompanying me as I see beyond what is. Yes, I didn't find an answer but even in this admission there is a growing peace. There is no need for me now to arrive at a specific answer. I accept and embrace the vagueness of it all. To be secure in life's insecurity because I am beginning to know in my heart that life's meaning and goal is beyond the events that seemingly shatters our life.

It's a mystery why Eugene was not graced with the same Light I encountered and continue to encounter but I know this is just my own thinking. God deals with each of us differently. God's seeming absence in his life does not necessarily imply that He was not there. There may never be complete healing but the journey goes on, with a deeply scarred heart but with deep hope, inner strength and assurance that God is with us always even in his seeming absence.

New horizons

My brother's short life opened for me new horizons on the meaning of life, suffering and compassion. His death marked me for life in terms of my own vocation as a contemplative nun. I am growing in compassion for all whimpering, fragile people all over, including that part of me who goes through life with my own share of brokenness. There is a Eugene in me in my own fragmented and wounded spirit. There are millions of "EUGENES" out there. They are in our homes, in our prayer communities, in our workplaces.

Eugene's life and death continue to invite me to a deeper understanding of my own pilgrimage in life. I do not believe in suicide but Eugene does not need my opinion on this, he just wants me to continue loving him and to continue being his sister all my life.

God's infinite mercy

Even from the start I never doubted God's infinite mercy on my brother and on all the people who took their own lives. I do not judge Eugene. He had enough of that as he spent his whole life here on earth being labeled by people. My little, big brother is now free from all his darkness, basking in the love and infinite mercy of our One Father. He, who alone, can heal Eugene's fragile heart. I cannot conceive of a God who would punish Eugene in the after life after all that he had been through in his 28 years of earthly life. I believe that Eugene is home with God, his mind freed from all the distortions that he had lived with all his life. He is now in a new realm of existence where he is completely restored and healed.

My letter to Eugene (On the tenth anniversary of his death)

Okay, Eugene. I am letting you go. It is not healthy to keep remembering you hanging, scaring me for years in my endless nightmares, hating you for what you did and at the same time crying my heart out in pity. I survived your death, the family survived your death. But it wasn't easy. We were immensely scarred by what you did. We never really get over your death, we continue to live with it but the healing is ongoing.

I dreamt of you walking in a field of flowers a year after your death. You showed me your neck cleared of that horrific black mark. Yet the hanging image seems much, much imprinted in my mind. Did you mean to hurt us too in choosing to die that way? Was it a sort of punishment for the whole family? Or where you in such an abyss of sorrow that none of these matter to you that very moment? Even now there's still much I wish I could discuss with you. But it's over. I have come to a point where life is asking me to choose my own meaning, to believe in what I believe and to go ahead choosing life and not just plain existence.

There were times, you know, when I feel guilty that I am feeling peaceful now. It sounds like I have stopped feeling bad or guilty about your death. It's like I might forget you. Never. For years I beat myself up for what you did. I need you to forgive me but more than that I know I need to forgive myself. I need to forgive myself that I wasn't able to stay home for you. There are regrets but I choose not to let these regrets define who I am now.

Where you are now is all LIGHT and PEACE. The moment you slipped in eternity I have no doubt that you have forgiven us all for the many ways we failed you. You have forgiven life too for all its wounding strike at you. Still I wish I can hear you telling me that you have forgiven me already. I have forgiven you, Eugene. There is nothing to forgive though because my heart understands the scared little boy inside you. I wish I was there to cry with you. I wish I was there to hold your trembling hands. I wish I was there to embrace you, my brother. I wish we said good-bye and I wish, yes, I wish I loved you more. It feels good to be able to tell you all these even if my eyes are now filled with tears. It's like when I begun to tell God everything and I allowed myself to finally weep for hours and hours.

When you died I thought of leaving the convent because it all seemed useless. I had a difficult time too adjusting with the convent life with all the raw wounds I am carrying. I thought I wouldn't last here. I was just nine months as a sister when you died. It was a tsunami experience.

I doubted God at that time, I was terribly angry at him. I was grieving but I didn't know I was grieving. I blamed myself and so many others. I blamed God, too. My beliefs about life and God crumbled. A God who cannot take care of you is not worth spending my whole life with. But in my heart I knew I was just acting out and was intensely confused and dis-oriented with the inner chaos I could not name. It was a huge sense of fail-ure for me. I was hoping I could make life different for you through my prayers. I was so naïve. I finally told God everything with torrents of tears and there I saw God in my heart crying with me, feeling my pain and your pain too.

Looking back now I'm so grateful that God allowed me to deeply feel my feelings and to rant my anger at him. I felt like He wanted me to be ut-terly honest with Him. It was my Jacob-experience of wrestling with him. He didn't get mad at me for the questions I shouted at Him in my heart, for all sorts of ugly feelings I have, for allowing myself to stand in front of Him and angrily demanding clear answers. It took time but I know now, in a way I cannot describe, that He was in pain too that you had to end your own life. I told Him that He could have stopped you. It took time before I started talking to Him again. Our relationship was never the same again after that. I caught a glimpse of a God different from the one I knew in my younger days. That was the most precious gem in the rubble you know. But I wish there were other ways to receive this gem.

With all that I had to go through as I come to grips with the pain of your death, especially at the crucial time of my novitiate, I never opted to leave the convent. In faith, I held on. I'm so grateful to God that he gave me the grace to trust even if it was pitch dark. Looking back I see that pe-riod of fire and hell as the best teacher I ever had as a young religious.

Thank you, Eugene for all the lessons I am continuously learning through you. Thank you for being my brother. I know you tried your best to be the good elder brother that you wanted to be. You taught me how to ride the bike and how to skate. You saved me when I almost drowned when I was ten. You allowed me to hang out with your friends as a kid even if I was the only girl. Remember the many times I helped you with your kites? We used to catch tadpoles, too. Don't worry, I also have good memories of you and I will keep them in my heart always.

How I wish life was different for you back then. I wish you weren't so fragile. I take great consolation in my belief that you are in God's arms now and has found the joy that you were not able to find here with us. You will always be loved and remembered. It is now peace time for both of us.

Your little sister, Lee-len

WE LOVED HIM

Gina Rusche

He was our hope, our dreams, and our vision to make so many of the wrong things right. He had tremendous promise as he was on the threshold of realizing his overwhelming potential.

I remember when my sister was pregnant awaiting the arrival of this first baby into our lives. Vividly, I remember the day he was born. I adored him instantly. I was incredibly honored when I was asked to be his God-mother. As often as I could I would race to Cherie and Ron's home right after work just to hold that baby. Or shall I say, walk the floors with that new baby, as he sure was a feisty little guy. When he was nine months old, Cherie and Ron decided to return to the place of Ron's upbringing, "Up North." I was devastated. Eric began receiving care packages at an early age and he also became accustomed to hearing the phone ring, as I called constantly.

When Eric was very small, I would make his Halloween costumes so that he could drive around the North Woods to go trick-or-treating. On a couple of Halloween holidays my sister succumbed to my begging and brought him back to Chicago land to trick-or-treat, suburban style. What memories we made.

As Eric grew, he devoured books. Being a teacher, I fancied in making sure that his bookshelves included every title that his little heart could relate to. When I would visit we would sit and read for hours as I know his parents and grandparents did with him as well. He became a reader very early in life, which thrilled me to the core. He had perspective beyond his years at a very early age, perhaps because he experienced so many great stories while he was young. He loved literacy and eventually acquired quite a talent for writing. I would love to read his essays as he always spoke to me and he made me think.

As Eric grew, he made us proud through every aspect of his life. He did well in school and in sports. He had great manners, was compassionate, humble, handsome, as well as giving. He was always willing to lend a hand if someone needed help.

I remember some of the growing pains Eric experienced as he was on his way to becoming a young man. Some of us thought Eric would really find his niche at college, where he was apt to meet others who shared the depth he had for things. There is a quote that I once heard that so fits this situation: "The only thing worse than sending a kid off to college, is *not* sending a kid off to college." We all know firsthand right now how true that saying is.

I now have three boys of my own, each of whom adored their cousin, Eric. I remember someone saying to me years ago, prior to my having children, that the love I felt for Eric would never compare to what I would feel for my own child. I did not find this to be true. Eric was the first child that stole my heart and for as much as I love my own, he will always hold the most special spot in my heart. I have told him this through the years and I am grateful that he knew how much I loved him.

In recent years, Eric has driven on his own to come to see us at our home, outside of Chicago. My boys would await his arrival with such anticipation. During his visits, he would roughhouse with them, take them for rides in his car, and swim with them at the pool. The most cherished memory they have of him is when he would provide them with their own private concert as he would play his guitar and sing for what seemed like hours. Just as he would be finishing up, I would have yet another song that I would request him to play and he would graciously agree. It was always so enjoyable to hear his guitar and his voice throughout our house.

I struggle with having the faith that this tragedy was the right plan for Eric. It is hard for me to believe that Eric was done with his job here on Earth this quickly, as it seems to me that he had so much left to do here. I am finding comfort in knowing that he continues his job in Heaven. I believe he will find his true niche there.

We will always love him.

MY NAME IS R AND THIS IS MY STORY

On April 2nd, 2003 my momma's sister died from cancer. We buried her on April 5th, 2003. On April 15th, 2003 my first cousin, J, completed suicide. He was my age (44 years old), a devout Christian, a loving and devoted husband, a father of a 16 ½ year old daughter. J had worked for 23 years at the GM plant. We grew up together and were close. It was a shock for our entire family. J left no note and nobody had any idea that he would even consider doing this. His daughter had been home with him all day. (He was off that day.) Just around 5:30pm she told him she was going off with some friends to "hang out." He reached in his wallet, gave her twenty dollars and told her to be careful and that he loved her. D, his beautiful, sweet wife arrived home around 6:45pm. J's truck was in the garage.

When D entered the house, she didn't hear him. She thought he must be lying down taking a nap. She entered their master bedroom and found him lying back on the bed with a gunshot to his neck. She ran hysterically out of the room and two doors down to where J's parents (my aunt and uncle—my momma's sister) live. D collapsed on their front door step. My aunt called 911. She went down to J and D's home to see if J was alive. He was dead. My aunt called 911 back and told them. The police arrived immediately. I received the phone call around 4:00am. I rushed over there to be with D, her daughter and my aunt and uncle.

Nobody slept for days. Nobody ate for days. We don't know why it happened. J was so close to his wife, child, parents and especially the church. He was very dedicated to the church and was there every Sunday to help set up the music equipment. He hid his depression from everyone. D is dealing with life on a day-to-day basis. Her faith in God is stronger today. She and I have become very close. She is a beautiful lady and the loss she is enduring is tremendous!

On Friday, April 18th, 2003 the visitation was at 4:00pm. Only the immediate family was to be there at 4:00pm, everyone else came after 5:00pm. I had not been to work for those first two days. Nobody had! I returned to work on Friday, April 18th, 2003 for a few hours, because I had to do the salesmen payroll commission checks. I came in and did what I had to do.

Around 3:00pm, my nephew, C called me. He was in a frenzied state and totally beside himself. C lived just outside of Jefferson, Texas, about one mile from Lake O' Pines in a small community called Harleton, Texas. He had been seeing a married girl, L. He told me what was going on, and that E, L's husband, knew about the affair. He was worried that E would do something and he would get blamed for it or that E would try to kill him. He said he had been running up and down the road hollering at him telling him he was going to kill him. He said E had a gun. I told him to call the police and let them know what was happening. Just in case something *did* happen. I could not talk to him very long because I was an emotional wreck and I had to leave to get up to the funeral home. I told him I would call him later.

I didn't get to call C back that night. I left the funeral home around 10:00pm and got home around 11:00pm. I was tired and drained. I tried to go to sleep, but I couldn't. I should have called and checked on C. I feel so guilty because I didn't. I should have gone over there and gotten him. I had no idea what was going on at that time. I found out all that later.

On Saturday, April 19th, 2003 we buried J. When I got home after his funeral, I lay down and slept for five hours. I woke up around 7:00pm that Saturday evening. Immediately, C was on my mind. I had not called him back and I had not heard from him. I called his cell phone and he answered it right away. I apologized to him for not calling him back sooner. And I let him know why I couldn't and didn't. While I was talking, he interrupted me and said, "I am waiting on an important phone call. Can I call you right back?" I sensed the urgency in his voice. I said, "Yeah, is everything okay?" He said, "Yeah, it's just that I am afraid being on the phone I will miss my important phone call. I'll call you back, I promise." I said, "Okay, I love you, Buddy." He said, "I love you, too, Aunt R." That was the last time I talked to him. Again, I never went to bed and slept that night. Later, I found out the "important phone call" he was waiting on was from L. I didn't feel like going to church the next day (Sunday, April 20th, 2003) because I was emotionally tired and I knew I would cry anyway all during the service. So I stayed home. I didn't feel like being around people.

The police called my house sometime around noon or 1:00pm. I am not sure because when I received the call most of everything went to pieces for me. My husband was not home, but he said when he returned from the store he found me on the floor crying hysterically. He called my momma, who was just a few miles down the road from our house, at my uncle's house celebrating their 65th Wedding Anniversary. She came to my house immediately. They could not get much out of me. I was in pretty bad shape. My momma looked at the caller ID and found the number on it. She called back at that point. After she spoke to the police, we drove to Marshall. On the way, my momma was on the phone to the police station. All they would tell us was to come there.

Once we got there, the lead investigator was still investigating the incident. We spoke to another man, who was extremely nice and showed concerned. He led us over to the funeral home, because they had C there. We were allowed to see him. He was still a mess. There was no exit wound. The bullet was lodged in his brain. He was in full rigor mortise and had blood all over his face and the front of his shirt. When I saw him lying there, I collapsed. This was real! C was gone!

When we left the funeral home, we asked the police to escort us to C's trailer. They said they couldn't, so we drove out there. At this point we still had no idea where it all had happened. When we got to C's trailer we noticed his car was not there. We went into the trailer. We entered wondering if we would find a crime scene. As we went from one room to another, we realized that he had not done "it" there. Mother wanted to know where the vehicle was, so she and my husband drove down to C's friend and boss's place. While they were gone, I began to look for reasons why this happened. Mother found out from his friend and boss that C had gone down to L's trailer, sat at her picnic table and put E's 22 pistol in his mouth and pulled the trigger. L and E were gone that Saturday night to a motel. They did not return home until early that Sunday morning, when they found C in their front yard laying across their picnic table with the fatal gunshot wound. I searched through the trailer looking for anything that would tell me. I went outside searching. While I was outside, I found a purple Crown Royal bag filled with 22 rifle shells. They were in their boxes but some of the bullets wee missing. I found this at the front of the trailer where the tong was facing his friend and boss's house. It didn't look like it had been there for long, just like it was dropped there recently. Mother and my husband didn't come back immediately.

At that point, I walked down the dusty driveway towards L's trailer. (I was still unaware where this happened). As I neared her trailer, she came outside. At first I did not know who she was. I had only met her one time and spoken to her on the phone a couple of times. During all this, you have to realize that I was in so much pain, so much despair, and in total shock. I was angry! I was angry at everyone and anyone who ever hurt my nephew physically, emotionally and spiritually. I was like Sally Field in *Steel Magnolias*, when Sally Field was at her daughter's funeral and she was grieving and weeping from her loss. L stood up and suddenly shouted, "I'm mad. I'm so mad I just want to hit something." That is how I felt. Haven't you ever gotten so mad at someone when you seen how hurt your child was and just wanted to hit them for hurting your child that you loved with all your heart? That was how I was feeling then and for months afterwards. L walked out of the house and began to come towards me. When I realized who she was, after she said she was L, I said, "Do not come any closer to me. I cannot console you because I am mad!" She made a smart-alecky remark something to the effect for me to leave and get off her property. As I turned away and began walking towards the trailer C lived in, I remember her saying, "C was f_ _ _ed up before I even met him." That hurt me! I thought about that ever since C's death. It has tormented me ever since. How could someone who claimed to love him so much, say something like that about him? Especially when they know he killed himself because he loved them! I don't understand it. I still cannot find a reason why anyone would say that about anyone that they claimed to love. If she thought he was so f _ _ _ ed up, why did she have an affair with him?

L was married to E, who had also been C's best friend for 12 years. She knew the "affair" was not C's idea! I talked about it to her on the telephone one day. C even wrote in his suicide note of how much he loved L *and* E. I know that, because I am the one who found the suicide note and I still have it. I know better than anyone else that C had some problems. But he had a great big tender heart. His *problems* were not with me, his MeeMaw, but with his mother, Y, (my sister), his father, and even his sister, N. I remember, I turned around, and in a fit of rage and complete madness because of that statement, and screamed back to L, "As far as I am concerned, you killed C. He may have pulled the trigger, but you killed him." I was so consumed with grief and despair.

That night, we (myself, my mother and my husband) stayed in C's trailer. I stayed up all night. I could not sleep. I cried all night long! Mother had called my sister (C's mother), who lives in Missouri, and she was on her way. I kept trying to get my sister on the cell phone she borrowed from a friend to travel with, but could not reach her. I called my best friend, who, bless her heart, stayed on the phone with me all night long. I remember at 2:00am, while I was still on the phone to my friend, I heard a gunshot go off. Mother was asleep in C's bed, and my husband was asleep in the smaller bedroom that had the twin mattress on the floor. When I heard the gunshot, Momma woke up and said, "What was that?" She heard it too. We never found out where it came from. It wasn't hunting season. I told my sister about it the next day. She asked the neighbors and even E and L about it and nobody knew anything about (or so they claim!) It was if C was giving us a sign. It kind of spooked us. In the morning, sometime around 10 o'clock, my sister showed up. We went to the funeral home. I don't remember much after that. Everything was, and still is, a fog. I was not doing well at all.

It wasn't until sometime in June, that I was told that C had previously tried to kill himself, that Friday night, by cutting his wrists. Because I was so consumed with grief, I hadn't noticed the bandages on his wrists. All I could see was him lying there, lifeless and not breathing. He was gone. And nothing else seemed to matter to me (at that time). I have been told that L and her Daddy bandaged him up. I became angrier! Why didn't they call me? I have been tormenting myself with anger over why someone *did not* call us when he was in that state of mind on Friday night? They were able to call us on Sunday when he was dead? I guess that is something they will have to live with.

I know how C felt about E and L. He loved E so much! So many times he told me how much he cared for E. He was his buddy, his pal and his best friend. He looked up to him. I know that he did not pursue L in the manner that E may think or have been told. I have the letters he wrote to me while he was in Texas. C was very vulnerable. He wanted someone to love him so badly and unconditionally! He found that in both E and L. The affair with L was literally killing him. He would call me and cry over the phone. He told me he knew he was wrong and how much he did not want to hurt E, his best friend! So many times he would tell me that he was going to call it off, but he said every time he would, L cried and he could not stand to see her cry. He even started to see another girl, but L would tell him she wasn't good enough for him, that she loved him. All the while, L was just playing a head game. She came to C many times and told him she didn't have any money for this or that. And that E was going to be mad at her because she used the bill money to buy this or that. As good-hearted as C was, he would hand her over a hundred dollars here and there to her, so E would not be mad at her.

E still does not know the whole story. He knows what L told him and wants him to know. I read and reread the letters C wrote to me and so many of them were about E and L. His friendship with E meant more than anyone will ever possibly know. I know that E is grieving for him too. We all are, even now. I know E cared about him. I have a lot of sympathy for E. As far as I know, E is still with L. He did leave her for a little while directly after C's death. He had a lot to deal with during that time. Not only did he lose his best friend, he had to deal with the fact that his best friend was having an affair with his wife and his best friend killed himself because of it. He suffered a tremendous amount. He second-guessed everything C said or did. He even second-guessed L and he second-guesses her actions even to this day. Wouldn't you? I believe he is only with L because they have two children. His pain is far deeper than L's pain. C didn't confide in many people about his feelings. He didn't want to seem "tender" to any one. He did confide to me, my husband and his Meemaw. But he had a great big heart and would work his butt off for anyone. He never asked for anything, he did the best he could with what he had.

My loss is so big that I will never be the same without C in my life. I have wonderful memories with him but I miss him so much everyday! I go into his room here at our house and sometimes I am consumed with so much grief that I don't know how I will make it through the day. When I hear a song on the radio on the way to work, I can't stop crying. C liked the group "3 Doors Down" and their song "Ticket To Heaven." I cry when I hear that song. It makes me think of how sad and full of despair C was that Saturday night. He couldn't see living with all his pain. His light was not shining anymore. He was lost. I don't have to have any of C's things to re-mind myself of him and his life here. I have my memories. They are deeply embedded in my heart and in my mind. Some days, I sit and close my eyes and remember! We were very close. He was always so special to me. I love him and I miss him so terribly *everyday*.

At the funeral home, C's mother, Y., was embarrassing to the whole family. She acted horribly. She cussed at my mother. She and her daughter, N, had a fistfight in the funeral home while trying to make preparations for C's funeral. N hit my mother with the funeral director sitting right there beside them. She just turned around and socked my mother right in the face. My mother paid for the entire funeral. (C was cremated). We were able to see him once again, after the autopsy and they bathed him. He didn't have anything disfiguring about him. It was as if he was just sleeping.

At the funeral home, during all the fighting with Y, N and my mother (who was grieving just as badly as me), all I could do was sit there and cry. Finally, I had to get up and I walked outside. On my way out, I told the funeral people to just call the police. Y and N were both on drugs during the entire event that surrounded C's death! At the memorial service, Mother handed the pastor a letter that she wrote for him to read. Y walked over and snatched the letter away from the pastor and ripped it up and threw it in the trash. Momma was crying. My husband walked over and pulled the letter out of the trash can, went into the Funeral Director's office, taped it back together and handed it to the pastor to read, anyway. The whole scene was an emotional fiasco! I had written a letter to God, thanking him for giving me this beautiful precious child; my husband read the letter for me.

After C's memorial service, my husband took me home. My momma went out to C's trailer. She had given C her old El Camino. He had another El Camino parked there that he was using as parts to fix up the one Mother gave to him. Mother had not put the El Camino in C's name yet. She was going to do that on his birthday, September 6th. She went there to try to get that other El Camino moved. She was met by Y, who was portraying a devil's demon! Y said a lot of ugly things to my mother. She also said a lot of ugly things to me through my answering machine. She wanted everything that I had that belonged to C.

Sometimes, I found myself sitting in my bedroom with all the lights in the house off and all the doors locked. I was just sitting there on the bed, crying. I was losing it. The phone rang and I knew it was Y. I was afraid of her for the first time in my life. She was controlling my sanity! Finally, after listening to this crap on the answering machine for days, I knew I had to make it stop. I placed a call to the lead investigator in C's death. I didn't know who else to call. You can't block out of state calls. I was in Louisiana and she was in Texas, only 45 miles away. The investigator was a very compassionate man. He was a Christian and even had family that went to my church. He told me to not worry about Y calling me again. He said he was going to speak to his immediate supervisor and handle the situation. He called Y and told her that as long as she remained in the state of Texas, that if she called me or my mother again harassing us, he would arrest her. He was such a nice man. He knew Y and N were on drugs. He was very compassionate towards me, my mother and my husband during the whole ordeal. He reached out to me when he didn't have to. C would have hated all the crap that Y and N were saying and doing. He would have run them off from there.

My mother did not speak to Y for months afterwards. She blocked her email so that she would not receive anything from Y. She still checks her caller I.D. box before she answers her phone. My mother loves Y because she is her daughter but she realizes Y cannot be trusted where your heart is concerned. When things do not go her way, Y blames everyone else for her failures. She did it to C his whole life. If a boyfriend left her, she blamed C. Everything that ever went wrong in her life was always C's fault. Like my mother told her, "Y, who are you going to blame now for all you bad choices and all your problems." Momma doesn't want to get hurt by Y anymore. It is too much for her. She has forgiven Y for everything, but she doesn't trust her. Y's moods flip-flop and anyone who gets in her was gets blamed for things that go wrong in her personal life. I have found out a lot of things just by talking to some of C's friends there and elsewhere.

Some things that happened while C and his mother lived in Harleton. C never told me, my husband or his MeeMaw these things because he did not want us to know. They were horrible things. Y allowed her boyfriend to tie C to a tree when he was only 10 years old and whip him. All the while C was crying with Y standing just a few feet away screaming at him that he deserved it. What kind of mother would allow this to happen to her child?

The same boyfriend molested her own daughter and then C later. (I think she is evil.) Yet she still stayed with him, claiming she "loved" him. I found myself even angrier with Y for allowing these things to happen to him and for doing a lot of them herself to him. I have my own regrets. I regret not taking C away from Y and I told her this in my 25-page letter to her. C and I had talked about that and I told him many times sitting at our kitchen table that I should have gotten him away from Y and her craziness. He told me it didn't matter. He didn't want me to know some of the things she did. He told me then he would never tell me some of the stuff he had to put up with, because he knew it would hurt me. I stood up, crying, hugged him and told him I loved him! C would call us all the time. No matter where he was or what he was doing, he would always call to say he loved us, tell us he was okay or just keep in touch. He did this all his life. That's the kind of relationship I had with C. He knew I loved him and I would defend him. He was saving me the grief and pain that Y caused!

I confronted Y with my anger towards her in my letter to her. One day, she called my house. I had not accepted any phone calls from her, but on this particular day, I forgot to check the caller I.D. box and just picked up the phone. It was my sister. She began by asking how I was and went right on in with her reason for calling. She went on to apologize to me for all the nasty things she said during the death of her son. She apologized for all the wrong she did to C growing up as a child and as a young adult. She said she received my letter. After I hung up the phone with her, I started to cry. I cried really hard that day. I had wanted her to apologize, but I really wanted her to do it to C. But it was too late for him. I hope that her heart was sincere and I hope that C heard her.

C was a beautiful artist. He loved to draw. When he was just a little boy, instead of going outside to play with friends he always wanted to go with me to the store and buy him "pretty pens." His artwork was wonderful. God gifted him with this talent. We have a few things he drew hanging in our home. People are in awe of some of the things he did.

Since C's death, with the help from my pastor, I *have* learned how to "forgive" my sister. I have to forgive her in order for God to *ever* forgive me of any of my own sins. The Bible tells me, "Bear with each other and forgive whatever grievances you may have against one another. Forgive as the Lord forgave you of all your sins (Colossians 3:13). "Get rid of all bitterness, rage and anger, brawling and slander along with every form of malice. Be kind and compassionate to one another, forgive each other, just as in Christ God forgives you (Ephesians 4:21 & 32). My pastor tells me "If someone hurts you, you are commanded by God to forgive them, but you are not expected to trust them immediately, and you are not expected to continue allowing them to hurt you. They must prove they have changed over time and they *can* be trusted." This is exactly how C was just before he died. He forgave his mother for all the crap she put him through, but he *did not* trust her. This is where I am and my *family* is where Y is concerned. My pastor goes on to tell me, "Forgiveness is letting go of the past. Trust has to do with future behavior." I even wrote to E and L. I knew that I had to "forgive" in order for me to heal. Am I healed? No! That is something that will take me a long time! But I still had to write them and Y. It is what I had to do!

On May 14th, after C's death, with my world already upside down, I had to take my best friend and sweet little girl to the vet and hold her while they put her to sleep. Her kidneys failed and she was dying. Nikki was 16 ½ years old. She was my kid, my baby! It butchered my soul when I had to do that. I went downhill from there. When I brought her home that day, we buried her in the back yard and made a marker for her little grave. I was devastated. That was the "straw that broke the camel's back" for me! I found myself in such a deep dark depression. Nobody and nothing could reach me. Everyone I loved was dying around me. I could not work. I could not function. I was only breathing in and out…and even that didn't matter to me. I shut myself off from everything and everyone. I wound up in the hospital. I did not eat. I did not sleep. I have not been able to return to work on a full-time basis. I had lost 30 pounds and when I dozed off I would have horrendous nightmares of C. I placed myself sitting at that picnic table with him and when he placed the gun in his mouth I could not reach him. I awake many times screaming. My husband had to wake me up and comfort me. My doctor gave me something to take at night to help me sleep, but I didn't take them like he prescribed. I was afraid I would become dependent on them. I have never liked taking medicine or anything.

I finally admitted myself to the hospital, at the urging of my family and my work. I was there for five days. I had to go to a group meeting everyday. Everyone all around me was there because they attempted suicide or, for the same reason I was, depression. After the second day of listening to each person state the reason they were there, it came my turn. I said my name, and why I was there. I remember standing up and telling these people that C completed suicide and my cousin, J, completed suicide and all within five days of each other. I raised my hand to them and said, "You think that nobody cares. I'm here to tell you that *somebody* does care. This is the mess you leave behind! I am a Survivor of Suicide. If by telling these people of my hell, I was able to stop one person from completing suicide, then I did what I was supposed to do. Maybe something good will come out of all this insanity.

While I was in the hospital, I began a journal. It helped me to "sort out" my feelings. It allowed me and still allows me to get rid of feelings I don't want to carry around with me. I don't worry if it makes "sense", but it allows me to sort out my thoughts that keep recurring in my mind. Nobody reads it. It is my outlet. When C did this, he did not "think" what this would do to me or anyone. His only thought was to get rid of his pain and sorrow. He didn't know that this would affect so many people. He knew we all loved him and cared about him. But at that very moment when he pulled that trigger, we were not in his mind. He didn't want to hurt us. He just could not see any reason for living. He "reacted".

It reminds me so much of how my sister is. Y "reacts" and does not think before hand. She has always been this way. Over the years, I learned to not "react" to her and her moods. I simply blew her off and went on about my business. If I had reacted to her every mood swing, fits of rage, etc., I would have ended up nuts or hurting her! I remember one time when I came to Y's place there in Harleton. It was C's eighteenth birthday. When I drove up to her trailer, she had spray painted on the door in black paint, "I'm not mad, I've just been in a bad mood for eighteen years." My thoughts on that were, and still are, "This is crazy!" I didn't "react" to it, I simply ignored it. I came in the trailer and she was in one of those crazy moods, ranting and raving, pissed off at C for one thing or another. I asked her where he was, and she said, "He's out back in the trailer *I* bought so he would stay out of *my* house!" I still did not react. I could have threw a fit and acted like she, but I didn't. Why fuel the fire? I went outside and spent a couple of hours out there with C. I now feel that I should have taken him home with me. But I didn't. (Another regret). We are all full of regrets. It comes with the whole "suicide" scenario.

I have since returned to work, (in September 2003). I have involved myself with a Survivors Of Suicide (SOS) group. I attend the group meetings, which are held every other Saturday. I also have a therapist who I see every two weeks. My therapist said to me on one of my visits to him, "R, the deaths you have endured remind me of something I read. I liked it so much. I wrote what he said down so that I could read it everyday. To remind ourselves that the reason we feel grief at a loved ones death is simply because we have the capacity to Love! If we never experienced love, then we would have no involvement that would be strong enough or deep enough to cause these unpleasant emotions. For that reason, we can accept grief as a testimony to our capacity to bond with and care for another. It means we have the ability to bond with and care for another. It means we have the ability to gain closeness with another, to feel affectionate, to dedicate part of our emotions and energies to another. Between grief and nothing, I will take grief!" I found those words to be a great comfort!

Going to the support group is like "confirmation" of what I feel is real! These people feel the same sorrow, sense of loss and despair and total isolation that I feel. They really know how and what I am feeling. They too are going through the same despair of loosing someone that they loved and cared about. They are asking themselves the same questions, "Why" and "What if?" When you are among others who have experienced this, you are able to relate and cope with it better. The name of the support group is "In Memory of Daniel ~ Survivors Of Suicide Support Group". I have also been in contact with the "Friends & Family of Suicide Survivors" in New York. They sent me, and many members of my family, information and books. I even had them send Y information. In my family, I have always been the "fixer." I was the "peacemaker." People like Y are "fixees". They seek out "Fixers" and "Fixers" seek out "fixees." I never really thought myself to be this, but as I have healed and received therapy for my grief. I have learned this to be true. I don't like fighting, I hate the turmoil, or as C always called it, "drama." C hated it too. When all that crap was going on at the funeral home with Y and N, it only made the hurt in losing C that much more intense. He could not even have a peaceful memorial service. I live everyday with a broken heart.

My husband and I got married on August 9th, 2003. We lived together for 19 years. I have no children and my husband has two daughters from a previous marriage. One is married, has our first grandchild and a second on the way and lives in Denver, Colorado. The other lives in North Carolina and is single.

Because I had lost so much weight, my wedding dress did not fit. It was a size 2 and fit fine when I bought it months before. The night before the wedding, my husband's cousins were there and wanted me to try it on. It was a strapless gown. When they zipped it up, it fell to my waist. I ended up having to wear two bras and pinning the bras to the dress to stay up. I didn't realize how thin I was. Looking back, I looked pretty pathetic. All of my family was at the wedding.

In March 2003, when I told C that we were going to get married, he was so excited. His exact words that day to me on the phone were, "Aunt R, you have made my day." Having a candle burning during the entire wedding ceremony and at the reception, we honored C, my cousin J, my aunt and my Nikki, along with my husband's parents, who died years ago. It was hard for us with them not being there, but they were there in spirit, watching and smiling.

Just when you "think" you are going to be all right and you begin to find hope…

On October 6th, 2005, my husband's nephew, M, was found hanging from his ceiling fan in his dorm room on Barksdale Air Force Base. He was 24 years old. M was a very intelligent kid. He graduated from high school with a 4.0 grade average. He went into the Air Force to further his education. He married and they had a little girl. While in Georgia, (after only two years being married), they divorced. M's daddy became ill and he transferred to Barksdale to be closer to him. When his daddy died he stayed on. In the meantime, his ex-wife became involved with a black man. She moved in with him with M's little girl. The black guy was a known drug pusher. In September, his ex-wife and the black man moved to Dallas, taking M's daughter with them. M was depressed about it. He did not leave a note. We don't know all the answers to why he chose suicide. We probably will never, just like with J and with C.

The Holidays were very hard on my family. C's birthday was the first hurdle we had to get through. Since we have gotten a birthday cake with his name printed on it and "celebrated" his life. We celebrated the day that God gave him to us. We will do this every year in praise of our C. Then there was Thanksgiving, Christmas and New Year's. Time *does* have a way of healing, but we never forget. The wounds are there forever. They hurt even today. I don't remember much about Spring/Summer 2003. It was a whirlwind of tragedy and emotions, unanswered questions and a whole lot of "what ifs." I still don't know what I am doing. The month of April is very tough, not just for myself but my family as well. I opt to take vacation time off during this month so that I can be by myself, so that other family members do not see my tears and cause them pain.

Spring is for "New Beginnings." I was hoping that this spring would be much kinder to me and my family. But it wasn't. My daddy's brother passed away on March 11th, 2004. A few weeks after my husband and I got married in 2003, my uncle found out he had cancer, a tumor in his brain. He suffered in his last days. He was a Christian man so full of life. We miss him dearly. On March 21st, 2004 my momma's only brother passed away also. He had just begun to recover from open-heart surgery when he took a turn for the worse. He was the caregiver in the family. Being the only brother and having seven sisters, he took care of everyone. He was the father of the family. He will be missed tremendously.

I have had death thrown at me in all directions. It is extremely hard for anyone to handle, but suicide is far more divergent. Suicide leaves those left behind with so *many* unanswered questions and so many regrets. We all ask ourselves, "If only I had…" Regardless of how good we were to our loved one, how much care we took and loved we showed, or how much time we spent with them, we still suffer from guilt. In my support group, the leader tells us "feeling guilty is our way of making ourselves believe that we had some control over the death. Fact of the matter is, we are *not* responsible." *Try making us believe that one!* It is hard for us to take this as the absolute truth. I also learned since all the deaths that have happened around me, three of which were by suicide, that the word s-u-i-c-i-d-e holds a huge stigma behind it. People look at all of us "survivors" as if we have a horrible disease and they might catch it, or that perhaps there is something wrong with our family. It's easier to tell folks that "Oh, he died in a car wreck…" As soon as you say he shot himself, they back away. They don't want to know! It is because of this stigma behind the "S" word that we are hindered from truly healing. Ignorance on those who have not been through it is the tragedy! We're not asking for sympathy, we just want understanding. Someone told me just the other day, "R, it has been a year. You need to get over it." I became angry. I didn't know that grief had a time limit. We all grieve in our own way, but I am here to tell you, GRIEF does not hold a time limit. One day everything is fine and the next you are a basket case. Nothing in particular triggers our grief; it just comes over us when we least expect it.

I have also learned since all this "insanity" *(that is what I have called this past year)*, that writing helps. I keep a journal. Sometimes I can't find anything to say, other times, you'd think I was writing a novel. It is my outlet for my fears, worries, prayers and blessings. I have poems in it, some I have written, some I have collected from other sources. I began writing it when all this happened with J, C and my Nikki. In the beginning, I was full of so much anger towards everyone and anyone who ever hurt C. As time has gone on, my journal entries have not been so aggressive. I have dealt with my anger and made peace with issues that I have no control over, especially now. Nobody reads it, and even I have not gone back and reread a lot of the "early" page entries. One day, I may. Who knows, I may even publish the thing. It certainly is full of the all the stuff one is looking for in a novel!

Just when you *think* you have survived…something happens that sends you back into that whirlwind of emotions. On August 10th, 2004, my husband's sister was found murdered in her home. Her husband had given her pills that didn't belong to him and she never woke up. Her murder is still under investigation. That is another "unknowing" that can drive you to insanity. In March 2005, I lost my wonderful loving step-father to open heart surgery and my mother's only brother from the same.

Since April 15th, 2003, I have dealt with three suicides, one murder, and seven illness related deaths. My life has changed forever. But the suicides are the hardest of all to deal with emotionally.

I want to make a difference in our society. I want people to know that there is help out there, for those who are contemplating suicide and for those who are grieving the loss of a loved by suicide. I look at people through a different set of eyes today. If I "think" someone is depressed or is sad, I don't just walk away and ignore it. I want them to know that someone does care. I care! The only thing that kept me from killing myself during all this insanity was I didn't want my family to have to go through another suicide. I knew how I was feeling, the loss and suffering, and I couldn't do that to them. That is what I want people to know. I want to make a difference for J, C and M, so that their deaths do not go unaccounted for. In memory of them, I want those left behind to know there is help and there are wonderful support groups to be able to go to release their anguish, to know that there are others that truly do understand all that they are going through, that they are not crazy.

CHARLIE'S EYES

"Bryan"

Charlie's eyes, large and intelligent if not always forgiving, were now limp slits watching me carefully, alert to my pain as well as hers. Finally she said, "I have to do this now. Soon I won't be able to. I can't wait until I'm that weak. Please understand."

When I could I answered, "I do, it's just hard to accept. Why now? Why can't we see what happens first. Maybe it'll get better."

When she was sad, Charlie had a way of making the world disappear for me, and for a moment even the birds outside our small apartment were quiet. "C'mon, Love," she said. "It's not going to get better, you know that. And now with this other thing flaring up...it's over. Accept that. It's finished. There's no more left."

"Please, give it a little longer...."

"I wish I could. But there's not much time."

The next day the doctor standing at the foot of her bed completed our trio. He watched her warily, and turning to leave said, "You take care of yourself," as though the previous half-hour had never taken place. Holding the hastily written prescription for Phenobarbital loosely in her hand, Charlie called after him, "How many will do it?"

"Just take one each night."

"Please stop that crap," she said. "You know what I'm saying."

He paused, eyes circling the room, uncomfortable wherever they landed. "Well," he said, after a time, "you want to be careful because too many of them could be lethal. I have to go now."

"How many?"

He still couldn't look directly at her. "Well, Phenobarbital is dangerous. I'm just guessing here, but I would imagine if someone took ten or twelve, it might prove fatal."

"So I should take at least twelve, right?" He didn't answer, busy as he was examining the floor. She pressed him, "Is that it, twelve or more?"

"I'm not comfortable with this," he finally said. "I don't like being put in this position. I'm going to leave." She smiled, waved weakly and said, "Sure. And thank you, I'm grateful for your help."

Clearly eager to escape an uncomfortable scene, he nodded then left the bedroom without comment. I was just behind him. His coat lay over the arm of the sofa where I had put it and he slipped it on while we both pointedly avoided eye contact. My aversion lay in the dread of what remained to be done—his, because he had just written a prescription for death and now wanted nothing more to do with it.

"She'll be okay," he said, still disclaiming responsibility.

"How long will it take?"

Again his eyes sought escape. "Those pills are strong, she should be asleep in no time."

"Please…! How long?"

He inhaled deeply. Then, despite obvious his discomfort with the subject said, "Depends. I would imagine 15 would kill a healthy man in a few hours." He paused before opening the door. "She shouldn't do this, you know. It's against the law. If I had known what she wanted I wouldn't have come."

"But I told you when I called!"

"That isn't my understanding. I gave her a prescription to help her sleep. That's all!" He pulled the front door open and stepped out.

As frustrating as it was, there was no sense in belaboring the point, he was just protecting himself and neither Charlie nor I could blame him. Existing laws are designed to accommodate lobbyists and those they represent, not people in distress. Besides, for all we knew he was placing himself at risk just writing the prescription, and what would we have done without it?

No doubt many things around the house are lethal, but our recent attempt at assisted suicide proved attaining a peaceful death took more knowledge and experience than we had. She tried to overdose with Valium and all that came of it was a good night's sleep. We needed something else, something guaranteed painless and certain. "Thank you, doctor," I said, and watched the door close behind him.

Once back in the bedroom, I took the vital script from Charlie's hand and kissed her on the forehead.

"Please fill it now," she murmured. I nodded, and before leaving asked, "Want anything before I go?"

Eyes closed, she wagged her head. "Nothing, thank you. I'm going to nap now, okay? But please wake me when you've got it."

I was back in 30 minutes. Before waking her I sat in the living room thinking about the last five years. Years of denial on my part, a narrow view permitting only hope and the best of possibilities. I had to wonder how that time added up in terms of help or hurt.

The first news of Charlie's cancer was devastating, but it was worse after her surgery. When the procedure was over, the surgeon came out saying he wished he could give me better news. All of her lymph nodes were affected and the consensus was she had a six percent chance of survival beyond a year or two.

I never let her know that.

For five years I insisted we beat this thing. And because she believed in me, and because I would consider no alternative, somehow we managed to steal those few extra inches of time. Now, a primary lung cancer had also developed.

Perhaps we could have fought it another month or two, and granted that was precious time, but all it would mean for Charlie was increased pain and a rapidly diminishing quality of life. She had already suffered beyond reason, mostly to please me. Now her wishes were clear and without qualification and I had no choice but to quiet my own in favor of hers.

So, once again we would have to face fear and the unknown, but this time when it was over she would be gone forever. This time she wouldn't be waking up in the morning, refreshed but disappointed. "Oh, God..." she had said, "Why am I still here?"

"It's all right, love..."

"No it's not! Why do they make this so hard? I could have committed some terrible crime and they'd have me meet death with less torment! Shame! Shame on the 'civilized' world. I'm ashamed to be part of it. And shamed in defying it."

That was hard. This was harder. I woke her up, and we sat for a long time talking about nothing.

The bed she lay on was bought early in our marriage, an expensive relic of a happier time. We discovered the rosewood gem in the back of a tiny Chinese antique shop in San Francisco and couldn't bring ourselves to leave without it. Now, with her right arm curled back over her head, she absently stroked the headboard, her fingers wandering lightly over its smoothly finished, deeply carved surface.

Her sigh brought us both up short. Weary but determined, it had the ring of something delicate and precious gathering courage to meet its fate.

264

She took the small brown vial from me and studied it carefully, then handed it back. "Sweetheart, take the lid off for me, okay?"

Designed for use by adults, the plastic phial was topped with a child-proof cap. I wrestled with it with trembling hands, all the while knowing any halfway intelligent toddler could probably open the damned thing with less trouble. Ultimately, I stumbled across the access code and the pills poured out onto my hand.

She was wasted and weak and when I raised my gaze to see her struggling to lift a glass of water from the nightstand, an involuntarily moan escaped me. She turned, her eyes clouding over seeing the tears in mine. "Come on, love," she said, "just do this for me and I'll never ask you for anything else."

Her off-the-wall humor rang hollow this time, just one pinch too painful. I placed a single sleeping pill in her outstretched hand. She tried again, "Look, fella, I don't know about your plans, but I don't have all day. Just hand me a bunch of them, all right?" I did; then lifted the water glass to her lips each time she put one of the colored capsules in her mouth.

Half an hour later, when about 16 of the sleeping pills had been swallowed this way, she asked for a cigarette. My stomach knotted. "My God, what's wrong with you?" I snapped. "Are you crazy? Look what smoking has done to us!"

Generously, she ignored the *us*. "What's the point in my quitting now?" she asked gently. "Last one, I promise." Deliberately giving her a cigarette was as devastating as helping her take those pills. But I gave in and pulled from beneath her pillow the small red and white pack we both pretended wasn't there. Reluctantly, I tapped out a soft ingot of tobacco.

Her eyes were glassy, unfocused now, and combined with my shaking hands made lighting that cigarette even more painful. An inhalation later, followed by a wracking cough, the cigarette dangled precariously from her dry lips. When finally it fell from them, I scooped it up quickly, hoping she wouldn't notice and ask for it again.

She forced herself to swallow another pill. Then, as though wanting her last comments to be worthy of our life together, focused momentarily and murmured, "You know, you gave me the best years of my life."

It was intended as a kindness, I knew that. Yet there, at that time, I just couldn't bring myself to be gracious, and I've regretted it ever since. I don't know what I should have said, but pain clouds your mind when you're helping your wife and best friend die.

When she spoke, it was almost as though she had already gone. "Thank you, sweetheart. Thank you." Her eyes moved slowly about the room. They seemed fascinated by something, and intent on capturing forever and committing to memory that which I could not see.

I watched those eyes slip finally closed. I never saw them opened again.

KEENING IN BANGOR

Carolyn Gage

On March 27, 1998, at 9:30pm on a Friday night, two sixteen-year-old girls, Cass Roberts and Emily Stupak, drove their car into a grove of birch trees at a speed estimated by police to have been over a hundred miles-an- hour, at "Dead Man's Curve" on Levant Road, just outside the town center of Levant, Maine, west of Bangor. Cass and Emily were in love with each other.

"Keening" is derived from the Irish word, "caoineadh," meaning to cry or lament. It is a deep, heartfelt vocalization over the dead, somewhere between a scream, a sob, and a wail. The sound of keening is profoundly disturbing to the human ear, which may be why it has been associated with supernatural traditions. It was believed that keening provided the soul of the recently deceased with a chaperone to the Otherworld. To keen too soon after death was to risk waking the devil's dogs, who could potentially intercept the soul in its passage. On the other hand, if the keening was too long delayed, there was the danger that the soul would have already departed for its journey in a perilously unchaperoned state.

Whether as a spirit escort or a catharsis for the living, keening was perceived by the Church as a political threat, and, for a time, it was banned as a pagan practice. Silence was officially instituted as the only dignified and appropriate response to grief. Apparently, those piercing, eerie, and peculiarly female-sounding wails were considered outside the bounds of Church decorum—and colonial occupation.

But grief itself lies on the extremity of human experience, and what more fitting expression than a sound situated on the boundary of human expression? Keening has been characterized as a way of emotionally purging an assimilable loss, in much the same way as vomiting (another indecorous act) can purge the stomach of potentially toxic content.

I practiced keening for the first time this year. It was in a small town in central Maine, about two hours north of Portland, where I live. I had gone there on a mission. One might even call it a pilgrimage. I wanted to visit the site where two sixteen-year-old girls had driven their car at what was estimated to be over a hundred-miles-an-hour into a grove of birch trees. The treacherous ninety-degree curve in the road was known locally as "Dead Man's Curve," but these deaths had been no accident. There were no skid marks, alcohol had not been involved, and a suicide note had been left on the seat of the car. The contents of the note were never disclosed to the public, because the police had chosen to turn it over to the parents. Their official explanation for their silence? "The families have already suffered enough."

No doubt the families suffered, although I am not sure what it means to "suffer enough." One thing is clear: The two girls had suffered beyond what they could bear. And nobody was allowed to talk about that. The silence was and still is deafening. By the unspoken rules of small-town preservation of family secrets, keening had again been banned.

The media gave the double suicide perfunctory, evasive coverage, either out of respect for the privacy of the families, or concern for their own reputation, or both. The disappeared note, which could have relieved the media of their temerity over ascribing the "L word" to the victims, had been ignorantly suppressed. In a small rural town in the middle of Maine, people would not have understood that lesbianism was an integral part of the story and that acknowledgement of it would have been a mark of respect for the dead. Instead, they would have taken their local newspaper to task for sensationalizing a tragedy and desecrating the memory of the girls. High school friends, possibly even more intimidated than the press, shuffled their feet and gave vague responses to reporters: "You never saw one without the other . . ." and "They were always pretty much together." One especially brave classmate, went so far as to say, "I hope this has made kids think . . . Did they know we loved them?"

Probably not. According to one recent study, 97% of students in a public high school hear homophobic remarks from their peers.[1] One reporter in Iowa found that the typical high school student hears anti-lesbian or anti-gay slurs more than twenty-five times a day.[2] In a fourteen-city study of gay, lesbian and bisexual youth, 80% reported verbal abuse, 44% reported threats of attack, 33% reported having objects thrown at them and 30% reported being chased or followed.[3] Lesbian and gay youth are two-to-six times more likely to attempt suicide, and this population may account for nearly a third of all completed suicides among teens.[4] In the Massachusetts study, 46% who identified as gay, lesbian or bisexual had attempted suicide in the past year compared to 8.8% of their peers. [5]

Despite the silence of the press, there were the rumors. According to a source close to one of the girls, they had both come out to their families just before the accident, and the members of one of the families had been Christian fundamentalists.

If it is the truth the girls had just come out to their parents, this paints us a painful picture of the girls' last day together. Had they been forbidden to see each other? Had they spent the day together anyway, knowing that they were defying their families? The day was a Friday. Were they unwilling to face their first weekend without any contact with each other? The time of death was 9:30pm. How long did they drive around? Had the suicide been planned earlier in the day, or was it a last-minute, panicked response to the approach of their curfew? Were they afraid to go home? Was this the first time they had ever violated curfew, openly defied their parents? Were they afraid of violence? Was lying an option? Wasn't there anyone, anywhere to whom they could turn? Was the note something they composed together, agonizing over the precise use of words that would enable the world to understand their love—or was it something hastily scrawled, just minutes before acceleration?

The accident was not reported until the next morning. Their car had been hidden from view under a canopy of branches bent low from the winter's ice storms. The tree that they hit was large for a birch, about two feet in diameter. Badly gashed, it did not fall. The police speculated, judging from the damage to the car, that the girls must have been traveling very fast and died immediately on impact.

I had difficulty at first locating this "Dead Man's Curve." There were two roads with the same name, more or less in the same county, and I had driven to the wrong one. Failing to locate any part of the road that could even remotely qualify as a "dead man's curve," I had given up and stopped at a coffee shop. Rechecking my sources, I realized my error and was soon on my way to the other road. This time there was no need to search for the site. It was impossible to miss. About a half-mile outside of town, at a right-angle bend and under a grove of birch trees, there were two white, wooden, hand-made crosses. A photograph of one of the girls was nailed above the gash on the tree that had been hit. Someone had lettered the names of the girls on the crosses and painted a tiny red heart on each of the opposing arms of the cross, where they touched—almost.

I had not really planned what I would do once I located the site, but suddenly here I was. I parked on the opposite side of the road and crossed to the birch grove. There were few cars on this country road, and I was alone. It was a fall day, rainy, and most of the leaves from the trees had already fallen. As I stood there, the idea of keening came to me. I felt a pain deep in my chest and a constriction in my throat. It was as if there was something stuck inside me that I couldn't get out. Strangled with grief, I was simultaneously choking from rage. And so I began. The sound came spontaneously. The constriction in my throat shaped the sound of my pain, and perhaps this is why keening is so cathartic. It gives voice to the unspeakable. I thought again of the Church's ban on keening, relating it to the silence and media blackout on the motivation for these girls' deaths, the censorship of their final words—words that may have been intended to change the world, and words that easily could have done just that.

What happens when people are not allowed the full expression of their grief? Is it true that an emotion not fully expressed, is one that is not fully felt? And when one does not feel one's feelings, what happens to them? In the case of these deaths, some of that taboo grief was transformed into fear. Fellow lesbians in the high school were deeply traumatized by this event, taking a giant step back into their closets. Some of the stifled grief was transmuted to anger directed at the dead girls that they could not work out their problems, that they should have shown more consideration toward their classmates than to kill themselves. Where was the anger toward the police who made the high-handed decision to protect the contents of the notes, clearly in opposition to the intention of the girls who martyred themselves in part to get their story out? Where was the anger toward a church that condemned them to hell? Toward parents who could not accept the sexual orientation of their own daughter? Toward the journalists who were too cowardly to challenge the codes of small-town homophobia, who were complicitous in covering up a story that could have galvanized the entire country around the issue of lesbian/gay-baiting and its horrendous consequences? Where was the anger toward school officials who have traditionally turned a blind eye to the sexual harassment and lesbian/gay-baiting that has made school a living hell for so many students?

There was nothing I could do for these two girls now. They were dead. But I could do something for myself. I could keen. I could stand by the side of this road, in front of these birch trees, and I could let out the sound of my pain until I was empty of it, until I was free of it, and it would not sour in my gut as fear, or guilt, or shame, or anger against myself. I could stand there and I could keen for all the unchaperoned spirits of lesbians and gays who have had to leave under similar pressures, similar torments, and with similar violence. And then I could leave that spot, the birch trees still resonating with the sound of my bitter keening, and I could drive away with a renewed commitment to social change, with a strengthened courage to stand up to oppressive institutions and individuals, with a deeper love for my own lesbianism.

References:

[1] *Making Schools Safe for Gay and Lesbian Youth: Report of the Massachusetts Governor's Commission on Gay and Lesbian Youth*, 1993.

[2] Carter, Kelley, "Gay Slurs Abound," in *The Des Moines Register*, March 7, 1997, p. 1.

[3] A. R. D'Augelli and S. L. Hershberger, Lesbian, gay and bisexual youth in community settings: Personal challenges and mental health problems, *American Journal of Community Psychology* 21:421, 1993

[4] Report of the Secretary's Task Force on Youth Suicide, U.S. Department of Health and

Human Services, 1989.

[5] Massachusetts Youth Risk Behavior Survey (MYRBS), Massachusetts Department of

Education, 1997.

(Statistics originally compiled by PFLAG)

SHE CHOSE DEATH
Pat McGrath Avery

She left a void...
a hole in our lives
that no number
of new faces
nor passing days
can ever fill.

She tore apart...
the puzzle of our lives,
threw away some of the pieces and
scattered bits of us in the wind.

She willed us...
wounded hearts,
lost opportunities,
unspoken words
and feelings of guilt
for the "might have beens."

She chose death...
she, whom we loved so much,
in her anguished soul,
felt unlovable.

About the Author

Karen Mueller Bryson, Ph.D. is a National Certified Counselor (NCC) and educator. She is also a fiction author, playwright and performer. She earned Master's degrees in both Human Development Counseling and Creative Writing with an Emphasis in Playwriting. She earned a doctoral degree in Human Science at Saybrook Graduate School. Dr. Bryson is currently an Assistant Professor of Psychology and Human Services at Ottawa University in Mesa, Arizona. This is her first nonfiction book.

Visit her website at: http://www.ahorsewithnoname.com.

About Transformational Stories

Transformational Stories uses a profit free publishing model to facilitate the telling of personal stories. Current projects include the enthnodrama, *Certain Expectations*, and the nonfiction book, *Those They Left Behind: A Collection of Interviews, Essays, Stories and Poems by Survivors of Suicide.*

Visit the website at: http://www.transformationalstories.com.

CPSIA information can be obtained at www.ICGtesting.com
Printed in the USA
LVOW041741100912

298201LV00007B/52/A